ENGLISH ILLUSTRATION

'THE SIXTIES': 1855-7o

BY GLEESON WHITE

WITH NUMEROUS ILLUSTRATIONS BY
FORD MADOX BROWN : A. BOYD HOUGHTON
ARTHUR HUGHES : CHARLES KEENE
M. J. LAWLESS : LORD LEIGHTON, *P.*R.A.
SIR J. E. MILLAIS, *P.*R.A. : G. DU MAURIER
J. W. NORTH, R.A. : G. J. PINWELL
DANTE GABRIEL ROSSETTI : W. SMALL
FREDERICK SANDYS : J. MᶜNEILL WHISTLER
FREDERICK WALKER, A.R.A. : AND OTHERS

KINGSMEAD REPRINTS

BATH.

First Published 1897.
Reprinted 1970.
SBN 901571 29 6

Reproduced and Printed in Great Britain by
Redwood Press Limited, Trowbridge and London.

TO

A. M. G. W. AND C. R. G. W.

IN MEMORY OF THE

MANY HOURS SPENT

UNGRUDGINGLY IN

PROOF READING

PREFACE

IN a past century the author of a well-digested and elaborately accurate monograph, the fruit of a life's labour, was well content to entitle it 'Brief Contributions towards a History of So-and-So.' Nowadays, after a few weeks' special cramming, a hastily written record of the facts which most impressed the writer is labelled often enough 'A History.' Were this book called by the earlier phrase, it would still be overweighted. Nor did an English idiom exist that would provide the exact synonym for *catalogue-raisonné*, could the phrase be employed truthfully. It is at most a roughly annotated, tentative catalogue like those issued for art critics on press-days with the superscription 'under revision'—an equivalent of the legal reservation 'without prejudice.' To conceal the labour and present the results in interesting fashion, which is the aim of the Chancellor of the Exchequer on a 'Budget' night, ought also to be that of the compiler of any document crammed with distantly unrelated facts. But the time required for rewriting a book of this class, after it has grown into shape, would be enough to appal a person who had no other duties to perform, and absolutely prohibitive to one not so happily placed.

In estimating the errors which are certain to have crept into this record of a few thousand facts selected from many thousands, the author is obviously the last person to have any idea of their number; for did he suspect their existence, they would be corrected before the work appeared. Yet all the same, despite his own efforts and those of kindly hands who have re-collated the references in the majority of cases, he cannot flatter himself he has altogether escaped the most insidious danger that besets a compilation of this kind,

vii

namely, overlooking some patently obvious facts which are as familiar to him as to any candid critic who is sure to discover their absence.

The choice of representative illustrations has been most perplexing. Some twenty years' intimacy with most of the books and magazines mentioned herein made it still less easy to decide upon their abstract merits. Personal prejudice— unconscious, and therefore the more subtle—is sure to have influenced the selection ; sometimes, perhaps, by choosing old favourites which others regard as second rate, and again by too reticent approval of those most appreciated personally, from a fear lest the partiality should be sentimental rather than critical. But, and it is as well to make the confession at once, many have been excluded for matters quite uncon- nected with their art. Judging from the comments of the average person who is mildly interested in the English illustrations of the past, his sympathy vanishes at once if the costumes depicted are 'old-fashioned.' Whilst I have been working on these books, if a visitor called, and turned over their pages, unless he chanced to be an artist by profession as well as by temperament, the spoon-bill bonnet and the male 'turban' of the 'sixties' merely provoked ridicule. As my object is to reawaken interest in work familiar enough to artists, but neglected at present by very many people, it seems wiser not to set things before them which would only irritate. Again, it is difficult to be impartial concerning the beauty of old favourites; whether your mother or sister happen to be handsome is hardly a point of which you are a trustworthy judge. Other omissions are due to the right, incontestable if annoying, every other person possesses in common with oneself, 'to do what he likes with his own'; and certain publishers, acting on this principle, prefer that half-forgotten engravings should remain so.

The information and assistance so freely given should be credited in detail, yet to do so were to occupy space already exceeded. But I cannot avoid naming Mr. G. H. Bough- ton, R.A., Mr. Dalziel, Mr. G. R. Halkett, Mr. Fairfax Murray, and Mr. Joseph Pennell for their kind response to various inquiries. Thanks are also due to the many holders of copyrights who have permitted the illustrations to be reproduced. As some blocks have changed hands since they

PREFACE

first appeared, the original source given below each picture
does not always indicate the owner who has allowed it to be
included. The artists' names are printed in many cases without titles bestowed later, as it seemed best to quote them as
they stood at the time the drawing was published. Lastly, I
have to thank Mr. Temple Scott for his elaborate index, prepared with so much care, which many interested in the subject
will find the most useful section of the book.

The claims of wood-engraving *versus* process have been
touched upon here very rarely. If any one doubts that
nearly all the drawings of the 'sixties' lost much, and that
many were wholly ruined by the engraver, he has but to
compare them with reproductions by modern processes from a
few originals that escaped destruction at the time. If this be
not a sufficient evidence, the British Museum and South Kensington have many examples in their permanent collections
which will quickly convince the most stubborn. If some few
engravers managed to impart a certain interest at the expense
of the original work, which not merely atones for the loss but
supplies in its place an intrinsic work of art, such exceptions
no way affect the argument. Wood-engraving of the first
order is hardly likely to die out. It is true that, as the craft
finds fewer recruits, the lessened number of journeymen,
experts in technique (whence real artist-engravers may be
expected to spring up at intervals), will diminish the supply.
Given the artist as craftsman, he may always be trusted to
distance his rival, whether it be mechanism or a profit-making
corporation which reduces the individuality of its agents to the
level of machines. For in art, still more than in commerce,
it is the personal equation that finally controls and shapes
the project to mastery, and the whole charm of the sixties
is the individual charm of each artist. The incompetent
draughtsman, then, was no less uninteresting than he is
to-day ; even the fairly respectable illustrators gain nothing
by the accident that they flourished in 'the golden decade.'
But the best of the work which has never ceased to delight
fellow-workers will, no doubt, maintain its interest in common
with good work of all schools and periods. Therefore,
this rough attempt at a catalogue of some of its most striking examples, although its publication happens to coincide
with a supposed 'boom,' may have more than ephemeral

ENGLISH ILLUSTRATION
value if it save labour in hunting up commonplace facts to many people now and in the future.   This plea is offered in defence of the text of a volume which, although cut down from its intended size, and all too large, is yet but a rough sketch.

Collectors of all sorts know the various stages which their separate hobbies impose on them.   First, out of pure love for their subject, they gather together chance specimens almost at haphazard.   Then, moved by an ever-growing interest, they take the pursuit more seriously, and, as one by one the worthier objects fall into their hands, they grow still more keen.   Later, they discover to their sorrow that a complete collection is, humanly speaking, impossible : certain unique examples are not to be obtained for love or money, or, at all events, for the amount at their personal disposal.   At last they realise, perhaps, that after all the cheapest and most easily procured are also the most admirable and delightful. This awakening comes often enough when a catalogue has been prepared, and on looking over it they find that the treasures they valued at one time most highly are only so estimated by fellow-collectors ; then they realise that the more common objects which fall within the reach of every one are by far the best worth possessing.

A homely American phrase (and the word homely applies in a double sense) runs : ' He has bitten off more than he can chew.'   The truth of the remark is found appropriate as I write these final words.   To mark, learn, and inwardly digest the output of ten to fifteen years' illustration must needs be predestined failure, if space and time for its preparation are both limited.   The subject has hitherto been almost un-touched, and when in certain aspects it has attracted writers, they have approached it almost always from the standpoint of artistic appreciation and criticism.   Here, despite certain unintentional lapses into that nobler path, the intention has been to keep strictly to a catalogue of published facts and with a few bibliographical notes added.

Setting out with a magnificent scheme—to present an iconography of the work of every artist of the first rank—the piles of manuscript devoted to this comprehensive task which are at my side prove the impracticability of the enterprise. To annotate the work of Sir John Gilbert or Mr. Birket Foster

PREFACE

would require for each a volume the size of this. But as *Punch, The Illustrated London News,* and the Moxon *Tennyson* have already been the subject of separate monographs, no doubt in future years each branch of the subject that may be worth treating exhaustively will supply material for other monographs. The chief disappointment in preparing a reference-book of this class belongs to the first compiler only ; the rest have the joy of exposing his shortcomings and correcting his errors, combined with the pleasure of indulging in that captious criticism which any overheard dialogue in the streets shows to be the staple of English conversation.

GLEESON WHITE.

10 THERESA TERRACE,
RAVENSCOURT PARK, W.,
October 1896.

CONTENTS

CHAPTER I

xiii

ENGLISH ILLUSTRATION

LIST OF ILLUSTRATIONS

(Where two or more illustrations follow each other with no text between, the references are given to the nearest page facing)

XV

ENGLISH ILLUSTRATION

xvi

LIST OF ILLUSTRATIONS

xvii

ENGLISH ILLUSTRATION

LIST OF ILLUSTRATIONS

xix

SCENE FROM "SHE STOOPS TO CONQUER."

ENGLISH ILLUSTRATION THE SIXTIES, 1855-1870

CHAPTER I: THE NEW APPRECIATION AND THE NEW COLLECTOR

THE borderland between the hallowed past and the matter-of-fact present is rarely attractive. It appeals neither to our veneration nor our curiosity. Its heroes are too recent to be deified, its secrets are all told. If you estimate a generation as occupying one-third of a century, you will find that to most people thirty-three years ago, more or less, is the least fascinating of all possible periods. Its fashions in dress yet linger in faded travesties, its once refined tastes no longer appeal to us, its very aspirations, if they do not seem positively ludicrous, are certain to appear pathetically insufficient. Yet there are not wanting signs which denote that the rush of modern life, bent on shortening times of waiting, will lessen the quarantine which a period of this sort has had to suffer hitherto before it could be looked upon as romantically attractive instead of appearing repulsively old-fashioned. For the moment you are able to take a man of a former generation, and can regard him honestly, not as a contemporary with all human weakness, but with the glamour which surrounds a hero ; he is released from the commonplace present and has joined the happy past. Therein he may find justice without prejudice. Of course the chances are that, be he artist or philosopher, the increased favour bestowed upon him will not extend to his subjects, or perhaps his method of work ; but so sure as you find the artists of any period diligently studied and imitated, it is almost certain that the costumes they painted, the furniture and accessories they admired, and the thought which infused their work, will be less intolerable, and possibly once again restored to full popularity.

Not very long ago anything within the limits of the century was called modern. Perhaps because its early years were passed in yearnings for the classic days of old Greece, and later in orthodox raptures over the bulls of Nineveh and

THE NEW APPRECIATION

the relics of dead Pharaohs. Then by degrees the Middle Ages also renewed their interest : the great Gothic revival but led the way to a new exploration of the Queen Anne and Georgian days. So in domestic life England turned to its Chippendale and Sheraton, America to its colonial houses, and the word 'antique,' instead of being of necessity limited to objects at least a thousand years old was applied to those of a bare hundred. Now, when the nineteenth century has one foot in the grave, we have but to glance back a few years to discover that what was so lately 'old-fashioned' is fast attaining the glamour of antiquity. Even our immediate progenitors who were familiar with the railway and telegraph, and had heard of photography, seem to be in other respects sufficiently unlike our contemporaries to appear quite respectably ancestral to-day. It is true that we have compensations : the new photography and electric lighting are our own joys ; and the new criticism had hardly begun, except perhaps in the Far West, during the time of this previous generation—the time that begins with a memory of the project for the Great Exhibition, and ends with an equally vivid recollection of the collapse of the Third Empire.

In those days people still preserved a sentimental respect for the artist merely because he was 'an artist,' quite apart from his technical accomplishment. It was the period of magenta and crinoline—the period that saw, ere its close, the twin domes of the second International Exhibition arise in its midst to dominate South Kensington before they were moved to Muswell Hill and were burnt down without arousing national sorrow—in short, it was 'the sixties.' Only yesterday 'the sixties' seemed a synonym for all that was absurd. Is it because most of us who make books to-day were at school then, and consequently surveyed the world as a superfluous and purely inconsequent background? For people who were children in the sixties are but now ripening to belief in the commonplace formulæ dear to an orthodox British citizen. To their amazement they find that not a few of the pupils of the 'seventies,' if not of the 'eighties,' have already ripened prematurely to the same extent. Have we not heard a youth of our time, in a mood not wholly burlesque, gravely discussing the Æsthetic movement of the 'eighties' as soberly as men heretofore discussed the move-

2

AND THE NEW COLLECTOR

ment of a century previous ?   Were the purpose of this book phrase-making instead of a dull record of facts, we might style this sudden appreciation of comparatively recent times the New Antiquity.   To a child the year before last is nearly as remote as the time of the Norman Conquest, or of Julius Cæsar.   Possibly this sudden erlightenment respecting the artistic doings of the mid-Victorian period may indicate the return to childhood which is part of a nonagenarian's equipment.   At seventy or eighty, our lives are spent in recollections half a century old, but at ninety the privilege may be relaxed, and the unfortunate loiterer on the stage may claim to select a far more recent decade as his Golden Age, even if by weakening memory he confuses his second childhood with his first.

To-day not a few people interested in the Arts find 'the sixties' a time as interesting as in the last century men found the days of Praxiteles, or as, still more recently, the Middle Ages appeared to the early pre-Raphaelites.   These few, however, are more or less disciples of the illustrator, as opposed to those who consider 'art' and 'painting' synonymous terms.   Not long since the only method deemed worthy of an artist was to paint in oils.   To these, perhaps, to be literally exact, you might add a few pedants who recognised the large aims of the worker in fresco, and a still more restricted number who believed in the maker of stained glass, mosaic, or enamel, if only his death were sufficiently remote.   Now, however, the humble illustrator, the man who fashions his dreams into designs for commercial reproduction by wood-engraving or 'process,' has found an audience, and is acquiring rapidly a fame of his own.

For those who recognise most sincerely, and with no affectation, the importance of the mere illustrator, this attempt to make a rough catalogue of his earlier achievements may be not without interest.   Yet it is not put forward as a novel effort.   One of the most hopeful auguries towards the final recognition of the pen-draughtsmen of the sixties quickly comes to light as you begin to search for previous notices of their work.   It was not Mr. Joseph Pennell who first appreciated them.   It is true that he carried the report of their powers into unfamiliar districts ; but, long before his time, Mr. J. M. Gray, Mr. Edmund Gosse, and many another had paid in public due

3

tribute to their excellence. Nor can you find that they were
unappreciated by their contemporaries. On the contrary, our
popular magazines were filled with their work. Despite Mr.
Ruskin's consistent 'aloofness' and inconsistent 'diatribes,'
many critics of their own day praised them; their names
were fairly well known to educated people, their works
sold largely, they obtained good prices, and commissions,
as the published results bear witness, were showered upon
them.

But, until to-day, the draughtsman for periodicals was
deemed a far less important person than the painter of
Academy pictures. Now, without attempting to rob the
R.A. of its historic glory, we see there are others without
the fold who, when the roll-call of nineteenth-century artists is
read, will answer 'Adsum.'

There are signs that the collector, always ready for a fresh
hobby, will before long turn his attention to the English
wood-engravings of this century, as eagerly as he has been
attracted heretofore by the early woodcuts of German and
Italian origin, or the copper-plates of all countries and
periods. It is true that Bewick already enjoys the distinction, and that Cruikshank and Leech have also gained a
reputation in the sale-rooms, and that Blake, for reasons
only partly concerned with art, has for some time past had
a faithful and devout following. But the prices realised, so
far, by the finest examples of the later wood-engravings, in
the Moxon edition of *Tennyson's Poems*, in *Once a Week*,
and Messrs. Dalziels' books, are not such as to inspire faith
in the collector who esteems his treasures chiefly for their
value under the hammer. But in this case, as in others, the
moderate prices demanded in 1896 may not be the rule a
few months hence. Already, although books rarely fetch
as much as the original published cost, they are getting scarce.
You may hunt the London shops in vain, and ransack the
second-hand stores in the big provincial towns and not
light on Jean Ingelow's *Poems*, 4to, Thornbury's *Legendary
Ballads*, or even *Wayside Poesies*, or a *Round of Days*, all
fairly common but a short time ago.

There are two great divisions of the objects that attract
collectors. In the first come all items of individual handiwork, where no two can be precisely alike (since replicas by

AND THE NEW COLLECTOR

the authors are too rare to destroy the argument), and each specimen cannot be duplicated. Into this class fall paintings and drawings of all sorts, gems, sword-guards, lacquer, and ivories, and a thousand other objects of art. In the second, where duplicates have been produced in large numbers, the collector has a new ideal—to complete a collection that contains examples of every variety of the subject, be they artistic :— coins, etchings, or engravings of any sort ; natural objects :— butterflies, or crystals, or things which belong neither to nature nor art : — postage - stamps, the majority of book-plates, and other trifles so numerous that even a bare list might extend to pages. The first class demands a long purse, and has, of necessity, a certain failure confronting it, for many of the best specimens are already in national collections, and cannot by any chance come into the market. But in the second class, no matter how rare a specimen may be, there is always a hope, and in many cases not a forlorn one, that some day, in some likely or unlikely place, its fellow may be discovered. And the chance of picking up a treasure for a nominal price adds to the zest of the collector, whose real delight is in the chase, far more than in the capture. Who does not hope to find a twopenny box containing (as once they did) a first edition of Fitzgerald's *Omar Khayyám* ? or a Rembrandt's *Three Trees* in a first state? Or to discover a *Tetradrachm* Syracuse, B.C. 317, 'with the superb head of Persephone and the spirited quadriga, on the obverse,' in some tray of old coins in a foreign market-place ?

Without more preamble, we may go on to the objects the new collector wishes to acquire ; and to provide him with a hand-book that shall set him on the track of desirable speci-mens. This desultory gossip may also serve to explain indirectly the aims and limits of the present volume, which does not pretend to be a critical summary, not a history of art, and neither a treatise on engravers, nor an anecdotal record of artists, but merely a working book of reference, whatever importance it possesses being due only to the fine examples of the subject, which those concerned have most kindly permitted to be reproduced.

It is quite true that in collecting, the first of the two classes demands more critical knowledge, because as it is not a collection but only a selection that is within the reach of

5

any one owner, it follows that each item must reflect his taste and judgment. In the second division there is danger lest the rush for comprehensiveness may dull the critical faculty, until, by and by, the ugly and foolish rarity is treasured far more than the beautiful and artistic items which are not rare, and so fail to command high prices.

In fact the danger of all collectors is this alluring temptation which besets other people in other ways. Many people prefer the exception to the rule, the imperfect sport to the commonplace type. If so, this discursive chatter is not wholly irrelevant, since it preludes an apology for including certain references to work distinctly below the level of the best, which, by its accidental position in volumes where the best occurs, can hardly be ignored completely.

Another point of conscience arises which each must decide for himself. Supposing that the collection of wood-engravings of the sixties assumes the proportion of a craze, must the collector retain intact a whole set of an illustrated periodical for the sake of a few dozen pictures within it, or if he decides to tear them out, will he not be imitating the execrable John Bagford, who destroyed twenty-five thousand volumes for the sake of their title-pages? Must he mutilate a Tennyson's *Poems* (Moxon, 1857) or *The Music-master*, or many of Dalziels' gift-books, for the sake of arranging his specimens in orderly fashion? The dilemma is a very real one. Even if one decides to keep volumes entire, the sets of magazines are so bulky, and in some cases contain such a small proportion of valuable work, that a collector cannot find space for more than a few of them. Possibly a fairly representative collection might be derived entirely from the back-numbers of periodicals, if any huge stores have yet survived the journey to the paper-mill or the flames; the one or the other being the ultimate fate of every magazine or periodical that is not duly bound before it has lost its high estate, as 'a complete set,' and become mere odd numbers or waste-paper.

So far the question of cost has not been raised, nor at present need it frighten the most economic. Taking all the subjects referred to in this book, with perhaps one or two exceptions (Allingham's *Music-master*, 1855, for instance), I doubt if a penny a piece for all the illustrations in the various volumes (counting the undesirable as well as the worthy specimens) would not be far above the market-price of the whole. But the penny each, like the old story of the horse-shoes, although not in this case governed by geometrical progression, would mount up to a big total. Yet, even if you purchase the books at a fair price, the best contain so many good illustrations, that the cost of each is brought down to a trifle.

Having decided to collect, and bought or obtained in other ways, so that you may entitle your treasures (as South Kensington Museum labels its novelties) 'recent acquisitions,' without scrupulous explanation of the means employed to get them, you are next puzzled how to arrange them. It seems to me that a fine book should be preserved intact. There are but comparatively few of its first edition, and of these few a certain number are doomed to accidental destruction in the ordinary course of events, so that one should hesitate before cutting up a fine book, and be not hasty in mutilating a volume of *Once a Week* or the *Shilling Magazine*. But if you have picked up odd numbers, and want to preserve the prints, a useful plan is to prepare a certain number of cardboard or cloth-covered boxes filled with single sheets of thick brown paper. In these an oblique slit is made to hold each corner of the print. By this method subjects can be mounted quickly, and, as the collection grows, new sub-divisions can be arranged and the subjects distributed among a larger number of boxes. This plan allows each print to be examined easily, the brown paper stands wear and tear and shows no finger-marks, and affords a pleasant frame to the engraving. Pasting-down in albums should be viewed with suspicion—either the blank leaves for specimens still to be acquired are constantly in evidence to show how little you possess, compared with your expectations; or else you will find it impossible to place future purchases in their proper order.

There is a process, known as print-splitting, which removes the objectionable printed back that ruins the effect of many good wood-engravings. It is a delicate, but not a very difficult operation, and should the hobby spread, young lady artists might do worse than forsake the poorly-paid production of nasty little head-pieces for fashion-papers and the like, and turn deft fingers to a more worthy pursuit. It needs an

7

artistic temperament to split the print successfully, and a market would be quickly opened up if moderate prices were charged for the new industry.

One could wish that representative collections of the best of these prints were gathered together and framed inexpensively, for gifts or loans to schools, art industrial classes, and other places where the taste of pupils might be raised by their study. The cheap process-block from a photograph is growing to be the staple form of black and white that the average person meets with in his daily routine. The cost of really fine etchings, mezzotints, lithographs, and other masterpieces of black and white prohibits their being scattered broadcast; but while the fine prints by Millais, Sandys, Hughes, Pinwell, Fred Walker, and the rest are still to be bought cheaply, the opportunity should not be lost.

CHAPTER II : THE ILLUSTRATED PERIODICALS BEFORE THE SIXTIES

HE more you study the position of illustrators during the last forty years, the more you are inclined to believe that they owe their very existence, as a class, to the popularity of magazines and periodicals. From the time *Once a Week* started, to the present to-day, the bulk of illustrations of any merit have been issued in serial publications. It is easy to find a reason for this. The heavy cost of the drawings, and, until recent times, the almost equally heavy cost of engraving them, would suffice to prohibit their lavish use in ordinary books. For it must not be forgotten that every new book is, to a great extent, a speculation ; whereas the circulation of a periodical, once it is assured, varies but slightly. A book may be prepared for twenty thousand buyers, and not attract one thousand ; but a periodical that sold twenty thousand of its current number is fairly certain to sell eighteen thousand to nineteen thousand of the next, and more probably will show a slight increase. Again, although one appears to get as many costly illustrations in a magazine to-day as in a volume costing ten times the price, the comparative sales more than readjust the balance. For a quarter of a million, although a record circulation of a periodical, is by no means a unique one ; whereas the most popular illustrated book ever issued—and *Trilby* could be easily proved to merit that title—is probably not far beyond its hundred thousand. This very book was published in *Harper's Magazine*, and so obtained an enormous advertisement in one of the most widely circulated shilling monthlies. One doubts if the most popular illustrated volumes published at one or two guineas would show an average sale of two thousand copies at the original price. Therefore, to regard the periodical, be it quarterly, monthly, or weekly—and quite soon the daily paper may be added to the list—as the legitimate field for the illustrator, is merely to accept the facts of the case. True, that here and there carefully prepared volumes, with all the added luxury of fine paper and fine printing, stand above the magazine of their time in this mechanical production. But things are rapidly changing.

9

THE ILLUSTRATED PERIODICALS

One may pick up some ephemeral paper to-day, to find it has process-blocks of better quality, and is better printed, than 'the art book of the season,' be it what it may. The illustrator is the really popular artist of the period—the natural product of the newer conditions. For one painter who makes a living entirely by pictures, there are dozens who subsist upon illustrating; while, against one picture of any reputable sort—framed and sold—it would be impossible to estimate the number of drawings made specially for publication. Nor even to-day—when either the demand for illustration is ahead of the supply, or else many editors artfully prefer the second best, not forgetting all the feeble stuff of the cheap weeklies—would it be safe to declare that the artistic level is below that of the popular galleries. Certainly, even in the thirties, there were, in proportion, as many masterpieces done for the engraver as those which were carried out in oil or water-colour. Waiving the question of the damage wrought by engraver, or process-reproducer, the artist—if he be a great man—is no less worthy of respect as an illustrator in a cheap weekly, than when he chooses to devote himself solely to easel pictures. It is not by way of depreciating paintings that one would exalt illustration, but merely to recognise the obvious truth that the best work of an artist who understands his medium can never fail to be of surpassing interest, whether he uses fresco, tempera, oil, or water-colour; whether he works with brush or needle, pen or pencil. Nobody doubts that most of these products are entitled, other qualities being present, to be considered works of art; but, until lately, people have not shown the same respect for an illustration. Even when they admired the work, it was a common form of appreciation to declare it was 'as good as an etching,' or 'a composition worthy of being painted.' Many writers have endeavoured to restore black-and-white art to its true dignity, and the labours of Sir F. Seymour Haden, who awakened a new popular recognition of the claims of the etcher, and of Mr. Joseph Pennell, who fought with sustained vigour for the dignity and importance of illustration, have helped to inspire outsiders with a new respect. For it is only outsiders who ever thought of making absurd distinctions between high art and minor arts. If the thing, be it what it may, is good—as good as it could be—at no age did it fail to win the regard of artists; even if it had to wait a few generations to charm the purchaser, or awaken the cupidity of the connoisseur. It is a healthy sign to find that people to-day are interesting themselves in the books of the sixties ; it should make them more eager for original contemporary work, and foster a dislike to the inevitable photograph from nature reproduced by half-tone, which one feared would have satisfied their love for black-and-white to the exclusion of all else.

If, after an evening spent in looking over the old magazines which form the subject of the next few chapters, you can turn to the current weeklies and monthlies, and feel absolutely certain that we are better than our fathers, it augurs either a very wisely selected purchase from the crowded bookstall, which, at each railway station as the first of the month approaches, has its hundreds of rival magazines, or else that it would be wiser to spend still more time over the old periodicals until a certain 'divine dissatisfaction' was aroused towards the average illustrated periodical of to-day.

Not that we are unable to show as good work perhaps, man for man, as they offer. We have no Sandys, no Millais, no Boyd Houghton, it is true; they had no E. A. Abbey, no Phil May, no . . ., but it would be a delicate matter to continue a list of living masters here. But if you can find an English periodical with as many first-rate pictures as *Once a Week, The Cornhill Magazine, Good Words*, and others contained in the early sixties, you will be . . . well . . . lucky is perhaps the most polite word.

That the cheapness and rapidity of 'reproduction by process' should be directly responsible for the birth of many new illustrated periodicals to-day is clear enough. But it is surprising to find that a movement, which relatively speaking was almost as fecund, had begun some years before photography had ousted the engraver. Why it sprang into existence is not quite so obvious; but if we assume, as facts indicate, that the system of producing wood-engravings underwent a radical change about this time, we shall find that again a more ample supply provoked a larger demand. Hitherto, the engraver had only accepted as many blocks as he could engrave himself, with the help of a few assistants ; but not very long before the date we are considering factories for the supply of wood-engravings had grown up. The

THE ILLUSTRATED PERIODICALS

heads of these, practical engravers and in some cases artists of. more than average ability, took all the responsibility for the work intrusted to them, and maintained a singularly high standard of excellence ; but they did not pretend that they engraved each block themselves.   Such a system not merely permitted commissions for a large quantity of blocks being accepted, but greatly increased speed in their production.

There can be little doubt that something of the sort took place ; it will suffice to name but two firms, Messrs. Dalziel and Messrs. Swain, who were each responsible often enough, not merely for all the engravings in a book, but often for all the engravings in a popular magazine.   Under the old system, the publisher had thrown upon him the trouble of discovering the right engraver to employ, and the burden of reconciling the intention of the artist with the product of the engraver.   This, by itself, would have been enough to make him very cautious before committing himself to the establish-ment of an illustrated magazine.   But if we also remember that, under such conditions, almost unlimited time would be required for the production of the engravings, and that, to ensure a sufficient quantity being ready for each issue, a very large number of independent engravers must needs have been employed, it is clear that the old conditions would not have been equal to the task.

When, however, the publisher or editor was able to send all his drawings to a reputable firm who could undertake to deliver the engravings by a given time, one factor of great practical importance had been established.   It is not surpris-ing to find that things went even further than this, and that the new firms of engravers not only undertook the whole of the blocks, but in several cases supplied the drawings also.

Without claiming that such a system is the best, it is but fair to own that to it we are indebted for the masterpieces of the sixties.   No doubt the ideal art-editor — a perfectly equipped critic, with the blank cheque of a millionaire at his back—might have done better ; but to-day there are many who think themselves perfectly equipped critics, and perhaps some here and there who are backed by millionaires, yet on neither side of the Atlantic can we find better work than was pro-duced under the system in vogue in the sixties.   But after all, it is not the system, then or now, that is praiseworthy, but

12

the individual efforts of men whose hearts were in their professions.

The more you inquire into the practice of the best engravers then and now, the more you find that ultimately one person is responsible for the good. In the sixties the engraver saw new possibilities, and did his utmost to realise them; full of enthusiasm, and a master of his craft, he inspired those who worked with him to experiment and spare no effort. That he did marvels may be conceded; and to declare that the merely mechanical processes to-day have already distanced his most ambitious efforts in many qualities does not detract from his share. But in this chapter he is regarded less as a craftsman than as a middleman, an art-editor in effect if not in name; one who taught the artists with whom he was brought in contact the limits of the material in which their work was to be translated, and in turn learned from them no little that was of vital importance. Above all, he seems to have kept closely in touch with draughtsmen and engravers alike; one might believe that every drawing passed through his hands, and that every block was submitted to him many times during its progress. When you realise the mass of work signed 'Dalziels' or 'Swain,' it is evident that its high standard of excellence must not be attributed to any system, but to the personal supervision of the acting members of the firms—men who were, every one of them, both draughtsmen and engravers, who knew not only the effect the artist aimed to secure, but the best method of handicraft by which to obtain it.

If, after acknowledging this, one cannot but regret that the photographic transfer of drawings to wood had not come into general use twenty years before it did, so that the master-pieces of the Rossetti designs to Tennyson's *Poems* and a hundred others had not been cut to pieces by the engraver; yet at the same time we must remember that, but for the enterprise of the engraver, the drawings themselves would in all probability never have been called into existence in many cases. This is especially true of the famous volumes which Messrs. Dalziel issued under the imprint of various publishers, who were really merely agents for their dis-tribution.

The Penny Magazine in 1832, and other of Charles

THE ILLUSTRATED PERIODICALS

Knight's publications, *Sharp's Magazine, The People's Journal, Howitt's Journal of Literature, The Illustrated Family Journal, The Mirror, The Parterre, The Casket, The Olio, The Saturday Magazine, Pinnock's Guide to Knowledge, Punch, The Illustrated London News*, had led the way for pictorial weekly papers, even as the old Annuals and the various novels by Ainsworth, Dickens, and Thackeray had prepared the way for magazines ; but the artistic movement of the 'sixties,' so far as its periodicals are concerned, need be traced back no further than *Once a Week*. Perhaps, however, it would be unfair to forget the influence of *The Art Journal* (at first called *The Art Union*), which, started in 1851, brought fine art to the homes of the great British public through the medium of wood-engravings in a way not attempted previously ; and certainly we must not ignore John Cassell, who, on the demise of *Howitt's Journal* and *The People's Journal* in 1850, brought out an illustrated chronicle of the Great Exhibition, which was afterwards merged in a *Magazine of Art*. As *The Strand Magazine* — the first monthly periodical to exploit freely the Kodak and the half-tone block—started a whole school of imitators, so *Once a Week*, depending chiefly on drawings by the best men of the day, engraved by the foremost engravers, was followed quickly by the *Cornhill Magazine, Good Words*, and the rest. Many of these were short-lived ; nor, looking at them impartially to-day, are we quite sure that the survivors were always the fittest. Certainly they were not always the best. But the number of new ventures that saw the light about this time can scarce be named here. Then, as now, a vast army of quite second-rate draughtsmen were available, and a number of periodicals, which it were gross flattery to call second-rate, sprang up to utilise their talents. Besides these, many weekly and monthly publications, ostensibly devoted to catering for the taste of the masses, gained large audiences and employed talented artists, but demand no more serious consideration as art, than do the 'snippet' weeklies of to-day as literature. But some of these popular serials—such as *The Band of Hope, The British Workman, The London Journal, The London Reader, Bow Bells, Every Week*, and the rest—are not, relatively speaking, worse than more pretentious publications. It is weary work to estimate the

14

place of the second and third bests, and whatever interest the subject possesses would be exhausted quickly if we tried to catalogue or describe the less important items. Yet, to be quite just, several of these, notably the cheap publications of Messrs. Cassell, Petter, and Galpin, Messrs. S. W. Partridge and Co., and many others, employed artists by no means second-rate and gave better artistic value for their money than many of their successors do at present.

It is well to face the plain fact, and own that at no time has the supply of really creative artists equalled the popular demand. Not all the painters of any period are even passable, nor all the illustrators. Much that is produced for the moment fulfils its purpose admirably enough, although it dies as soon as it is born. Nature shows us the prodigal fecundity of generation compared with the few that ripen to maturity. The danger lies rather in appreciating too much, whether of 'the sixties' or 'the nineties'; yet, if one is stoical enough to praise only the best, it demands not merely great critical acumen, but no little hardness of heart. The intention always pleads to be recognised. We know that accidents, quite beyond the artist's power to prevent, may have marred his work. Each man, feeling his own impotence to express his ideas lucidly, must needs be lenient to those who also stammer and fail to interpret their imaginings clearly and with irresistible power. Yet, although the men of the sixties survive in greatly reduced numbers and one might speak plainly of much of its trivial commonplace without hurting anybody's feelings, there is no need to drag the rubbish to light.

CHAPTER III : SOME ILLUSTRATED MAGAZINES OF THE SIXTIES. I. 'ONCE A WEEK'

NCE A WEEK.—On the second of July 1859 appeared the first number of *Once a Week*, 'an illustrated miscellany of Literature, Art, Science, and Popular Information.' Despite the choice of an extraordinary time of year, as we should now consider it, to float a new venture, the result proved fortunate. Not merely does the first series of this notable magazine deserve recognition as the pioneer of its class; its superiority is no less provable than its priority. The earliest attempt to provide a magazine with original illustrations by the chief artists of its time was not merely a bold and well-considered experiment but, as the thirteen volumes of its first series show, an instant and admirably sustained triumph. No other thirteen volumes of an English magazine, at any period, contain so much first-class work. The invention and knowledge, the mastery of the methods employed, and the superb achievements of some of its contributors entitle it to be ranked as one of the few artistic enterprises of which England may be justly proud.

When the connection of Dickens with his old publishers was severed, and *All the Year Round* issued from its own office, Messrs. Bradbury and Evans projected a rival paper that was in no sense an imitation of the former. The reasons for its success lie on the surface. Started by the proprietors of *Punch*, with the co-operation of an artistic staff that has been singularly fortunate in enlisting always the services of the best men of their day, it is obvious that few periodicals have ever been launched under happier auspices. Its aim was obviously to do for fiction, light literature, and *belles-lettres*, what *Punch* had accomplished so admirably for satire and caricature. At that time, with no rivals worth consideration, a fixed intention to obtain for a new magazine the active co-operation of the best men of all schools was within the bounds of possibility. To-day a millionaire with a blank cheque-book could not even hope to succeed in such a project. He would find many first-rate artists, whom no amount of money would attract, and others with connections that would be imperilled

16

ONCE A WEEK

if they contributed to a rival enterprise. There are many who prefer the safety of an established periodical to the risk which must needs attend any 'up-to-date' venture. Now *Once a Week* was not merely 'up-to-date' in its period, but far ahead of the popular taste. As we cannot rival it to-day in its own line, even the most ardent defender of the present at the expense of the past must own that the improvement in process-engraving and the increased truth of facsimile reproductions it offers have not inspired draughts-men to higher efforts. Why so excellent a magazine is not flourishing to-day is a mystery. It would seem as if the public, faithful as they are to non-illustrated periodicals, are fickle where pictures are concerned. But the memory of the third series of *Once a Week* relieves the public of the responsibility; changes in the direction and aim of the periodical were made, and all for the worse; so that it lost its high position and no more interested the artist. *Punch*, its sponsor, seems to have the secret of eternal youth, possibly because its original programme is still consistently maintained.

In another feature it resembled *Punch* more than any previous periodical. In *The London Charivari* many of the pictures have always been inserted quite independently of the text. Some have a title, and some a brief scrap of dialogue to explain their story; but the picture is not there to elucidate the anecdote, so much as the title, or fragment of conversation, helps to elucidate the picture. Unless an engraving be from a painting, or a topographical view, the rule in English magazines then, as now, is that it must illustrate the text. This is not the place to record an appreciation of the thorough and consistent way in which the older illustrators set about the work of reiterating the obvious incident, depicting for all eyes to see what the author had suggested in his text already, for it is evident that a design untrammelled by any fixed programme ought to allow the artist more play for his fancy. Nevertheless, the less frequent illustrations to its serial fiction are well up to the level of those practically independent of the text. In *Once a Week* there are dozens of pictures which are evidently purely the invention of the draughtsman. That a modest little poem, written to order usually, satisfies the conventions of established precedent, need not be taken as evidence that traverses the argument. *Once a*

17

Week ranked its illustrators as important as its authors, which is clearly an ideal method for an illustrated periodical to observe. To write up to pictures has often been attempted ; were not *The Pickwick Papers* begun in this way? But the author soon reversed the situation, and once more put the artist in a subordinate place. It is curious to observe that readers of light literature had been satisfied previously with a very conventional type of illustration. For, granting all sorts of qualities to those pictures by Cruikshank, 'Phiz,' and Thackeray, which illustrated the Dickens, Ainsworth, Lever, and Thackeray novels, you can hardly refer the source of their inspiration to nature, however remotely. Their purpose seems to have been caricature rather than character-drawing, sentimentality in place of sentiment, melodrama in lieu of mystery, broad farce instead of humour. These aims were accomplished in masterly fashion, perhaps ; but is there a single illustration by Cruikshank, 'Phiz,' Thackeray, or even John Leech, which tempts us to linger and return again and again purely for its art? Its 'drawing' is often slipshod, and never infused by the perception of physical beauty that the Greeks embodied as their ideal, that ideal which the illustrators of *Once a Week*, especially Walker, revived soon after this date. Nor are they inspired by the symbolists' regard for nature, which attracted the 'primitives' of the Middle Ages, and their legitimate followers the pre-Raphaelites. Indeed, as you study the so-called 'immortal' designs which illustrate the early Victorian novels, you feel that if many of the artists were once considered to be as great as the authors whose ideas they interpreted, time has wreaked revenge at last. If a boy happens to read for the first time Thackeray's *Vanity Fair* with its original illustrations, the humour and pathos of the masterpiece lose half their power when the ridiculously feeble drawings confront him throughout the book. This is not the case with Millais' illustrations to Trollope, or those by Fred Walker to Thackeray. The costume may appear grotesque, but the men and women are vital, and as real in the picture as in the literature.

Lacking the virility of Hogarth, or the coarse animal vigour of Rowlandson, these caricaturists kept one eye on the fashion-book and one on the grotesque. It was 'cumeelfo' to depict the English maiden a colourless vapid

nonentity, to make the villain look villainous, and the benevo-
lent middle-aged person imbecile. Accidental deformities
and vulgar personal defects were deemed worthy themes for
laughter. The fat boy in *Pickwick*, the fat Joe Sedley
in *Vanity Fair*, the *Marchioness and Dick Swiveller*, the
Quilps' Tea-Party, and the rest, all belong to the order of
humour that survives to-day in the 'knockabout artists,' or
the 'sketch' performances at second-rate music-halls. Even
the much-belauded *Fagin in the Condemned Cell* appears a
trite and ineffective bit of low melodrama to-day. We know
the oft-repeated story of the artist's despondency, his failure
to realise an attitude to express Fagin's despair, and how as
he caught sight of his own face in the glass he saw that he
himself, a draughtsman troubled by a subject, was the very
model for one about to be hanged. All the personality
of anecdote and the sentimental log-rolling which gathered
round the pictures, that by chance were associated with a
series of masterpieces in fiction, no longer fascinate us. We
recognise the power of the writers, but wish in our hearts
that they had never been 'illustrated,' or if so, that they had
enjoyed the good fortune which belongs to the novelists of
the sixties. But to refuse to endorse the verdict of earlier
critics does not imply that there was no merit in these designs,
but merely that their illustrators must be classed for the most
part (Leech least of all) with the exaggerators—those who
aimed at the grotesque—with Gilray or Baxter, the creator of
Ally Sloper, and not with true satirists like Hogarth or Charles
Keene, who worked in ways that are pre-eminently masterly,
even if you disregard the humorous element in their designs.

Without forcing the theory too far, it may be admitted
that the idea of *Once a Week* owes more to these serial
novels than to any previous enterprise. Be that as it may,
the plan of the magazine, as we find in a postscript (to vol. i.),
was at once 'ratified by popular acceptance.' Further, its
publishers admit that its circulation was adequate and its
commercial success established, after only thirty-six numbers
had appeared. It is no new thing for the early numbers of
magazines and papers to contain glowing accounts of their
phenomenal circulation ; but, in this case, there can be no
doubt that the self-congratulation is both well deserved and
genuine. To *Once a Week* may be accorded the merit of

initiating a new type of periodical which has survived with trifling changes until to-day. Its recognition of 'fiction' and 'pictures,' as the chief items in its programme, has been followed by a hundred others; but the editing, which made it readable as well as artistic, is a secret that many of its imitators failed to understand. Although *A Good Fight* (afterwards rewritten and entitled *The Cloister and the Hearth*) is the only novel within its pages that has since assumed classic rank, yet the average of its art—good as it was—is not as far above the standard of its literature, as the illustrations of its predecessors fell below the text they professed to adorn.

In sketching the life-history of other illustrated magazines it seemed best to follow a chronological order, because the progress of the art of illustration is reflected more or less faithfully in the advance and retrogression they show. But the thirteen volumes which complete the first series of *Once a Week* may be considered better in a different way. For to-day it is prized almost entirely for its pictures, and they were contributed for the most part by the same artists year after year. While in other periodicals you find, with every new volume, a fresh relay of artists, *Once a Week*, during its palmy days, was supported by the same brilliant group of draughtsmen, who admitted very few recruits, and only those whose great early promise was followed almost directly by ample fulfilment.

The very first illustration is a vignette by John Leech to a rhymed programme of the magazine by Shirley Brooks. But Leech, who died in 1864, cannot be regarded as a typical illustrator of 'the sixties'—not so much because his work extended only a few years into that decade, as that he belonged emphatically to the earlier school, and represented all that is *not* characteristic of the period with which this book is concerned.

It is unnecessary to belittle his art for the sake of glorifying those who succeeded him in popularity. That he obtained a strong hold upon English taste, lettered and unlettered, is undeniable. It has become part and parcel of that English life, especially of the insular middle-class, whose ideal permitted it to regard the exhibition building of 1851 not as a big conservatory, but as a new and better Parthenon, and to believe honestly enough that the millennium of universal peace with art, no less than morals, perfected to the '*n*th' degree (on purely British lines), was dawning upon

20

humanity. That the efforts of 1851 made much possible to-day which else had been impossible may be granted.

The grace and truth of John Leech's designs may be recognised despite their technical insufficiency, but at the same time we may own that, in common with Cruikshank and the rest, he has received infinitely more appreciation than his artistic achievement merited, and leave his share unconsidered here, although no doubt it was a big commercial factor in the success. To vol. i. of *Once a Week* he contributed no less than thirty-two designs, to vol. ii. forty-six, to vol. iii. seven, to vol. iv. one, and to vol. v. four.

John Tenniel, although he began to work much earlier, and is still an active contemporary, may be considered as belonging especially to the sixties, wherein he represents the survival of an academic type in sharply accentuated distinction to the pre-Raphaelism of one group or to the romantic naturalism of a still larger section. On page 4 of vol. i. we find his first drawing, a vignette, and page 5 a design, *Audun and the White Bear*, no less typically 'a Tenniel' in every particular than is the current cartoon in *Punch*. Those on pages 21, 30, 60, 90, 101, 103, and 170 are all relatively unimportant. *The King of Thule* (p. 250) is an illustration to Sir Theodore Martin's familiar translation of Goethe's poems. Others are on pp. 285, 435, 446. To vol. ii. he is a less frequent contributor. The designs, pp. 39, 98, 99, and 103 call for no comment. The one on p. 444 (not p. 404 as the index has it), to Tom Taylor's ballad *Noménoë*, is reprinted in *Songs and Ballads of Brittany* (Macmillan, 1865). In vol. iii. there is one (p. 52) of small value. On pp. 533, 561, 589, 617, 645, 673, and 701 are pictures to Shirley Brooks's *The Silver Cord*, showing the artist in his less familiar aspect as an illustrator of fiction. The one on p. 589 is irresistibly like a 'Wonderland' picture, while that on p. 225 (vol. iv.) suggests a *Punch* cartoon ; but, on the whole, they are curiously free from undue mannerism in the types they depict. In vol. iv. are more illustrations to *The Silver Cord* (pp. 1, 29, 57, 85, 113, 141, 169, 197, 225, 253, 281, 309, 337, 365, 393, 421, 449, 477, 505, 533, 561, 589, 617, 645, 673, and 701), and illustrations to Owen Meredith's poem, *Fair Rosamund* (pp. 294, 295). In volume v. *The Silver Cord* is continued with ten more designs (pp. 1, 29, 57, 85,

SOME ILLUSTRATED MAGAZINES

113, 141, 169, 197, 225, 253), and there is one to *Mark Bozzari* (p. 659), translated from Müller by Sir Theodore Martin.

In volume vi. Tenniel appears but four times : *At Crutchley Prior* (p. 267), *The Fairies* (p. 379), a very delicate fancy, *Prince Lulu* (p. 490), and *Made to Order* (p. 575). From the seventh and eighth volumes he is absent, and reappears in the ninth with only one drawing, *Clytè* (p. 154), and in the tenth (Dec. 1863-June 1864) with one, *Bacchus and the Water Thieves* (p. 658). Nor does he appear again in this magazine until 1867, with *Lord Aythan*, the frontispiece to vol. iii. of the New Series. Sir John Tenniel, however, more than any other of the *Punch* staff, seems never thoroughly at home outside its pages. The very idea of a Tenniel drawing has become a synonym for a political cartoon; so that now you cannot avoid feeling that all his illustrations to poetry, fiction, and fairy-tale must have some satirical motive underlying their apparent purpose.

It is difficult to record Sir John Everett Millais' contributions to this magazine with level unbiassed comments. Notwithstanding the palpable loss they suffered by translation under the hands of even the most skilful of his engravers, the impressions belong to a higher plane than is reached by their neighbours save in a very few instances. The Millais wood-engravings deserve a deliberately ordered monograph as fully as do the etchings by Rembrandt and Whistler, or Hokousaï's prints. It is true that not quite all his many illustrations to contemporary literature are as good as the best works of the great artist just named ; but if you search through the portfolios of the past for that purpose, you will find that even the old masters were not always adding to a cycle of masterpieces. The astounding fact remains that Sir John Millais, dealing with the hair-net and the Dundreary whiskers, the crinoline and peg-top trousers, imparted such dignity to his men and women that even now they carry their grotesque costumes with distinction, and fail to appear old-fashioned, but at most as masqueraders in fancy dress. For in Millais' work you are face to face with actual human beings, superbly drawn and fulfilling all artistic requirements. They possess the immense individuality of a Velasquez portrait, which, as a human being, appeals to you no less surely, than its handling arouses your æsthetic appreciation. At this period it seems as if the

J. E. MILLAIS

GRANDMOTHER'S
APOLOGY

THE PLAGUE OF
ELLIANT

artist was overflowing with power and mastery—everything he touched sprang into life. Whether he owed much or little to his predecessors is unimportant—take away all, and still a giant remains. It is so easy to accept the early drawings of Millais as perfect of their kind, beyond praise or blame, and yet to fail to realise that they possess the true vitality of those few classics which are for all time. The term monumental must not be applied to them, for it suggests something dead in fact, although living in sentiment and admired by reason of conventional precedent. The Millais drawings have still the power to excite an artist as keenly as a great Rembrandt etching that he sees for the first time, or an early Whistler that turns up unexpectedly in a loan collection, or an unknown Utamaro colour print. The mood they provoke is almost deprived of critical analysis by the overwhelming sense of fulfilment which is forced on your notice. In place of gratified appreciation you feel appalled that one man should have done over and over again, so easily and with such certainty, what dozens of his fellows, accomplished and masterly in their way, tried with by no means uniform success. If every canvas by the artist were lost, he might still be proved to belong to the great masters from his illustrations alone ; even if these were available only through the medium of wood-engraving.

The first volume of *Once a Week* contains, as Millais' first contribution, *Magenta* (p. 10), a study of a girl who has just read a paper with news of the great battle that gave its name to the terrible colour which typifies the period. It is badly printed in the copy at my side, and, although engraved by Dalziels, is not an instance of their best work. In *Grandmother's Apology* (p. 41) we have a most delightful illustration to Tennyson, reproduced in his collected volume, but not elsewhere. *On the Water* (p. 70) and *La Fille bien gardée* (p. 306) may be passed without comment. But *The Plague of Elliant* (p. 316), a powerful drawing of a woman dragging a cart wherein are the bodies of her nine dead children, has been selected, more than once, as a typical example of the illustrator at his best. *Maude Clare* (p. 382), *A Lost Love* (p. 482), and *St. Bartholomew* (p. 514), complete the Millais' in vol. i.

In the second volume we find *The Crown of Love* (p. 10), a poem by George Meredith. This was afterwards painted and exhibited under the same title in the Royal Academy

SOME ILLUSTRATED MAGAZINES

of 1875. *A Wife* (p. 32), *The Head of Bran* (p. 132), *Practising* (p. 242), (a girl at a piano), and *Musa* (p. 598), complete the list of the five in this volume. In vol. iii. there are seven : *Master Olaf* (p. 63), *Violet* (p. 140), *Dark Gordon's Bride* (p. 238), *The Meeting* (p. 276), *The Iceberg* (pp. 407, 435), and *A Head of Hair for Sale* (p. 519). In vol. iv. but two appear, *Iphis and Anaxarete* (p. 98) and *Thorr's Hunt for the Hammer* (p. 126), both slighter in execution than most of the *Once a Week* Millais'.

Volume v. also contains but two, *Tannhäuser* (p. 211) and *Swing Song* (p. 434), a small boy in a Spanish turban swinging. Volume vi. houses a dozen : *Schwerting of Saxony* (p. 43), *The Battle of the Thirty* (p. 155), *The Child of Care* (pp. 2, 39), five designs for Miss Martineau's *Sister Anne's Probation* (pp. 309, 337, 365, 393, 421), *Sir Tristem* (p. 350), *The Crusader's Wife* (p. 546), *The Chase of the Siren* (p. 630), and *The Drowning of Kaer-is* (p. 687). The seventh volume contains eleven examples by this artist : *Margaret Wilson* (p. 42), five to Miss Martineau's *Anglers of the Don* (pp. 85, 113, 141, 169, 197), *Maid Avoraine* (p. 98), *The Mite of Dorcas* (p. 224), (which is the subject of the Academy picture, *The Widow's Mite* of 1876 ; although in the painting the widow turns her back on the spectator), *The Parting of Ulysses* (p. 658), *The Spirit of the Vanished Island* (p. 546), and *Limerick Bells* (p. 710), a design of which a eulogist of the artist says : 'the old monk might be expanded as he stands into a full-sized picture.'

In the eighth volume *Endymion on Latmos* (p. 42), a charming study of the sleeping shepherd, is the only independent picture ; the other nine are by way of illustration to Miss Martineau's *The Hampdens* (pp. 211, 239, 267, 281, 309, 337, 365, 393, 421, 449). These are delightful examples of the use of costume by a great master. Neither pedantically correct, nor too lax, they revivify the period so that the actors are more important than the accessories.

The ninth volume, like the eighth, has only one picture by Millais not illustrating its serial. This is *Hacho the Dwarf* (p. 504). The others represent scenes in Miss Martineau's *Sir Christopher* (pp. 491, 519, 547, 575, 603, 631, 659, 687), a seventeenth-century story. The illustrators of to-day should study these and other pictures where the artist

24

TANNHÄUSER

J. E. MILLAIS

SISTER ANNE'S
PROBATION

THE HAMPDENS

J. E. MILLAIS

DEATH DEALING
ARROWS

was hampered by the story, and imitate his loyal purpose to
expound and amplify the text, accomplishing it the while with
most admirably dramatic composition and strong character-
drawing. In the remaining volume of the first series there
are no other examples by Millais ; nor, with the exceptions
Death Dealing Arrows (Jan. 25, 1868, p. 79), one in the
Christmas Number for 1860, and *Taking his Ease*, 1868
(p. 65), does he appear as a contributor to the magazine. It
must not be forgotten that high prices are often responsible for
the desire, or rather the necessity, of using second-rate work.
When an artist attains a position that monopolises all his
working hours, it is obvious that he cannot afford to accept
even the highest current rate of payment for magazine illustration ; nor, on the other hand, can an editor, who conducts
what is after all a commercial enterprise, afford to pay enormous sums for its illustrations. For later drawings this artist
was paid at least five times as much as for his earlier efforts,
and possibly in some cases ten or twelve times as much.

Charles Keene, the great illustrator so little appreciated
by his contemporaries, whose fame is still growing daily, was
a frequent contributor to *Once a Week* for many years. Starting with volume i. he depicted, in quasi-mediæval fashion,
Charles Reade's famous *Cloister and the Hearth*, then called,
in its first and shorter form, *A Good Fight* (pp. 11, 31, 51,
71, 91, 111, 131, 151, 171, 191, 211, 231, 251, 254, 273).
Coincidently he illustrated also *Guests at the Red Lion* (pp.
61, 65), *A Fatal Gift* (p. 141), *Uncle Simkinson* (pp. 201,
203), *Gentleman in the Plum-coloured Coat* (p. 270), *Benjamin
Harris* (pp. 427, 449, 471), *My Picture Gallery* (p. 483), and
A Merry Christmas (p. 544). In volume ii. there are only
five illustrations by him (pp. 1, 5, 54, 111, and 451) to shorter
tales ; but to George Meredith's *Evan Harrington*, running
through this volume and the next, he contributes thirty-nine
drawings, some of them in his happiest vein, all showing
strongly and firmly marked types of character-drawing, in
which he excelled. Volume iii. contains also, on pages 20, 426,
608, 687, and 712, less important works : *The Emigrant
Artist* on p. 608 is a return to the German manner which distinguished the *Good Fight*. The drawings for *Sam Bentley's
Christmas* commence here in (pp. 687, 712), and are continued
(pp. 19, 45, 155, 158) in vol. iv., where we also find *In re*

SOME ILLUSTRATED MAGAZINES

Mr. Brown (pp. 330, 332), *The Beggar's Soliloquy* (p. 378), *A Model Strike* (p. 466), *The Two Norse Kings* (pp. 519, 547), and *The Revenue Officer's Story* (p. 713). In volume v. are: *The Painter Alchemist* (p. 43), *Business with Bokes* (p. 251), *William's Perplexities* (pp. 281, 309, 337, 365, 393), also a romantic subject, *Adalieta* (p. 266) : a poem by Edwin Arnold, and *The Patriot Engineer* (p. 686). To the sixth volume, the illustrations for *The Woman I Loved and The Woman who loved me* (pp. 85, 113, 141, 169, 197, 225, 253, 281) are by Keene, as are also those to *My Schoolfellow Friend* (p. 334), *A Legend of Carlisle* (p. 407), a curiously Germanic *Page from the History of Kleinundengreich* (p. 531), *Nip's Daimon* (p. 603), and *A Mysterious Supper-Party* (659). In vol. vii. and vol. viii. *Verner's Pride*, by Mrs. Henry Wood, supplies motives for seventeen pictures. In vol. viii. *The March of Arthur* (p. 434), *The Bay of the Dead* (p. 546), and *My Brother's Story* (p. 617). In vol. ix. *The Viking's Serf* (p. 42), *The Station-master* (pp. 1, 69), and *The Heirloom* (pp. 435, 463) complete Charles Keene's share in the illustration of the thirteen volumes of the first series.

Fred Walker is often supposed to have made his first appearance as an illustrator in *Once a Week*, vol. ii. with *Peasant Proprietorship* (p. 165) ; and, although an exception of earlier date may be discovered, it is only in an obscure paper (of which the British Museum apparently has no copy) barely a month before. For practical purposes, therefore, *Once a Week* may be credited with being the first-established periodical to commission a young artist whose influence upon the art of the sixties was great. This drawing was quickly followed by *God help our Men at Sea* (p. 198), *An honest Arab* (p. 262), *Après* (p. 330), *Lost in the Fog* (p. 370), *Spirit Painting* (p. 424), and *Tenants at No. 27* (p. 481), and *The Lake at Yssbrooke* (p. 538). Looking closely at these, in two or three only can you discover indications of the future creator of *Philip*. Those on pages 424 and 481 are obviously the work of the Fred Walker as we know him now. But those on pp. 165, 198, 330, and 538 would pass unnoticed in any magazine of the period, except that the full signature ' F. Walker ' arouses one's curiosity, and almost suggests, like Lewis Carroll's re-attribution of the *Iliad*, ' another man of the same name.'

In vol. iii. a poem, *Once upon a Time*, by Eliza Cook, has

CHARLES KEENE

'A GOOD FIGHT'

two illustrations (pp. 24, 25), which, tentative as they are, and not faultless in drawing, foreshadow the grace of his later work. In *Markham's Revenge* (pp. 182-184) the artist is himself, as also in *Wanted a Diamond Ring* (p. 210). *A Noctuary of Terror* (pp. 294, 295), *First Love* (p. 322), *The Unconscious Bodyguard* (p. 359), are unimportant. *The Herberts of Elfdale* (pp. 449, 454, 477, 505, 508), possibly the first serial Walker illustrated, is infinitely better. *Black Venn* (p. 583), *A Young Wife's Song* (p. 668), and *Putting up the Christmas*, a drawing group, complete the examples by this artist in vol. iii. Volume iv. contains: *Under the Fir-trees* (p. 43), *Voltaire at Ferney* (p. 66), a very poor thing, *The Fan* (p. 75), *Bring me a light* (pp. 102-105), *The Parish Clerk's Story* (p. 248), *The Magnolia* (pp. 263, 267), *Dangerous* (p. 416), *An Old Boy's Tale* (p. 499), *Romance of the Cab-rank* (p. 585), and *The Jewel Case* (p. 631). In vol. v. we find *Jessie Cameron's Bairn* (p. 15), *The Deserted Diggings* (p. 83), *Pray, sir, are you a Gentleman?* (pp. 127, 133), *A Run for Life* (p. 306), *Cader Idris* (p. 323), and a series of illustrations to *The Settlers of Long Arrow: a Canadian Story* (pp. 421, 449, 477, 505, 533, 561, 589, 617, 645, 673, and 701). To volume vi. Walker contributes *Patty* (pp. 126, 127), *A Dreadful Ghost* (p. 211), and nine to Dutton Cook's *The Prodigal Son* (pp. 449, 477, 505, 533, 561, 589, 617, 673, 701), which story, running into volume vii., has further illustrations on pp. 1, 29, and 57. *The Deadly Affinity* (pp. 421, 449, 477), and *Spirit-rapping Extraordinary* (p. 614) are the only others by the artist in this volume. The eighth volume has but one, *After Ten Years* (p. 378), and *The Ghost in the Green Park* (p. 309) is the only one in volume ix., and his last in the first series. Vol. i. of the New Series has the famous *Vagrants* (p. 112) for one of its special art supplements.

Amid contemporary notices you often find the work of M. J. Lawless placed on the same level as that of Millais or Sandys; but, while few of the men of the period have less deservedly dropped out of notice, one feels that to repeat such an estimate were to do an injustice to a very charming draughtsman. For the sake of his future reputation it is wiser not to attempt to rank him with the greatest; but in the second order he may be fitly placed. For fancy and feeling, no less

27

than for his loyal adherence to the Dürer line, at a time it found little favour, Lawless deserves to be more studied by the younger artists of to-day. A great number of decorative designers are too fond of repeating certain mannerisms, and among others, Lawless in England and Howard Pyle in America, two men inspired by similar purpose, should receive more attention than they have done. *Once a Week* contains the largest number of his drawings. In vol. i., to *Sentiment from the Shambles*, there are three illustrations attributed to him. Those on pp. 505 and 509 are undoubtedly by Lawless, but that on p. 507 is so unlike his method, and indeed so unimportant, that it matters not whether the index be true or in error.

In vol. ii. are ten examples, two on the same page to *The Bridal of Galtrim* (p. 88), *The Lay of the Lady and the Hound* (p. 164), a very pre-Raphaelite composition, *Florinda* (p. 220), (more influenced by the later Millais), *Only for something to say* (p. 352), a study of fashionable society, which (as Mr. Walter Crane's attempts show) does not lend itself to the convention of the thick line, *The Head Master's Sister* (pp. 386, 389, 393), *The Secret* (p. 430), and *A Legend of Swaffham* (p. 549). In vol. iii. *Oysters and Pearls* (p. 79) is attributed to Lawless, but one hopes wrongly; *The Betrayed* (p. 155), *Elfie Meadows* (p. 304), *The Minstrel's Curse* (p. 351), *The Two Beauties* (unsigned and not quite obviously a Lawless) (p. 462), and *My Angel's Visit* (p. 658) are the titles of the rest. In the fourth volume there are: *The Death of Œnone* (pp. 14, 15), *Valentine's Day* (p. 208), *Effie Gordon* (pp. 406, 407), and *The Cavalier's Escape* (687), all much more typical. In vol. v. we find *High Elms* (p. 420), *Twilight* (p. 532), *King Dyring* (p. 575), and *Fleurette* (p. 700). In the sixth volume there are only three: *Dr. Johnson's Penance* (one of the best drawings of the author), (p. 14), *What befel me at the Assizes* (p. 194), and *The Dead Bride* (p. 462). In the seventh volume there is one only to a story by A. C. Swinburne, *Dead Love* (p. 434). Despite the name of Jacques d'Aspremont on the coffin, the picture is used to a poem with quite a different theme, *The White Witch*, in Thornbury's *Legendary Ballads*, which contains no less than twenty of Lawless's *Once a Week* designs. In vol. viii. are two, *The Linden Trees* (p. 644) and *Gifts* (p. 712). In vol. ix. three only: *Faint heart never won fair lady* (p. 98),

EFFIE GORDON

DR. JOHNSON'S PENANCE

JOHN OF PADUA

ONCE A WEEK
Heinrich Frauenlob (p. 393), and *Broken Toys* (p. 672). In vol. x. appears the last of Lawless's contributions, and, as some think, his finest, *John of Padua* (p. 71).

The first work by Frederick Sandys in *Once a Week* will be found in vol. iv. : it is not, as the index tells you, *The Dying Hero*, on page 71, which is wrongly attributed to him; *Yet once more on the Organ play* (p. 350) is by Sandys, as is also *The Sailor's Bride* (p. 434) in the same volume. In vol. v. are three, *From my Window* (p. 238), *The three Statues of Ægina* (p. 491), and *Rosamund, Queen of the Lombards* (p. 631). In vol. vi. we find *The Old Chartist* (p. 183), *The King at the Gate* (p. 322), and *Jacques de Caumont* (p. 614). In vol. vii. *Harold Harfagr* (p. 154), *The Death of King Warwolf* (p. 266), and *The Boy Martyr* (p. 602). Thence, with the exception of *Helen and Cassandra*, published as a separate plate with the issue of April 28, 1866 (p. 454), no more Sandys are to be found.

To *Once a Week* Holman Hunt contributed but three illustrations: *Witches and Witchcraft* (ii. p. 438), *At Night* (iii. p. 102), and *Temujin* (iii. p. 630); yet this very scanty representation is not below the average proportion of the work of this artist in black and white compared with his more fecund contemporaries.

A still more infrequent illustrator, J. M'Neill Whistler, is met with four times in *Once a Week*, and, I believe, but twice elsewhere. Speaking of the glamour shed upon the magazine by its Sandys drawings, it is but just to own that to another school of artists these four 'Whistlers' were responsible for the peculiar veneration with which they regarded an old magazine. The illustrations to *The Major's Daughter* (vi, p. 712), *The Relief Fund in Lancashire* (vii. p. 140), *The morning before the Massacre of St. Bartholomew* (vii. p. 210), and *Count Burckhardt* (vii. p. 378), a nun by a window, are too well known to need comment. That they show the exquisite sense of the value of a line, and have much in common with the artist's etchings of the same period, is evident enough.

G. J. Pinwell first makes his appearance in *Once a Week*, in the eighth volume, with *The Saturnalia* (p. 154), a powerful but entirely untypical illustration of a classical subject by an artist who is best known for pastoral and bucolic scenes, *The Old Man at D. 8* (p. 197), *Seasonable Wooing* (p. 322),

SOME ILLUSTRATED MAGAZINES

A Bad Egg (p. 392), and *A Foggy Story* (p. 477); but only in the latter do you find the curiously personal manner which grew to a mannerism in much of his later work. These, with *Blind* (p. 645) and *Tidings* (p. 700), are all well-thought-out compositions. To volume ix. he contributes *The Strong Heart* (p. 29), *Not a Ripple on the Sea* (p. 57) (a drawing which belies its title), *Laying a Ghost* (p. 85), *The Fisherman of Lake Sunapee* (p. 225), *Waiting for the Tide* (p. 281), *Nutting* (p. 378), and *The Sirens* (p. 616). In volume x. he is represented by *Bracken Hollow* (pp. 57, 85), *The Expiation of Charles V.* (p. 99), *The Blacksmith of Holsby* (pp. 113, 154), *Calypso* (p. 183), *Horace Winston* (p. 211), *Proserpine* (p. 239), *A Stormy Night* (p. 253), *Mistaken Identity* (p. 281), *Hero* (p. 350), *The Vizier's Parrot* (406), *A Pastoral* (p. 490), *A'Beckett's Troth* (p. 574), and *The Stonemason's Yard* (p. 701). The eleventh volume contains only four : *Hettie's Trouble* (p. 26), *Delsthorpe Sands* (p. 586), *The Legend of the Bleeding Cave* (p. 699), and *Rosette* (p. 713); and volume xii. has three : *Followers not allowed* (p. 71), *Homer* (p. 127), and *Dido* (p. 527). The last volume of the first series (1866) has but one, *Achilles* (p. 239). Pinwell's work bulks so largely in the sixties that a bare list of these must suffice; but this period, before he developed the curiously immobile manner of his later years, is perhaps the most interesting.

The index asserts that George Du Maurier is responsible for the pictures in *Once a Week*, vol. iii. pp. 378-379, signed M.B., and as you find others unmistakably Du Maurier's signed with various monograms, its evidence must not be gainsaid ; but neither these nor others, to *My Adventures . . . in Russia* (pp. 553, 557), *The Two Hands* (p. 640), and *The Steady Students* (pp. 691, 695), betray a hint of his well-known style. But *Non Satis* (p. 575) is signed in full, and obviously his, as a glance would reveal. In vol. iv., *Indian Juggling* (p. 41), *The Black Spot* (p. 134), *A Life Story* (p. 165), *In search of Garibaldi* (p. 210), and *The Beggar's Soliloquy* (p. 378, more like a Charles Keene) are from his hand. In the picture here reproduced, *On her Deathbed* (p. 603), the artist has found himself completely, yet *A Portuguese Tragedy* (p. 668) has no trace of his manner. In vol. v. *Recollections of an English Gold Miner* (p. 361), *Monsieur the Governor* (p. 445), *A man who fell among thieves* (p. 463), *Sea-Bathing*

FREDERICK SANDYS

THE THREE STATUES
OF ÆGINA

THE OLD CHARTIST

HAROLD HARFAGR

ROSAMUND, QUEEN
OF THE LOMBARDS

ONCE A WEEK

in France (p. 547), and *The Poisoned Mind,* are his only con-
tributions. In vol. vi. are three illustrations to *The Admiral's
Daughters* (pp. 1, 29, 57), *The Hotel Garden* (p. 24), *The
Change of Heads* (p. 71), *The latest thing in Ghosts* (p. 99),
Metempsychosis (p. 294), *Per l'Amore d'una Donna* (p. 390),
A Parent by Proxy (p. 435), and *Threescore and Ten* (p. 644).
Vol. vii. contains *Miss Simons* (p. 166), *Santa* (pp. 253, 281, 309,
337), *Only* (p. 490), and the *Cannstatt Conspirators* (p. 561).
A Notting Hill Mystery is pictured on pages 617, 645, 673,
and 701 of the seventh volume, and in vol. viii. is continued
on pages 1, 5, 7, 85 ; *Out of the Body* (p. 701), is also here.
Eleanor's Victory is illustrated on pages 295, 351, 407, 463,
519, 575, 631, and 687, and continued in vol. ix on pages
15, 71, 127, 183, 239, 295, 351, 407. Vol. x. contains *The
Veiled Portrait* (p. 225), *The Uninvited* (p. 309), *My Aunt
Tricksy* (p. 393), *The Old Corporal* (p. 462), and *Detur
Digniori* (pp. 505 and 533). In vol. xi. we find two illustrations only by this artist, *Philip Fraser's Fate,* and vols. xii.
and xiii. contain no single example.

A few illustrations by T. Morten appear, and these are
scattered over a wide space. The first, *Swift and the
Mohawks* (iv. p. 323), is to a ballad by Walter Thornbury ;
The Father of the Regiment (v. p. 71), *Wish Not* (x. p. 421),
The Coastguardsman's Tale (x. p. 561), *Late is not Never* (xi.
p. 141), *The Cumæan Sibyl* (xi. p. 603), and *Macdhonuil's
Coronach* (xii. p. 161), make one regret the infrequent appear-
ance of one who could do so well.

Edward J. Poynter (the present director of the National
Gallery) is also sparsely represented : *The Castle by the Sea*
(vi. p. 84), a very pre-Raphaelite decoration to Uhland's
ballad, *Wife and I* (vi. p. 724), *The Broken Vow* (vii.
p. 322), *A Dream of Love* (vii. pp. 365, 393), *A Fellow-
Traveller's Story* (vii. pp. 699, 722), *My Friend's Wedding-
day* (viii. p. 113), *A haunted house in Mexico* (viii. p. 141),
Ducie of the Dale (viii. p. 476), and *A Ballad of the Page to
the King's Daughter* (viii. p. 658), are all the examples by this
artist in *Once a Week.*

Charles Green, of late known almost entirely as a painter,
was a fecund illustrator in the sixties. Beginning with vol. iii.,
in which seven of his works appear (pp. 246, 327, 330, 375,
472, 612, 633), he contributed freely for several years; in vol. iv.

31

SOME ILLUSTRATED MAGAZINES

there are examples on pp. 41, 52, 53, 357, 359, 361, and 529, and on pp. 518, 519 of the fifth volume, and 206 and 255 of the sixth, on pp. 306, 505, 589, and 670 of the seventh. But not until the eighth volume, with *The Wrath of Mistress Elizabeth Gwynne* (p. 169), do we find one that is of any importance. Whether spoilt by the engraver, or immature work, it is impossible to say; but the earlier designs could scarcely be identified except for the index. In the same volume *The Death of Winkelried* (p. 224), *Milly Leslie's Story* (p. 225), *The Countess Gabrielle* (p. 253), *Corporal Pietro Micca* (p. 364), *Damsel John* (p. 490), *My Golden Hill* (p. 505), *Five Days in Prison* (p. 533), *The Queen's Messenger* (p. 561), *The Centurion's Escape* (p. 589), and *The Cry in the Dark* (p. 673), are so curiously unlike the earlier, and so representative of the artist we all know, that if the ' C. Green ' be the same the sudden leap to a matured style is quite remarkable. In volume ix. but three appear: *Paul Garrett* (p. 1), *A Modern Idyll* (p. 322), and *My Affair with the Countess* (p. 337); but in the tenth are nine: *Norman's Visit* (pp. 1, 43), *Legend of the Castle* (p. 14), *A Long Agony* (p. 127), *The Lady of the Grange* (p. 141), *The Gentleman with the Lily* (pp. 169, 197), *The Mermaid* (p. 295), and *T' Runawaa Lass* (p. 630). *The Hunt at Portskewitt* (p. 126) is in vol. xi., the last appearance of the artist I have met with in this magazine.

F. J. Shields, so far as I can trace his drawings, is represented but three times: *An hour with the dead* (iv. p. 491), *The Risen Saint* (v. p. 378), and *Turberville* (x. p. 378). As reference to this comparatively infrequent illustrator appears in another place no more need be said of these, except that they do not show the artist in so fine a mood as when he illustrated Defoe's *History of the Plague*. Simeon Solomon contributes a couple only of drawings of Jewish ceremonies (vii. pp. 192, 193). J. Luard, an artist, whose work floods the cheaper publications of the time, shows, in an early drawing, *Contrasts* (iii. p. 84), a pre-Raphaelite manner, and a promise which later years did not fulfil, if indeed this be by the Luard of the penny dreadfuls.

M. E. Edwards, a most popular illustrator, appears in the last volume of the first series, with *Found Drowned* (xiii. pp. 14, 42, 70, 98, 253, 281, 309, 337, 365, 393, 442, 471), in which volume J. Lawson has three: *Ondine* (p. 351), *Narcissus* p.

THE MAJOR'S DAUGHTER

THE RELIEF FUND

IN LANCASHIRE

J. M'NEILL WHISTLER

THE MORNING BEFORE THE
MASSACRE OF ST. BARTHOLOMEW

E

COUNT BURCKHARDT

ONCE A WEEK

463), and *Adonis* (686). Of a number of more or less frequent contributors, including F. Eltze, R. T. Pritchett, P. Skelton, F. J. Slinger, J. Wolf (the admirable delineator of animals), space forbids even a complete list of their names.

Among other occasional contributors to the first thirteen volumes are: J. D. Watson with *The Cornish Wrecker's Hut* (viii. p. 602), *No Change* (ix. p. 210), and *My Home* (ix. 266); A. Boyd Houghton :—*The Old King Dying* (xii. p. 463), *The Portrait* (xiii. p. 209), *King Solomon* (xiii. p. 603), *The Legend of the Lockharts* (xiii. p. 715), and *Leila and Hassan* (xiii. p. 769); Walter Crane :—*Castle of Mont Orgueil* (ix. p. 713) and *The Conservatory* (xiii. p. 763); J. W. North :—*Bosgrove Church* (ix. p. 447), *The River* (xii. p. 15), and *St. Martin's Church, Canterbury* (xii. p. 713)—the two latter being worthy to rank among his best work; Paul Gray with *Hans Euler* (xii. p. 322), *Moses* (xiii. p. 55), *The Twins* (xiii. pp. 378-406), *Two Chapters of Life* (xiii. p. 519), and *Quid Femina Possit* (xii. pp. 491, 517, 547, 575); A. R. Fairfield (x. pp. 546, 589, 617, 686, 712); W. S. Burton, *Romance of the Rose* (x. p. 602), *The Executioner* (xi. p. 14), *Dame Eleanor's Return* (xi. p. 210), and *The Whaler Fleet* (xi. p. 638); T. White (viii. p. 98); F. W. Lawson, *Dr. Campany's Courtship* (xii. pp. 351, 390, 407, 446), and others on pp. 586, 631, 722); (xiii. pp. 127, 141, 169, *Lucy's Garland*, p. 516); C. Dobell (vi. p. 420); *Our Secret Drawer*, by Miss Wells (v. p. 98); and four by Miss L. Mearns, which are of genuine interest (xiii. pp. 85, 153, 657, 742).

The New Series of *Once a Week*, started on January 6, 1866, was preceded by a Christmas number, wherein one of the most graceful drawings by Paul Gray is to be found, *The Chest with the Silver Mountings* (p. 30). It contains also a full-page plate by G. B. Goddard, *Up, up my hounds* (p. 34), and designs by W. Small, *A Golden Wedding* (p. 37); G. Du Maurier, *The Ace of Hearts* (p. 56); J. Lawson, *A Fairy Tale* (p. 44), and others of little moment.

The New Series announced, as a special attraction, 'extra illustrations by eminent artists, printed separately on toned paper.' Those to the first volume include *Little Bo Peep*, a delightful and typical composition by G. Du Maurier (*Frontispiece*); *The Vagrants* (p. 112), by Fred Walker; *Helen and Cassandra* (p. 454), by F. Sandys; *The Servants' Hall*

33

SOME ILLUSTRATED MAGAZINES

(p. 560), by H. S. Marks; *Alonzo the Brave* (p. 359), by Sir John Gilbert, and *Caught by the tide*, by E. Duncan (p. 280).

'A specimen of the most recent application of the versatile art of lithography' which is also given, dates the popular introduction of the coloured plate by which several magazines, *Nature and Art, The Chromo-lithograph*, etc., were illustrated entirely; others, especially *The Sunday at Home, Leisure Hour, People's Magazine*, etc., from 1864 onwards issued monthly frontispieces in colours and gold—a practice now confined almost wholly to boys' magazines. The pictures by artists already associated with *Once a Week* include (in vol. i. p. 8) two by A. Boyd Houghton, *The Queen of the Rubies* (p. 177) and *A Turkish Tragedy* (p. 448); four by Paul Gray, *The Phantom Ship* (p. 43), *Blanche* (pp. 291, 317), and *The Fight on Rhu Carn* (p. 713); two by T. Morten, *The Dying Viking* (p. 239), a drawing curiously like Sandys's *Rosamunda*, and *King Eric* (p. 435); six by W. Small, *Billy Blake's Best Coffin* (p. 15), *Kattie and the Deil* (p. 99), *The King and the Bishop* (p. 183), *The Staghound* (p. 295), *Thunnors Slip* (p. 351), and *Larthon of Inis-Huna* (p. 575); five by J. Lawson: *The Watch-tower* (p. 121), *Theocritus* (p. 211), *In statu quo* (p. 463), *Ancient Clan Dirge* (p. 491), and *Wait On* (p. 631); one by F. W. Lawson, *A Sunday a Century ago* (p. 671), and others. Among recruits we find R. Barnes with *Lost for Gold* (p. 407), B. Bradley with *A Raid* (p. 659), eleven by Edward Hughes, and many by G. Bowers, R. T. Pritchett, F. J. Slinger, and others. Altogether the New Series started bravely. In vol. ii. New Series, the so-called 'extra illustrations' include *The Suit of Armour (Frontispiece)*, by Sir John Gilbert; *Evening* (p. 97), by Basil Bradley; *Poor Christine* (p. 245), by Edward Hughes; *Among the Breakers* (p. 344), by E. Duncan; *The Nymph's Lament* (p. 476), by G. Du Maurier; and *The Huntress of Armorica* (p. 706), by Paul Gray. Of 'old hands' Du Maurier has another of his graceful drawings, *Lady Julia* (p. 239), and Paul Gray has, besides the special plate, eleven to *Hobson's Choice* (pp. 169, 197, 225, 253, 281, 309, 337, 365, 393, 421, and 449); three by A. Boyd Houghton are *A Dead Man's Message* (p. 211); and *The Mistaken Ghost* (pp. 687, 723); T. Morten has only a couple, *The Curse of the Gudmunds* (p. 155) and *On the Cliffs* (p. 308); and G. J.

G. DU MAURIER

ON HER
DEATHBED

G. DU MAURIER

PER L'AMORE
D'UNA DONNA

T. MORTEN

'ONCE A WEEK'
VOL. XI. p. 603

THE CUMÆAN SIBYL

Pinwell one, *The Pastor and the Landgrave* (p. 631); J. W
North's *Luther's Gardener* (p. 99) is a curious drawing to
a curious poem; W. Small, with *Eldorado* (p. 15), *Dorette*
(p. 379), *The Gift of Clunnog Vawr* (p. 463), *The Prize Maiden*
(pp. 491, 519, 560), and *Tranquillity* (p. 575), shows more
and more that strong personality which by and by influenced
black and white art, so that men of the seventies arc far more
disciples of Small than even were the men of the sixties of
Millais.　M. E. Edwards's *Avice and her Lover* (p. 141); six
by Basil Bradley (pp. 140, 252, 279, 532, 603, and 659),
Charles Green's *Kunegunda* (p. 71), *Hazeley Mill* (p. 85),
and *Michael Considine's Daughter* (p. 351); five by Edward
Hughes (pp. 183, 407, 547, 585, and 599); three by J.
Lawson: *Ariadne* (p. 127), *The Mulberry-tree* (p. 323), and
Gabrielle's Cross (p. 699).　F. W. Lawson's *A Midshipman's
Yarn* (p. 113) and *Grandmother's Story* (p. 223) deserve to be
noted.　Others by G. Bowers, F. Eltze, R. T. Pritchett,
P. J. Skelton, E. Wimpress (*sic*), and J. Wolf among the rest,
call for no comment.　For the Christmas number for this year
1866, W. Small has *The Brown Imp* (p. 12); J. Lawson, *The
Birth of the Rose* (p. 20); E. Hughes, *The Pension Latoque*
(p. 25); Ernest Griset, *Boar Hunting* (p. 57); G. B. Goddard,
Christmas Eve in the Country (p. 58); and Basil Bradley, *A
Winter Piece* (p. 62); John Leighton contributes a frontispiece and illustrations to *St. George and the Dragon*, a poem
by the author of *John Halifax*.

In volume iii. 1867 the extra illustrations are still distinguished by a special subject index; they include *Lord Aythan*
(*Frontispiece*), by J. Tenniel; *Coming through the Fence* (p.
112), by R. Ansdell, A.R.A.; *Feeding the Sacred Ibis* (p. 238),
by E. J. Poynter; *Come, buy my pretty windmills* (p. 360),
by G. J. Pinwell; *Hide a Stick* (p. 569), by F. J. Shields; and
Highland Sheep (p. 692), by Basil Bradley.　Another extra
plate, a drawing by Helen J. Miles, 'given as an example of
graphotype,' is not without technical interest.　In the accompanying article we find that the possibilities of mechanical
reproduction are discussed, and the writer adds, as his highest
flight of fancy, 'who shall say that graphotype may not be
the origin of a daily illustrated paper?'　It would be out of
place to pursue this tempting theme, and to discuss the *Daily
Graphic* of New York and succeeding illustrated dailies, for

SOME ILLUSTRATED MAGAZINES

all these things were but dreams in the sixties. Yet, undoubtedly, graphotype set people on the track of process-work. By and by the photographer came in as the welcome ally, who left the draughtsman free to work upon familiar materials, instead of the block itself, and presently supplanted the engraver also, and the great rival of wood-cutting and wood-engraving sprang into life. Among the ordinary illustrations A. Boyd Houghton is represented by *The Mistaken Ghost* (p. 15), *A Hindoo Legend* (p. 273), and *The Bride of Rozelle* (p. 663); G. J. Pinwell by *Joe Robertson's Folly* (p. 225) and *The Old Keeper's Story* (p. 483); J. W. North by *The Lake* (p. 303); W. Small by *A Queer Story about Banditti* (pp. 55, 83); S. L. Fildes by a strongly-drawn design, *The Goldsmith's Apprentice* (p. 723); Ernest Griset by a slight yet distinctly grotesque *Tale of a Tiger* (p. 7); M. Ellen Edwards by *Wishes* (p. 633) and Kate Edwards by *Cherry Blossom* (p. 543); J. Lawson by *The Legend of St. Katherine* (p. 127), *Sir Ralph de Blanc-Minster* (p. 168), and *Hymn to Apollo* (p. 406); F. W. Lawson by *The Singer of the Sea* (p. 603). The various examples by F. A. Fraser, T. Green, T. Scott (a well-known portrait engraver), E. M. Wimpress, and the rest may be dismissed with bare mention. In vol. iv., New Series, we find Charles Keene with a frontispiece, *The Old Shepherd*; *The Haymakers* (p. 105), E. M. Wimpress; *Cassandra* (p. 345), S. L. Fildes; *Fetching the Doctor* (p. 494), H. S. Marks; *Imma and Eginhart* (p. 644), W. Small; and *The Christmas Choir* (p. 762), F. A. Fraser, are the other separate plates. Those printed with the text include *The Child Queen* (p. 135) and *Feuilles d'Automne* (p. 285), by S. L. Fildes; *Evening Tide* (p. 255), a typical pastoral, by G. J. Pinwell; *Zoë Fane* (p. 705), by J. Mahoney; and others by B. Bradley, E. F. Brewtnall, F. Eltze, T. Green, E. Hughes, F. W. Lawson, E. Sheil, L. Straszinski, T. Sulman, E. M. Wimpress, etc. Despite the presence of many of the old staff, the list of names shows that the palmy days of the magazine are over. The Christmas number contains, *inter alia*, a frontispiece by John Gilbert; *My Cousin Renie* (p. 13), by J. Mahoney; *Scotch Cattle*, by Basil Bradley; and *The Maiden's Test*, by M. E. Edwards (p. 49).

In 1868 another new series starts. A notable feature has disappeared: the illustrations no longer figure in a separate

36

list, but their artists' names are tacked on to the few articles and stories which are illustrated in the ordinary index. Yet the drawings by Du Maurier to Charles Reade's *Foul Play* (pp. 12, 57, 140, 247, 269, 312, 421, 464, 530) would alone make the year interesting. People, who regard Du Maurier as a society draughtsman only, must be astonished at the grim melodramatic force displayed in these. 'John Millais, R.A.,' also appears as a contributor with *Death Dealing Arrows* (p. 79); S. L. Fildes has *The Orchard* (p. 396); F. W. Lawson, *The Castaway* (p. 242); Basil Bradley is well represented by *The Chillingham Cattle* (p. 100), and *Another day's work done* (p. 346); F. S. Walker appears with *A Lazy Fellow* (p. 211), John Gilbert with *The Armourer* (p. 364), and M. E. Edwards with the society pictures, *The Royal Academy* (p. 409) and *A Flower Show* (p. 516). In the second volume for 1868 we find *Salmon Fishing* (p. 292) and *Daphne* (p. 397), both by S. L. Fildes; *Found Out* (p. 31), *A Town Cousin* (p. 150), *Left in the Lurch* (p. 230), and *Blackberry Gatherers* (p. 213), by H. Paterson; *Sussex Oxen* (p. 110) and *The Foxhound* (p. 355), by Basil Bradley; *The Picnic* (p. 270), by F. W. Lawson, who has also *The Waits*, the frontispiece of the Christmas number, which contains *Taking his ease* (p. 264), the last Millais in the magazine; a clever gallery study; *Boxing Night*, by S. L. Fildes, and a capital domestic group, *The Old Dream* (p. 48), by M. E. Edwards.

In 1869, vol. iii., New Series, contains a single example by G. J. Pinwell, *A seat in the park* (p. 518); five by S. L. Fildes: *The Duet* (p. 56), *The Juggler* (p. 188), *Hours of Idleness*, the subject of a later Academy picture (p. 475), *Led to Execution* (p. 540), and *Basking* (p. 562); and others by Fred Barnard (pp. 166, 254, 346, 450), B. Bradley (pp. 78, 210, 496), Val Prinsep (p. 298), F. W. Lawson (p. 34), and Ford Madox Brown, *The Traveller* (p. 144). To state that vol. iv., New Series, is absolutely without interest is to let it off cheaply.

In the volume for 1870 the names of artists are omitted, and if we follow the editor's example no injustice will be done, despite a few clever drawings by R. M[acbeth]; the work, not merely in date but in spirit, is of the new decade, and as it is exceptionally poor at that for the most part, it no longer belongs to the subject with which this volume is concerned.

CHAPTER IV: SOME ILLUSTRATED MAGAZINES OF THE SIXTIES: II. 'THE CORNHILL,' 'GOOD WORDS,' AND 'LONDON SOCIETY'

HE CORNHILL MAGAZINE, which began in 1860 with Thackeray as editor, showed from the very first that the aim of the Magazine was to keep the level of its pictures equal to that of its text. In looking through the forty-seven volumes of the first series it is gratifying to find that this purpose was never forgotten. Many a rival magazine has been started since under the happiest auspices, with the most loyal intention to have the best and only the very best illustrations; but in a few years the effort has been too exacting, and the average commonplace of its padding in prose and verse has been equalled by the dull mediocrity of its pictures. Only those who have experienced the difficulty which faces an editor firmly resolved to exclude the commonplace of any sort can realise fully what a strain a successful effort, lasting over twenty years, must needs impose on the responsible conductors. Thackeray, as we know, soon found the labour too great; but his successors kept nobly to their purpose, and few magazines show more honourable fulfilment of their projected scheme than the classic *Cornhill*, which has introduced so many masterpieces in art and literature to the public.

Curiously enough, the weakest illustrations under the *régime* he inaugurated so happily are those by the editor himself. Thackeray's designs to *Lovel the Widower*, and the one example by G. A. Sala in the first volume, link the new periodical with the past. They belong to the caricature type of illustrations which had been accepted by the British public as character-drawing. Like the 'Phiz' plates for Dickens's works, and many of John Leech's sketches, they have undoubtedly merit of a sort, but not if you consider them as pictures pure and simple. Later experience shows that an illustration to a story, which catches the spirit of the writer, and realises in another medium the characters he had imagined, may also be fine art—art as self-sufficient and as wholly beautiful as that of a Dürer wood-cut or a Rembrandt etching. The

38

masterpieces of modern illustrations to fiction which the *Cornhill Magazine* contains would by themselves suffice to prove this argument up to the hilt. The collection of drawings chiefly by Millais, Walker, and Leighton, in a volume of carefully-printed impressions, from one hundred of the original wood-blocks, issued under the title of the *Cornhill Gallery* in 1864, may in time to come be prized as highly as *Bible Wood-cuts, The Dance of Death*, or the *Liber Studiorum.* It is true that the pictures aimed only to fulfil their actual purpose, and it may be argued, reasonably enough, that a picture which illustrates a story is for that very reason on a different level to a self-contained work—inspired solely by the delight of the artist in his subject. But, in their own way, they touched high-water mark. Upon one of Dürer's blocks he is said to have written in Latin, ' Better work did no man than this,' and on many a *Cornhill* design the same legend might have been truly inscribed.

It is true that most of the etchings and wood-cuts beside which they deserve to be ranked are untrammelled autograph work throughout, and that here the drawing done direct on the block was paraphrased by an engraver. Not always spoilt, sometimes (as even the draughtsman himself admitted), improved in part, but still with the impress of another personality added. And this argument might be extended to prove that an engraving by another craftsman can never be so interesting as an etching from a master's hand, or a block cut by its designer. Yet, without forcing such comparison, we may claim that the engravings in *Once a Week, Good Words*, and the *Cornhill* enriched English art to lasting purpose.

Although sets of the *Cornhill Magazine* are not difficult to procure, and a large number of people prize them in their libraries, yet by way of bringing together those scattered facts of interest which pertain to our subject, it may be as well to indicate briefly the principal contents of the first thirty-two volumes which cover the period to which this book is limited.

In 1860 we find six full-page illustrations to *Lovel the Widower*, three to *The Four Georges*, two to *Roundabout Papers*, all by Thackeray, to whom they are all formally attributed in the *Cornhill Gallery*. Possibly one, entirely unlike the style of the rest to *The Four Georges*, is from another hand—the fact that it is not included in the reprint seems to confirm this suspicion. Millais' first contributions included *Unspoken Dialogue*, ' *Last Words*,' and the beginning of the illustrations to *Framley Parsonage*, which he equalled often but never excelled. F. Sandys is represented by *Legends of the Portent* (i. p. 617), and Frederick Leighton by *The Great God Pan* (ii. p. 84) to Mrs. Browning's poem. *Ariadne in Naxos*, an outline-drawing in a decorative frame, is unsigned, and so strangely unlike the style of the magazine that it provokes curiosity.

In 1861 Thackeray started illustrating his serial story, *The Adventures of Philip*, but, after four full-page drawings, relinquished the task to Fred Walker, who at first re-drew Thackeray's compositions, but afterwards signed his work with the familiar ' F. W.' We may safely attribute eight solely to him. Millais continued his series of drawings to illustrate *Framley Parsonage*, and has besides one other, entitled *Temptation* (iii. p. 229). A series of studies of character, *The Excursion Train*, by C. H. Bennett, is a notable exception to the practice of the magazine, which printed all its ' pictures ' on plate-paper apart from the text, the blocks in the text (always excepting the initial letters) being elsewhere limited to diagrams elucidating the matter and obviously removed from consideration as pictures. This year Doyle began those outline pictures of Society which attained so wide a popularity.

In 1862 Walker concludes his *Philip* series with eight full-page drawings, including the superb *Philip in Church*, of which he made a version in water-colours that still ranks among his most notable work. The first two illustrations to Miss Thackeray's *Story of Elizabeth* are also from his hand. Millais is represented by *Irené*, a kneeling figure (v. p. 478), and by the powerfully conceived *Bishop and the Knight* (vi. p. 100), and the first four illustrations to Trollope's *Small House at Allington*. Richard Doyle continues the series of *Pictures of English Society*; but now that their actuality no longer impresses, we fail to discover the special charm which endeared them to contemporaries. F. Sandys is represented by *Manoli* (vi. p. 346), the second of his three contributions, which deepens the regret that work by this fine artist appeared so seldom in this magazine. But the most notable feature this year is found in the drawings contributed by Frederick

FREDERICK SANDYS

LEGEND OF
THE PORTENT

MANOLI

THE CORNHILL MAGAZINE

Leighton, then not even an Associate of the Royal Academy, which illustrate George Eliot's *Romola*. With these the *Cornhill* departed from its ordinary custom, and gave two full-page illustrations to each section of the serial month by month. Consequently in the volumes in 1862 and 1863 the usual two-dozen plates are considerably augmented.

In 1863 twelve more of the *Romola* series complete Leighton's contributions to the magazine. Millais has twelve more to *The Small House at Allington*, Walker is represented by one drawing, *Maladetta*, another to *Mrs. Archie*, two to *Out of the World*, and one more to *The Story of Elizabeth*. Du Maurier, destined to occupy the most prominent position in later volumes, appears for the first time with *The Cilician Pirates, Sibyl's Disappointment, The Night before the Morrow*, and *Cousin Phillis*. Possibly a drawing entitled 'The First Meeting' to a story, *The . . . in her Closet*, is from his hand ; but the style is not clearly evident, nor is it included in the *Cornhill Gallery* which, published in the next year, drew its illustrations from the few volumes already noticed, with the addition of five others from the early numbers of 1864. Another drawing, signed A. H., to *Margaret Denzil*, is by Arthur Hughes.

In 1864 two other illustrations complete *The Small House at Allington*, and Millais has also two others for *Madame de Monferrat*. Sir Noel Paton appears for the only time with a fine composition, *Ulysses* (ix. p. 66). *Margaret Denzil* has its three illustrations signed R. B., probably the initials of Robert Barnes, who did much work in later volumes. Charles Keene, a very infrequent contributor, illustrated *Brother Jacob*, a little-known story by George Eliot. Du Maurier supplies the first four illustrations to Mrs. Gaskell's unfinished *Wives and Daughters*, and Fred Walker contributes five to the other serial, also interrupted by its author's death, the delightful *Denis Duval*. Here we see the artist employed on costume-work, and hampered somewhat by historical details, yet infusing into his designs the charm which characterises his idyllic work. G. J. Pinwell is represented by *The Lovers of Ballyvookan*. G. H. Thomas starts Wilkie Collins's *Armadale* with two pictures that do not accord with the rest of the *Cornhill* work, but belong to a differently considered method, popular enough elsewhere, but rarely employed in this

41

SOME ILLUSTRATED MAGAZINES

magazine. The volume contains also a portrait of Thackeray engraved on steel, by J. C. Armytage, after Laurence.

In 1865 the *Armadale* illustrations take up twelve full pages, and Du Maurier supplies the remaining twelve stories to *Wives and Daughters*.

In 1866 six *Armadale* and one *Wives and Daughters* are reinforced by eleven illustrations to *The Claverings* by M. Ellen Edwards. Fred Walker is again a contributor with five drawings for Miss Thackeray's *Village on the Cliff*, and Frederick Sandys, with a fine composition illustrating Swinburne's *Cleopatra* (xiv. p. 331), makes his last appearance in the magazine.

In 1867 M. E. Edwards signs five of *The Claverings* and seven to *The Bramleighs of Bishop's Folly*. *The Satrap*, an admirable composition, is signed F. W. B., but for whom these initials stand is not clear. Fred Walker completes his illustrations to the *Village on the Cliff*, and adds one other to *Beauty and the Beast*, and two to *A Week in a French Country House* and one to *Red Riding Hood*. F. W. Lawson makes his *entrée* with the four drawings to *Stone Edge*, and Du Maurier has a curiously massive *Joan of Arc*.

In 1868 Walker has three illustrations to *Jack the Giant Killer*, '*I do not love you*,' and *From an Island* respectively. M. Ellen Edwards is responsible for ten to *The Bramleighs*, one to a story, *The Stockbroker*, and the first two to *That Boy of Norcott's*. F. W. Lawson has four to *Avonhoe*, and two to *Lettice Lisle*, and Du Maurier two to *My Neighbour Nelly*, and one to *Lady Denzil*.

In 1869 *That Boy of Norcott's* supplies the subjects for three others by M. E. Edwards, and *Lettice Lisle* for four by F. W. Lawson. The first chapters of *Put yourself in his place*, Charles Reade's trades-union novel, are illustrated by ten drawings by Robert Barnes, F. Walker has one to *Sola*, for which tale Du Maurier supplies another, as well as one to the *Courtyard of the Ours d'Or*, and the three for *Against Time*.

In 1870 Robert Barnes continues illustrating Charles Reade's novel with seven full pages. Du Maurier contributes ten to *Against Time*, and four to George Meredith's *Adventures of Harry Richmond*, and S. L. Fildes (more familiar to-day as Luke Fildes) comes in with three admirable compositions to Charles Lever's *Lord Kilgobbin*.

CLEOPATRA

THE CORNHILL MAGAZINE

In 1871 the latter story engages twelve full pages, and *Harry Richmond* and eleven others, Du Maurier has the first to a *Story of the Plébiscite*.

In 1872 Du Maurier continues *The Plébiscite* with one full page (the others to the same story are signed ' H. H.'), and has four others to Francillon's *Pearl and Emerald,* and ten to *The Scientific Gentleman.* Fildes concludes his embellishment of *Lord Kilgobbin* with three full pages. Hubert Herkomer (the ' H. H.' of *The Plébiscite* probably) appears as a recruit with two most satisfactory designs to *The Last Master of the Old Manor-House,* and G. D. Leslie, also a fresh arrival, finds, in Miss Thackeray's *Old Kensington,* the themes for nine graceful compositions.

In 1873 to Du Maurier are devoted twelve subjects illustrating *Zelda's Fortune.* G. D. Leslie has four others concluding *Old Kensington.* S. L. Fildes illustrates *Willows* with two, and Marcus Stone is represented by half-a-dozen idyllic and charming, if somewhat slight, designs for *Young Brown.*

In 1874 H. Paterson, W. Small, and Du Maurier contribute all the pictures excepting one by Marcus Stone. *Far from the Madding Crowd* by Thomas Hardy, illustrated by the first artist, and *A Rose in June,* and Black's *Three Feathers* by the second.

In 1875 H. Allingham supplies most graceful pictures to *Miss Angel.* Du Maurier is the artist chosen for another Hardy novel, *The Hand of Ethelberta.* A. Hopkins illustrates Mr. Henley's wonderful achievement, *Hospital Outlines,* as the poems were called when they appeared in July 1875. From this date to the last number of the shilling series, June 1883, the artists are limited to Small and Du Maurier for the most part, and as this record has already exceeded its limits, no more need be said, except that until the last, the high standard of technical excellence was never abandoned. Although the rare mastery of Millais and the charm of Walker were hardly approached by their successors, yet the magazine was always representative of the best work of those of its contemporaries who devoted themselves to black and white, and not infrequently, as this notice shows, attracted men who have made few, if any other, attempts to draw for publication. It is curious to find that, notwithstanding the evident importance it attached to its pictorial department, no artist's name is ever mentioned in the index or elsewhere. In a graceful and discriminative essay 'S. C.' speaks feelingly and appreciatively of Fred Walker just after his death ; but that seems to be the only time when the anonymity imposed on the artists was divulged in the magazine itself. It is but fair to add that the literary contents were never signed, or attributed in the index, except that a few articles bear the now familiar initials, 'L. S.', 'W. E. H.', 'R. L.S.', 'G. A.', and others.

GOOD WORDS

This popular, semi-religious, sixpenny magazine, established in 1860, achieved quickly a circulation that was record-breaking in its time. Edited by Dr. Norman Macleod, it was printed by Thomas Constable, and published (at first) in Edinburgh by Alexander Strahan and Co. Although, viewed in the light of its later issues, one cannot help feeling disappointed with the first volume, yet even there the pictures are distinctly interesting as a forecast, even if they do not call for any detailed notice by reason of their intrinsic merit. They rarely exceed a half page in size, and were engraved none too well by various craftsmen. Indeed, judging from the names of the artists, then as afterwards, given fully in the index of illustrations, it might not be unfair to blame the engravers still more strongly. The very fact that the illustrations are duly ascribed in a separate list is proof that, from the first, the editor recognised their importance. Such honourable recognition of the personality of an illustrator is by no means the rule, even in periodicals that have equal right to be proud of their collaborators. Where the artists' names are recorded it is rare to find them acknowledged so fully and thoroughly as in *Good Words*. In other magazines they are usually referred to under the title of the article they illustrate and nowhere else ; or their name is printed (as in *Once a Week*) with a bare list of numerals showing the pages containing their pictures ; but in *Good Words* the subject, titles, and artists' names have always been accorded a special index.

In the first volume, for 1860, W. Q. Orchardson—not then even an Associate of the Royal Academy—supplies nine drawings, engraved by F. Borders. Admirable in their own way, one cannot but feel that the signature leads one to

G. DU MAURIER

'GOOD WORDS'
1861, p. 579

A TIME TO
DANCE

expect something much more interesting; and, knowing the quality of Mr. Orchardson's later work, it is impossible to avoid throwing the blame on the engraver. Keeley Halswelle contributes six; in these you find (badly drawn or spoilt by the engraver) those water-lilies in blossom, which in after years became a mannerism in his landscape foregrounds. J. W. M'Whirter has four—one a group of *Autumn Flowers* (p. 664), cut by R. Paterson, that deserves especial notice as a much more elaborate piece of engraving than any other in the volume. Erskine Nicol supplies two *genre* pieces, the full-page, *Mary Macdonell and her friends* (p. 216), being, most probably, a thoroughly good sketch, but here again the translator has produced hard scratchy lines that fail to suggest the freer play of pencil or pen, whichever it was that produced the original. Others by 'J. B.,' J. O. Brown, C. A. Doyle, Clarence Dobell, Jas. Drummond, Clark Stanton, Gourlay Steell, and Hughes Taylor, call for no particular comment.

From 1861 the chief full-page illustrations were printed separately on toned paper. A series of animal subjects by 'J. B.,' twelve 'Illustrations of Scripture,' engraved by Dalziel Brothers, were announced in the prospectus as a special feature. Somewhat pre-Raphaelite in handling they are distinctly interesting, but hardly masterly. But the volume will be always memorable for its early work by Frederick Walker and G. Du Maurier. *A Time to Dance*, by the latter, shows a certain decorative element, which in various ways has influenced his work at different periods, although no one could have deduced from it the future career of its brilliant author as a satirist of society, a draughtsman who imparted into his work, to a degree no English artist has surpassed, and very few equalled, that 'good form' so prized by well-bred people. The drawing unsigned *The Blind School* (p. 505), attributed to Fred Walker in the index, suggests some clerical error. Like one attributed to Sandys in a later volume, you hesitate before accepting evidence of the compiler of the list of engravings, which the picture itself contradicts flatly. *Only a Sweep* (p. 609) is signed, and, although by no means a good example, is unquestionably attributed rightly. John Pettie has two designs, *Cain's Brand* (pp. 376, 422); J. M'Whirter and W. Q. Orchardson, one each; H. H. Armstead, a pre-Raphaelite composition, *A Song which none but the Redeemed ever sing*,

45

which is amongst the most interesting of the comparatively few illustrations by the Royal Academician, who is better known as a sculptor, as his *Music, Poetry, and Painting* in the Albert Memorial, the panels beneath Dyce's frescoes at Westminster Palace, and a long series of works shown at the Academy exhibitions suffice to prove. T. Morten, a draughtsman who has missed so far his due share of appreciation, is represented by *The Waker, Dreamer, and Sleeper* (p. 634), a powerful composition of a group of men praying at night by the side of a breaking dyke. John Pettie has two drawings; and J. D. Watson, six subjects—the first, *The Toad*, being singularly unlike his later style, and suggesting a closer discipleship with the pre-Raphaelites than he maintained afterwards. Two by Clarence Dobell, and three by T. Graham—one, *The Young Mother*, a charming arrangement in lines; with others by J. Wolf, Zwecker, W. M'Taggart, J. L. Porter, A. W. Cooper, A. Bushnell, W. Fyfe, W. Linney, and C. H. Bennett, are also included. Altogether the second volume shows marked advance upon the first, although this admirable periodical had not yet reached its high-water mark.

In 1862 we find added to its list of artists, Millais, Keene, Sandys, Whistler, Holman Hunt, E. Burne-Jones, A. Boyd Houghton, Tenniel, S. Solomon, and Lawless, a notable group, even in that year when so many magazines show a marvellous 'galaxy of stars.' To Millais fell the twelve illustrations to *Mistress and Maid*, by the author of *John Halifax*, and two others, *Olaf* (p. 25) and *Highland Flora* (p. 393). That these maintain fully the reputation of the great illustrator, whose later achievements in oil have in popular estimation eclipsed his importance as a black-and-white artist, goes without saying. If not equal to the superb *Parables* of the following year, they are worthy of their author. Indeed, no matter when you come across a Millais, it is with a fresh surprise each time that one finds it rarely falls below a singularly high level, and is apt to seem, for the moment, the best he ever did.

The two illustrations by J. M'Neill Whistler seem to be very little known. Those to *Once a Week*, possibly from the fact of their being reprinted in Thornbury's *Legendary Ballads*, have been often referred to and reproduced several times; but no notice (so far as I recollect) of these, to *The First*

SIMEON SOLOMON

'GOOD WORDS'
1862, p. 592

THE VEILED
BRIDE

FREDERICK WALKER

'GOOD WORDS'
1862, p. 657

OUT AMONG THE
WILD-FLOWERS

GOOD WORDS

Sermon, has found its way into print. The one (p. 585) shows a girl crouching by a fire, with a man, whose head is turned towards her, seated at a table with his hand on a lute. The other (p. 649) is a seated girl in meditation before a writing-table. Not a little of the beauty of line, which distinguishes the work of the famous etcher, is evident in these blocks, which were both engraved by Dalziel, and as whatever the original lost cannot now be estimated, as they stand they are nevertheless most admirable works, preserving the rapid touch of the pen-line in a remarkable degree.

The Charles Keene drawing to *Nanneri the Washerwoman* is another Dalziel block which merits praise in no slight measure; as here again one fancies that the attempt has been to preserve a facsimile of each touch of the artist, and not to translate wash into line. The *King Sigurd* of Burne-Jones has certainly lost a great deal; in fact, judging by drawings of the same period still extant, it conveys an effect quite different from that its author intended. Certainly, at the present time, he regards it as entirely un-representative; but no doubt then as now he disliked drawing upon wood. To-day it has been said that his Chaucer drawings in pencil were practically translated by another hand in the course of their being engraved on wood. Certainly technique of lead pencil is hardly suggested, much less reproduced in facsimile in the entirely admirable engravings by the veteran Mr. W. H. Hooper. But if the designs were photographed on the block such translation as they have undergone is no doubt due to the engraver.

A drawing by Simeon Solomon, *The Veiled Bride* (p. 592), seems also much less dainty than his pencil studies of the same period. Many artists, when they attempt to draw upon wood, find the material peculiarly unsympathetic. Rossetti has left his opinion on record, and it is quite possible that in both the Burne-Jones and Solomon, as in the Tennyson drawings, although the engravers may have accomplished miracles, what the artist had put down was untranslatable. For the delicacies of pencil may easily produce something beyond the power of even the most skilful engraver to reproduce. The Sandys, *Until her Death* (p. 312), illustrating a poem, loses much as it appeared in the magazine; you have but to compare a proof from the block itself, in a reprinted collection of

SOME ILLUSTRATED MAGAZINES

Messrs. Strahan's engravings, to realise how different a result was secured upon good paper with careful printing. A. Boyd Houghton is represented by four subjects: *My Treasure* (p. 504), *On the Cliff* (p. 624), *True or False* (p. 721), and *About Toys* (p. 753); they all belong to the manner of his *Home Scenes*, rather than to his oriental illustrations. *The Battle of Gilboa* (p. 89), by Tenniel, is typical. M. J. Lawless is at his best in *Rung into Heaven* (p. 135), and in the *Bands of Love* (p. 632) shows more grace than he sometimes secured when confronted by modern costume.

T. Morten has a finely-engraved night-piece, *Pictures in the Fire* (p. 200), besides *The Christmas Child* (p. 56) and *The Carrier Pigeon* (p. 121). The Holman Hunt, *Go and Come* (p. 32), a weeping figure, is not particularly interesting. *Honesty* (p. 736), by T. Graham, gives evidence of the power of an artist who has yet to be 'discovered' so far as his illustrations are concerned. H. H. Armstead's *Seaweeds* (p. 568), and eight by J. D. Watson (pp. 9, 81, 144, 201, 209, 302, 400, 433) need no special comment, nor do the ten by J. Pettie (pp. 264-713). Fred Walker is represented by *The Summer Woods*, a typical pastoral (p. 368), *Love in Death*, a careworn woman in the snow (p. 185), and *Out among the wild flowers* (p. 657), the latter an excellent example of the grace he imparted to rustic figures. These, with a few diagrams and engravings from photographs, complete the record of a memorable, if not the most memorable, year of the magazine.

In 1863 we find less variety in the artists and subjects, which is due to the presence of the superb series of drawings by Millais, *The Parables*, wherein the great illustrator touched his highest level. To call these twelve pictures masterpieces is for once to apply consistently a term often misused. For, though one ransacked the portfolios of Europe, not many sets of drawings could be found to equal, and very few to excel them. The twelve subjects appeared in the following order: *The Leaven* (p. 1), *The Ten Virgins* (p. 81), *The Prodigal Son* (p. 161), *The Good Samaritan* (p. 241), *The Unjust Judge* (p. 313), *The Pharisee and Publican* (p. 385), *The Hid Treasure* (p. 461), *The Pearl of Great Price* (p. 533), *The Lost Piece of Money*[1] (p. 605), *The Sower* (p. 677), *The*

---

[1] Engraved by Dalziels about double the size of this page, the subject was issued afterwards in *The Day of Rest* (Strahan).

HONESTY

M. J. LAWLESS

'GOOD WORDS'
1862, p. 153

RUNG INTO HEAVEN

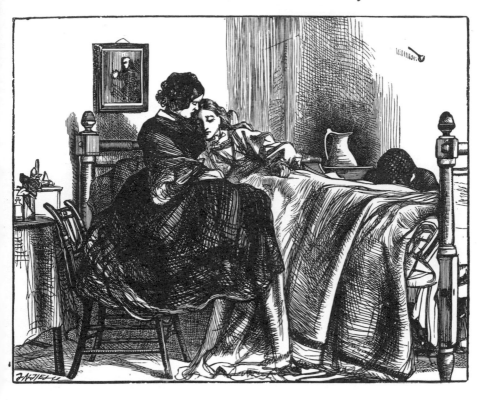

'GOOD WORDS'
1862, p. 632

THE BANDS
OF LOVE

J. PETTIE

THE MONKS AND
THE HEATHEN

FREDERICK SANDYS

FREDERICK SANDYS

THE NORSE
PRINCESS

GOOD WORDS

Unmerciful Servant (p. 749), and *The Labourers in the Vineyard* (p. 821). To F. Sandys two drawings are attributed; one is obviously from another hand, but *Sleep* (p. 589) undoubtedly marks his final appearance in this magazine. T. Morten is represented by *Cousin Winnie* (p. 257), *Hester Durham* (p. 492), *The Spirit of Eld* (p. 629, unsigned), a powerful composition that at first glance might almost be taken for a Sandys, and *An Orphan Family's Christmas* (p. 844). In *Autumn Thoughts* (p. 743) we have an example of J. W. North, more akin to those he contributed to the Dalziel tablebooks, a landscape, with a fine sense of space, despite the fact that it is enclosed by trees. John Tenniel, in *The Norse Princess* (p. 201) and *Queen Dagmar* (p. 344), finds subjects that suit him peculiarly well. The *Summer Snow* (p. 380), attributed to 'Christopher' Jones, is by Sir Edward Burne-Jones of course, and the final contribution of the artist to these pages. H. J. Lucas, a name rarely encountered, has one drawing, *The Sangreal* (p. 454). A. Boyd Houghton, in *St. Elmo* (p. 64), *A Missionary Cheer* (p. 547), and *Childhood* (p. 636), is showing the more mature style of his best period. G. J. Pinwell has but a single drawing, *Martin Ware's Temptation* (p. 573), and that not peculiarly individual; John Pettie appears with six, *The Monks and the Heathen* (p. 14), *The Passion Flowers of Life* (p. 141), a study of an old man seated in a creeper-covered porch with a child on his lap, *The Night Walk over the Mill Stream* (p. 185), and *Not above his Business* (p. 272), *A Touch of Nature* (p. 417), and *The Negro* (p. 476). To a later generation, who only know the pictures of the Royal Academician, these come as a surprise, and prove the versatility of an artist whose painting was somewhat mannered. Walter Crane's— a fine group of oriental sailors—*Treasure-trove* (p. 795), and J. D. Watson's six drawings are all capable and accomplished; *A Pastoral* (p. 32), a very elaborate composition which looks like a copy of an oil-painting, *Fallen in the Night* (p. 97), *The Curate of Suverdsio* (p. 333), *The Aspen* (p. 401), *Rhoda* (p. 520), and *Olive Shand's Partner* (p. 774), with the not very important *Sheep and Goats* wrongly attributed to Sandys, two decorated pages by John Leighton, one drawing by E. W. Cooke and five by T. Graham, complete the year's record.

49

SOME ILLUSTRATED MAGAZINES

The volume for 1864 is distinctly less interesting. Nevertheless it holds some fine things. Notably five Millais', including *Oh ! the Lark* (p. 65), *A Scene for a Study* (p. 161), *Polly* (p. 248), (a baby-figure kneeling by a bed, which has been republished elsewhere more than once), *The Bridal of Dandelot* (p. 304), and *Prince Philibert* (p. 481), another very popular childish subject, a small girl with a small boy holding a toy-boat. Frederick Walker, in his illustrations to Mrs. Henry Wood's novel, *Oswald Cray* (pp. 32-129, 202, 286, 371, 453, 532, and 604), shows great dramatic insight, and a certain domestic charm, which has caused the otherwise not very entrancing story to linger in one's memory in a way quite disproportionate to its merits. The remaining illustrations to *Oswald Cray* are by R. Barnes (pp. 691, 761, 827), the same artist contributing also *Grandmother's Snuff*, (p. 411), *A Burn Case* (p. 568), *A Lancashire Doxology*, (p. 585), *Blessed to Give* (p. 641), and *The Organ Fiend* (p. 697). M. J. Lawless is responsible for only one subject, a study of a man and a harpsichord, *The Player and the Listeners*; in this case, as, on turning over the pages, you re-read a not very noteworthy poem, you find it has lingered in memory merely from its association with a picture. Arthur Hughes has a graceful design, *At the Sepulchre* (p. 728), which seems to have lost much in the engraving; John Tenniel is also represented by a solitary example, *The Way in the Wood* (p. 552); G. J. Pinwell, in five full-page drawings, *A Christmas Carol* (p. 30), *The Cottage in the Highlands* (p. 427), *M'Diarmid explained* (p. 504), *Malachi's Cove* (p. 729), and *Mourning* (p. 760), sustains his high level. Other subjects, animal pictures by J. Wolf, and figures and landscapes by R. P. Leitch, Florence Claxton, F. Eltze, J. W. Ehrenger, R. T. Pritchett, and W. Colomb, call for no special mention. To John Pettie is attributed a tail-piece of no importance.

With 1865 comes a sudden cessation of interest, as seventy of the illustrations are engraved 'from photographs of oriental scenes to illustrate the editor's series of travel papers,' *Eastward*. This leaves room merely for pictures to the two serials. Paul Gray contributed those to Charles Kingsley's novel, *Hereward, the Last of the English*; but the twelve drawings are unequal, and in few show the promise which elsewhere he exhibited so fully. Robert Barnes

M. J. LAWLESS

'GOOD WORDS'
1864, p. 168

THE PLAYER AND
THE LISTENERS

GOOD WORDS
supplies nine for the story, *Alfred Hagart's Household*, by
Alexander Smith of *City Poems* fame. These, like all the
artist's work, are singularly good of their kind, and show at
once his great facility and his comparatively limited range of
types.

In 1866, although engravings after photographs do not
usurp the space to the extent they did in the previous year,
they are present, and the volume, in spite of many excellent
drawings, cannot compare in interest with those for 1862-64.
The frontispiece, *Lilies*, is a most charming figure-subject
by W. Small, who contributes also three others : *The Old
Yeomanry Weeks* (p. 127), *Deliverance* (p. 663), a typical example of a landscape with figures in the foreground, which,
in the hands of this artist, becomes something entirely distinct
from the ' figure with a landscape beyond ' of most others ; and
Carissimo (p. 736), a pair of lovers on an old stone bench, 'just
beyond the Julian gate,' which seems as carefully studied as
if it were intended for a painting in oils. To compare the
average picture to a poem to-day, with the work of Mr.
Small and many of his fellows, is not encouraging. Thirty
years ago it seemed as if the draughtsman did his best to
evolve a perfect representation of the subject of the verses ;
now one feels doubtful whether the artist does not keep on
hand, to be supplied to order, a series of lovers in attitudes
warranted to fit, more or less accurately, any verses by any
poet. Of course for one picture issued then, a score, perhaps
a hundred, are published to-day, and it might be that numer-
ically as many really good drawings appear in the course of a
year now, as then ; but, while our average rarely descends to
the feeblest depths of the sixties, it still more rarely comes
near such work as Mr. Small's, whose method is still followed
and has influenced more decidedly a larger number of draughtsmen than has that of Millais, Walker, Pinwell, or Houghton.

Studying his work at this date, you realise how very strongly
he influenced the so-called ' *Graphic* School ' which supplanted
the movement we are considering in the next decade. Despite
the appreciation, contemporary and retrospective, already
bestowed upon his work, despite the influence—not always
for good—upon the younger men, it is yet open to doubt if
the genius of this remarkable artist has received adequate
recognition. In a running commentary upon work of all
51

degrees of excellence, one is struck anew with its admirably
sustained power and its constantly fresh manner.

This digression, provoked by the four delightful 'Small'
drawings, must not lead one to overlook the rest of the
pictures in *Good Words* for 1866. They include *The Island
Church*, by J. W. North (p. 393), *The Life-Boat*, by J. W.
Lawson (p. 248), *Between the Showers*, by W. J. Linton,
(p. 424), six illustrations to *Ruth Thornbury*, by M. E.
Edwards, and one by G. J. Pinwell, *Bridget Dally's Change*.
Perhaps the most notable of the year are the five still to be
named: A. Boyd Houghton's *The Voyage*, and a set of four
half-page drawings, *Reaping, Binding, Carrying, Gleaning*,
entitled *The Harvest* (pp. 600, 601). These have a decorative
arrangement not always present in the work of this clever
artist, and a peculiarly large method of treatment, so much so
that if the text informed you that they were pen-sketches
from life-size paintings, you would not be surprised. Whether
by accident or design, it is curious to discover that the landscapes in each pair, set as they are on pages facing one another,
have a look of being carried across the book in Japanese
fashion.

1867 might be called the Pinwell year, as a dozen of his
illustrations to Dr. George Mac Donald's *Guild Court*, and
one each to *A Bird in the Hand* and *The Cabin Boy*, account
for nearly half the original drawings in the volume. W.
Small is seen in five characteristic designs to Dr. Macleod's
The Starling, and one each to *Beside the Stile* (p. 645) and
The Highland Student (p. 663). Arthur Boyd Houghton
contributes *Omar and the Persian* (p. 104) and *Making Poetry*
(p. 248); the first a typical example of his oriental manner,
the latter one of his home scenes. S. L. Fildes appears
with *In the Choir* (p. 537), a church interior showing the
influence of William Small. F. W. Lawson illustrates *Grace's
Fortune* with three drawings, also redolent of Small, and Fred
Walker has *Waiting in the Dusk*, a picture of a girl in a
passage, which does not illustrate the accompanying verses,
and has the air of being a picture prepared for a serial some
time before, that, having been delayed for some reason, has
been served up with a poem that chanced to be in type.

In 1868 Pinwell and Houghton between them are
responsible for quite half the separate plates, and Small

contributes no less than thirty-four which illustrate delightfully *The Woman's Kingdom*, a novel by the author of *John
Halifax*, together with a large number of vignetted initials, a
feature not before introduced into this magazine. Without
forgetting the many admirable examples of Mr. Small's power
to sustain the interest of the reader throughout a whole set of
illustrations to a work of fiction, one doubts if he has ever
surpassed the excellence of these. The little sketches of
figures and landscapes in the initials show that he did not
consider it beneath his dignity to study the text thoroughly,
so as to interpret it with dramatic insight. Your modern
chic draughtsman, who reads hastily the few lines under-
scored in blue pencil by his editor, must laugh at the pains
taken by the older men. Indeed, a very up-to-date illustrator
will not merely refuse to carry out the author's idea, but
prefer his own conception of the character, and say so. That
neither course in itself produces great work may be granted,
but one cannot avoid the conclusion that if it be best to
illustrate a novel (which is by no means certain) that artist is
most worthy of praise who does his utmost to present the
characters invented by the author. True, that character-
drawing with pen and pencil is out of date,—subtle emotion
has taken its place,—it is not easy to make a picture of a
person smiling outwardly, but inwardly convulsed with conflicting desires ; the smile you may get, but the conflicting
desires are hard to work in at the same time. Appreciation
of Mr. Small's design need not imply censure of the work of
others ; but, all the same, the cheap half-tone from a wash-
drawing, in the current sixpenny magazine, looks a very feeble
thing after an hour devoted to the illustrations to *Guy Water-
man's Maze*, *The Woman's Kingdom*, *Griffith Gaunt*, and the
rest of the serials he illustrated. In this volume two others,
The Harvest Home (p. 489) and *A Love Letter* (p. 618), are
also from the same facile hand.

The first of the Boyd Houghtons is a striking design to
Tennyson's poem of *The Victim* (p. 18) ; neither picture nor
poem shows its author at his best. Others signed A. B. H.
are : *The Church in the Cevennes* (pp. 56, 57), *Discipleship*
(p. 112), *The Pope and the Cardinals* (p. 305), *The Gold Bridge*
(p. 321), *The Two Coats* (p. 432), *How it all happened* (seven
illustrations), *Dance my Children* (p. 568), a typical example

of the peculiar mannerism of its author, and a *Russian Farm-yard* (p. 760); also a number of small designs to *Russian Fables*, some of which were illustrated also by Zwecker. G. J. Pinwell illustrates *Notes on the Fire* (pp. 47, 49), *Much work for Little Pay* (p. 89), *A Paris Pawn-shop* (p. 233), *Mrs. Dubosq's Daughter* (four pictures), *Una and the Lion* (p. 361), *Lovely, yet unloved* (pp. 376, 377), *Hop Gathering* (p. 424), *The Quakers in Norway* (p. 504). S. L. Fildes has *The Captain's Story*, a good study of fire-light reflected on three seated figures. Other numbers worth noting are an excellent example of J. Mahoney, *Yesterday and To-day* (p. 672), Briton Riviere's *At the Window* (p. 630), R. Buckman's *The White Umbrella* (p. 473), and seven by Francis Walker to *Hero Harold*, and one each to *Glenalla* (p. 384), *The Bracelet* (p. 753), and *Thieves' Quarter* (p. 553).

With 1869 we lose sight of many of the men who did so much to sustain the artistic reputation of this magazine. W. Small has but one drawing, *The Old Manor-House* (p. 849). Hubert Herkomer is represented by *The Way to Machaerus* (pp. 353, 497), J. Mahoney by five designs to *The Staffordshire Potter*, Francis Walker by nine to *The Connaught Potters* and *A Burial at Machaerus* and *Holyhead Breakwater*. Arthur Hughes, an infrequent contributor so far, contributes two illustrations to *Carmina Nuptialia*. F. Barnard has two to *House-hunting*; F. A. Fraser has no less than seventy-five : thirty-five to *Debenham's Vow*, and thirty-three to *Noblesse Oblige*, with seven others, none of them worth reconsideration, although they served their purpose no doubt at the time.

With 1870 we reach the limit of the present chronicle, to which Francis Walker and F. A. Fraser contribute most of the pictures. The most interesting are : Arthur Hughes's *Fancy* (p. 777) and *The Mariner's Cave* (p. 865); J. D. Linton, *Married Lovers* (p. 601); J. Mahoney, *The Dorsetshire Hind* (p. 21), *Ascent of Snowdon* (p. 201); and *Dame Martha's Well* (p. 680), and G. J. Pinwell's three very representative drawings, *Rajah playing Chess* (p. 211), *Margaret in the Xebec* (p. 280), and *A Winter Song* (p. 321).

1871 is memorable for three of Arthur Hughes's designs, made for a projected illustrated edition of Tennyson's *Loves of the Wrens*, a scheme abandoned at the author's wish; the three drawings cut down from their original size, *Fly Little*

FANCY

LONDON SOCIETY

Letter (p. 33), *The Mist and the Rain* (p. 113), and *Sun Comes, Moon Comes* (p. 183), are especially dear to collectors of Mr. Hughes's work, which appeared here with the lyrics set to Sir Arthur Sullivan's music; another by the same artist, *The Mother and the Angel* (p. 648), is also worth noting. One Boyd Houghton, *Baraduree Justice* (p. 464), twenty-one drawings by W. Small to Katharine Saunders, *The High Mills*, and one by the same artist to *An Unfinished Song* (p. 641) are in this volume, besides four by Pinwell, *Aid to the Sick* (p. 40), *The Devil's Boots* (p. 217), *Toddy's Legacy* (p. 336), and *Shall we ever meet again?* (p. 817).

Without discussing the remaining years of this still flourishing monthly one can hardly omit mention of the volume for 1878, in which William Black's *Macleod of Dare* is illustrated by G. H. Boughton, R.A., J. Pettie, R.A., P. Graham, R.A., W. Q. Orchardson, R.A., and John Everett Millais, R.A., a group which recalls the glories of its early issues.

LONDON SOCIETY

This popular illustrated shilling magazine, started in February 1862 under the editorship of Mr. James Hogg, has not received so far its due share of appreciation from the few who have studied the publications of the sixties. Yet its comparative neglect is easily accounted for. It contains, no doubt, much good work—some, indeed, worthy to be placed in the first rank. But it also includes a good deal that, if tolerable when the momentary fashions it depicted were not ludicrous, appears now merely commonplace and absurd. A great artist—Millais especially—could introduce the crino-line and the Dundreary whiskers, so that even to-day their ugliness does not repel you. But less accomplished draughts-men, who followed slavishly the inelegant mode of the sixties, now stand revealed as merely journalists. Journalism, useful and honourable as its work may be, rarely has lasting qualities which bear revival. Aiming as it did to be a 'smart' and topical magazine, with the mood of the hour reflected in its pages, it remains a document not without interest to the social historian. Amid its purely ephemeral contents there are quite enough excellent drawings to ensure its preservation in any representative collection of English illustrations.

55

SOME ILLUSTRATED MAGAZINES

In the first volume for 1862 we find a beautiful Lawless, *Beauty's Toilet* (p. 265), spoilt by its engraving, the texture of the flesh being singularly coarse and ineffectual. Fred Walker, in *The Drawing-room*, '*Paris*' (i. p. 401), is seen in the unusual and not very captivating mood of a 'society' draughtsman. *Ash Wednesday* (p. 150), by J. D. Watson, is a singularly fine example of an artist whose work, the more you come across it, surprises you by its sustained power. The frontispiece *Spring Days* and *A Romance* and *A Curacy* (p. 386), are his also. Other illustrations by T. Morten, H. Sanderson, C. H. Bennett, Adelaide Claxton, Julian Portch, and F. R. Pickersgill, R.A., call for no special comment. In the second volume there are two drawings by Lawless, *First Night at the Seaside* (p. 220) and *A Box on the Ear* (p. 382); several by Du Maurier, one *A Kettledrum* (p. 203), peculiarly typical of his society manner; others, *Refrezzment* (p. 110), *Snowdon* (p. 481), *Oh sing again* (p. 433), *Jewels* (p. 105), and a *Mirror Scene* (p. 107), which reveal the cosmopolitan student of nature outside the artificial, if admirable, restrictions of 'good form.' *The Border Witch* (p. 181), by J. E. Millais, A.R.A., is one of the very few examples by the great illustrator in this periodical. J. D. Watson, in *Moonlight on the Beach* (p. 333), *Married*[1] (p. 449), *A Summer Eve* (p. 162), *On the Coast* (p. 321), *Holiday Life* (p. 339), and *How I gained a Wife* (p. 551), again surprises you, with regret his admirable work has yet not received fuller appreciation by the public. Walter Crane contributes some society pictures which reveal the admirable decorator in an unusual, and, to be candid, unattractive aspect. *Kensington Gardens* (p. 172), *A London Carnival* (p. 79), and *Which is Fairest?* (p. 242), are interesting as the work of a youth, but betray little evidence of his future power. Robert Barnes, in *Dreaming Love and Waiting Duty* (p. 564), shows how early in his career he reached the level which he maintained so admirably. A. Boyd Houghton's *Finding a Relic* (p. 89) is a good if not typical specimen of his work. The designs by E. J. Poynter, *Tip Cat* (p. 321), *I can't thmoke a pipe* (p. 318), and *Lord Dundreary* (pp. 308, 472), are singularly unlike the usual work of the accomplished author of *Israel in Egypt*. To these one must add the names of C. H. Bennett (*Beadles*,

---

[1] This is entitled *Too Soon*, in *Pictures of Society*, 1867.

J. D. WATSON

TOO LATE

three), W. M'Connell, C. A. Doyle, George H. Thomas,
E. K. Johnson, F. J. Skill, F. Claxton, H. Sanderson, and
A. W. Cooper.   So that 1862 offers, at least, a goodly list of
artists, and quite enough first-rate work to make the volumes
worth preserving.
   In vol. iii. 1863 there is a drawing, *The Confession* (p. 37),
engraved by Dalziel, that is possibly by Pinwell.   Three by
T. Morten, *After the Opera* (p. 39), *A Struggle in the Clouds*
(p. 287), and *Ruth Grey's Trial* (p. 59), are good, if not the
best of this artist's work.   Two by George Du Maurier (pp. 209,
216) employ, after the manner of the time, a sort of pictured
parable entitled *On the Bridge* and *Under the Bridge.   Our
Honeymoon*, by Marcus Stone, is interesting.   *Struck Down*
(p. 106) and *The Heiress of Elkington* (p. 345), both by J. D.
Watson, are as good as his work is usually.   *A May Morning*
(p. 428), by George H. Thomas, is also worthy of mention, but
the rest, by E. K. Johnson, E. H. Corbould, W. Brunton, W.
Cave Thomas, Louis Huard, etc., are not peculiarly attractive.
   The concluding volume for 1863 has a very dainty figure,
Honey-Dew, by M. J. Lawless (p. 554).   The three Du
Mauriers are *A Little Hop in Harley St.* (p. 469), *Lords* :
University Cricket Match (p. 161), and the *Worship of Bacchus*
(p. 192) at first sight so curiously like a Charles Keene that,
were it not for the signature, one would distrust the index.
Nine drawings by T. Morten to *The First Time* are good,
especially those on p. 180, and *A First Attempt*, Charles
Green (p. 205), is also worth notice.   Two drawings by G. J.
Pinwell, *Wolsey* (p. 311) and another (p. 319), are charac-
teristic.   For the rest, C. H. Bennett, Louis Huard, Felix
Darley, W. M'Connell, W. Brunton, Matt Morgan, Florence
Claxton, T. Godwin, Waldo Sargent, George Thomas, and
C. A. Doyle, provide *entrées* and sweets a little flavourless
to-day, although palatable enough, no doubt, at the time.
   In 1864, M. J. Lawless's *Not for You* (p. 85) ; a fine J. D.
Watson, *The Duet* (p. 268) ; *Charley Blake*, by G. Du Maurier
(p. 385) ; *At Swindon* (p.41), M. E. Edwards, and *Little Golden
Hair*, by R. Barnes, are the only others above the average.
Adelaide Claxton, W. M'Connell, H. Sanderson, and J. B.
Zwecker provide most of the rest.   The second half of the
year (vol. vi.) is far better, contains some good work by the
' talented young lady,' M. E. E. (to quote contemporary praise);

SOME ILLUSTRATED MAGAZINES

that her work was talented all students of the 'sixties' will agree. *A Holocaust* (p. 433), *Dangerous* (p. 353), *Gone* (p. 185), *Magdalen* (p. 553), *Milly's Success* (p. 269), and *Unto this Last* (p. 252) are all by Miss Edwards. A fine Millais, *Knightly Worth* (p. 247), and a good J. D. Watson, *Blankton Weir* (p. 416), would alone make the volume memorable. C. A. Doyle has some of his best drawings to *A Shy Man*, and G. H. Thomas and others maintain a good average. Rebecca Solomon has a good full page (p. 541). In the extra Christmas number you will find E. J. Poynter's *A Sprig of Holly* (p. 28), J. D. Watson's *Story of a Christmas Fairy* (p. 24), a notable design, besides capital illustrations by Du Maurier, R. Dudley (*The Blue Boy*), R. Barnes, and Marcus Stone.

1865 is a Du Maurier year. In vol. vii. eleven drawings by this fecund artist on pp. 38, 193, 202, 289, 296, 428, 430, 481, 488, and 697, all excellent examples of his early manner. Arthur Hughes, with *The Farewell Valentine* (p. 188), makes his first appearance within the pages of *London Society*. A. W. Cooper, J. Pasquier, T. R. Lamont, and A. Claxton are to the fore, and C. H. Bennett has a series of typical members of various learned societies, which, characteristic as they are, might have their titles transposed without any one being the wiser. In vol. viii. 1865, Paul Gray appears with *My Darling* (p. 253). T. Morten has three capital drawings : *Two Loves and a Life* (p. 400), *A Romance at Marseilles* (p. 549), and *Love and Pride* (p. 16) ; and Du Maurier has *Codlingham Regatta* (p. 284), *How not to play Croquet* (p. 61), *Where shall we go?* (p. 17), *Old Jockey West* (p. 288), *The Rev. Mr. Green* (p. 122), *Furnished Apartments* (p. 481), and *Ticklish Ground* (p. 488). G. J. Pinwell is represented by a solitary example, *The Courtship of Giles Languish* (p. 384), J. D. Watson by *Green Mantle* (pp. 385, 388, 389), and M. E. Edwards by *Georgie's First Love-letter* (p. 152), *Faithful and True* (p. 263), *Firm and Faithful* (p. 60). The other contributors are A. W. Bayes (*To Gertrude*, p. 460), L. C. Henley, T. R. Lamont, J. A. Pasquier, Kate Edwards, W. Brunton, T. S. Seccombe, John Gascoine, etc.

In 1866, vol. ix., George Du Maurier signs the frontispiece, *Two to One*, and also two illustrations to *Much Ado About Nothing* (pp. 289, 296), two to *Second Thoughts* (pp. 385, 391), and two to *Queen of Diamonds* (pp. 481-488).

58

LONDON SOCIETY

T. Morten has again three designs : *Mrs. Reeve* (p. 135), *On the Wrekin* (p. 1), and *The Man with a Dog* (p. 239); R. Dudley supplies one, *The Tilt-Yard* (p. 441), and Kate Edwards one, *The June Dream* (p. 531). M. Ellen Edwards in three admirable examples, *In Peril* (p. 450), *Mutually Forgiven* (p. 228), and *The Cruel Letter* (p. 364), shows how cleverly she caught the influence in the air. Other artists contribute many drawings of no particular interest.

Vol. x. shows W. Small with two drawings, *Agatha* (p. 160) and *The Reading of Locksley Hall* (p. 8). It is curious to see how the sentimentality of the poem has influenced the admirable draughtsman, who is not here at his best. Paul Gray has also two, *An English October* (p. 289) and *To a Flirt* (p. 373); G. Du Maurier is represented by one only, *Life in Lodgings* (p. 516); J. G. Thompson by one also, *Caught at Last* (p. 80); T. Morten again contributes three : *Marley Hall* (p. 560), *May's Window* (p. 432), and *The Trevillians' Summer Trip* (p. 124); A. Boyd Houghton is represented by *Ready for Supper* (p. 146), and M. E. Edwards by two drawings to *Something to My Advantage* (pp. 481-488). The Christmas number contains one Boyd Houghton, *The Christmas Tree* (p. 80); a J. D. Watson, *Given back on Christmas Morn* (p. 63); a very good F. W. Lawson, *Did I Offend?* (p. 32); a delightful Charles Keene, *How I lost my Whiskers* (p. 27); *Sir Guy's Goblet* (p. 16), by M. E. Edwards, and one by George Cruikshank, *My Christmas Box*, looking curiously out of place here.

In the eleventh volume (1867) the four by W. Small are among the most important. They are *A Pastoral Episode* (p. 406), *Quite Alone* (p. 277), *The Meeting* (p. 163), and *Try to Keep Firm* (p. 361); a J. D. Watson, *Changes* (p. 373); a Paul Gray, *Goldsmith at the Temple Gate* (p. 392); a J. G. Thompson, *An Expensive Journey* (p. 36); M. E. Edwards's *Winding of the Skein* (p. 177), and L. C. Henley's *How I set about Paying my Debts* (p. 388), are all that need be mentioned. In the twelfth volume (1867) A. Boyd Houghton signs a couple of drawings to *A Spinster's Sweepstake* (pp. 376, 383), G. J. Pinwell supplies two to *Beautiful Mrs. Johnson* (pp. 136-248), F. W. Lawson two to *Dedding Revisited* (p. 433), *Without Reserve* (p. 440), and four to *Mary Eaglestone's Lover* (pp. 97, 103, 207, 362). Charles Green is

59

responsible for *The Meeting at the Play* (p. 276), and J. G. Thompson for a series, *Threading the Mazy at Islington.* The Christmas number is honoured by two fine drawings by Charles Keene (p. 18) and a good double page by J. D. Watson, *Christmas at an old Manor-House.* Sir John Gilbert, a rare contributor to these pages, is represented by *The Rowborough Hollies* (p. 41), M. E. Edwards by *The Christmas Rose* (p. 16), and F. W. Lawson by *My Turn Next* (p. 73).

With its thirteenth volume (1868) *London Society* still keeps up to the level it established. Among much that was intended for the moment only there is also work of far more sterling value. Charles Keene, in two drawings for *Tomkins' Degree Supper* (pp. 224, 232), is seen at his best, and how good that is needs no retelling. Sir John Gilbert, among a new generation, keeps his place as a master, and in four drawings (pp. 113, 249, 314, 429) reveals the superb qualities of his work, coupled, it must be said, with certain limitations which are almost inseparable from rapid production. G. Du Maurier is represented by two, *Lift her to it* (p. 324) and *The White Carnation* (p. 558). The inscription of *Expectation* (p. 360), by 'the late M. J. Lawless', marks the final discharge of an illustrator who did much to impart permanent interest to the magazine. It is always a regret to find that Mr. Sandys chose other fields of work, and that death withdrew Lawless so soon ; for these two, not displaying equal power, together with Walter Crane maintained the decorative ideal through a period when it was unpopular with the public and apparently found little favour in editors' eyes. M. E. Edwards's *My Valentine* (p. 114) and *Married on her tenth Birthday* (p. 206). To this list must be added W. Small, with a delightful out-of-doors study, '*You did not come*' (p. 368); G. B. Goddard with some capital 'animal' pictures : *Spring of Life* (p. 353), *Buck Shooting* (p. 72), and *Dogs of Note* (pp. 75, 179); Wilfrid Lawson, *A Spring-tide Tale* (p. 472); F. Barnard, *A Bracing Morning* (p. 60); A. W. Cooper, *The Old Seat* (p. 268); and others by Tom Gray, J. G. Thomson, W. L. Thomas, J. A. Pasquier, W. S. Gilbert, S. E. Illingworth, Rice, W. Brunton, H. French, A. Crowquill, Edwin J. Ellis, Fane Wood, and Isaac L. Brown. Vol. xiv., the second of 1868, contains J. D. Watson's *The Oracle* (p. 457); W. Small's *The Lights on Gwyneth's Head*

LONDON SOCIETY
(p. 165) ; A. Boyd Houghton, *The Turn of the Tide* (p. 458); John Gilbert's *Cousin Geoffrey's Chamber* (*Frontispiece*), and *Box and Cox in Bay of Bengal* (p. 392); Birket Foster's *The Falconer's Lay*, probably engraved from a water-colour drawing (p. 529); Wilfrid Lawson's *Crush-room* (p. 140); *For Charity's Sake* (p. 112); *Behind the Scenes* (p. 141), *The Gentle Craft* (p. 86), and *The Golden Boat* (p. 579), with many others by the regular contributors. In the Christmas number we find *Linley Sambourne*, whose work is encountered rarely outside the pages of *Punch*, with a design for a *Christmas Day Costume* (p. 17); Charles Keene, with two drawings for *Our Christmas Turkey* (pp. 44, 46); G. B. Goddard's full-page, *Knee-deep* (p. 32); J. D. Watson's *Aunt Grace's Sweetheart* (p. 19) and *The Two Voices* (p. 86) deserve noting.

In 1869 Wilfrid Lawson illustrates Whyte-Melville's *M. or N.*, and has several other full-page drawings in his best vein (pp. 8, 48, 89, 128, 152, 232, 307, 467, 540) ; J. Mahoney is first met here with *Officers and Gentlemen* (p. 284), and J. D. Watson supplies the frontispiece to vol. xv., *Bringing Home the Hay*, and also that to vol. xvi., *Second Blossom*. In this latter Wilfrid Lawson has illustrations to *M. or N.* (pp. 156, 193, 236, 386); T. Morten, a powerful drawing, *Winter's Night* (p. 550); G. B. Goddard, *The Sportman's Resolve* (p. 528). The other artists, including some new contributors, are M. A. Boyd, Horace Stanton, E. J. Ellis, T. Sweeting, James Godwin, F. Roberts, A. W. Cooper, L. Huard, and B. Ridley. The Christmas number for 1869 contains a good Charles Keene, *The Coat with the Fur Lining* (pp. 1, 6); Gilbert's *Secret of Calverly Court* (p. 4); M. E. Edwards's *How the Choirs were Carolling* (p. 84) ; and J. Mahoney's *Mr. Daubarn* (p. 49), with others of no particular importance.

The numbers for 1870 contain, *inter alia*, in the first half-year, a good J. D. Watson, *Going down the Road* (*Frontispiece*); *A Leaf from a Sketch-Book*, by Linley Sambourne (printed, like a series this year, on special sheets of thick white paper, as four-page supplements), which contained lighter work by artists of the hour, but none worth special mention.

J. Mahoney's *Going to the Drawing-room* (p. 321), and *Sir Stephen's Question* (p. 112), and *Spring-time*, drawn and engraved by W. L. Thomas (p. 375), are among the most

61

interesting of the ordinary full pages. In the second half of the year, volume 18, there is a full page, *Not Mine* (p. 501), by Arthur Hughes, which links 1855 to 1870; A. W. Small, *After the Season* (p. 338); the very unimportant drawing by M. J. Lawless, *An Episode of the Italian War* (p. 97), has interest as a relic; J. Mahoney contributes two to *The Old House by the River* (pp. 67, 172), and many others by H. Paterson, Wilfrid Lawson, A. Claxton. This year a Holiday number appeared, with a not very good J. D. Watson, *A Landscape Painter* (p. 47), and two Francis Walkers, *A Summer Holiday* and *Rosalind and Celia*, and other seasonable designs by various hands. The Christmas number has a coloured frontispiece and other designs by H. D. Marks; J. D. Watson illustrates *What might have happened* (pp. 8, 17, 19); and Charles Keene, *Gipsy Moll* (pp. 39, 45); Francis Walker has *The Star Rider* (p. 59) and *A Tale* (p. 63); F. A. Fraser, typical of the next decade, and one might say, without undue severity, of the decadence also, and F. Gilbert, that facile understudy of *Sir John*, show examples of work differing as far as it well could; but 1870 is the last stage we need note here in the career of a magazine which did notable service to the cause of illustration, and brought a good many men into notice who have taken prominent part in the history of 'black and white.' Without placing it on a level with *Once a Week*, it is an interesting collection of representative work, with some really first-rate drawing.

Frederick Sandys, del.

"Oh, what's that in the hollow, so pale I quake to follow?
Oh, that's a thin dead body which waits th'eternal term."

Christina Rossetti.

CHAPTER V: OTHER ILLUSTRATED PERIODICALS OF THE SIXTIES. 'CHURCHMAN'S FAMILY MAGAZINE,' 'SUNDAY MAGAZINE,' ETC.

N devoting another chapter to periodicals one must insist upon their relative importance; for the time and money expended on them in a single year would balance possibly the cost of all the books mentioned in this volume. In a naïve yet admirable article in the Christmas *Bookseller*, 1862, written from a commercial standpoint, the author says, speaking of some pictures in *Good Words* : ' Some of these, we are informed, cost as much as £50 a block, a sum which appears marvellous when we look at the low price of the magazine'; he instances also the celebrated ' J. B.'[1], 'whose delineations of animals are equal to Landseer. The magazines to be noticed are those only which contain original designs; others, *The National Magazine*, the *Fine Arts Quarterly*, and the like, which relied upon the reproductions of paintings, are not even mentioned.

THE CHURCHMAN'S FAMILY MAGAZINE

Any periodical containing the work of Millais and Sandys is, obviously, in the front rank, but *The Churchman's Family Magazine*, which started in January 1863, did not long maintain its high level; yet the first half a dozen volumes have enough good work to entitle them to more than passing mention. This, like *London Society*, was published by Mr. James Hogg, and must not be confounded with another of the same price, with similar title, *The Churchman's Shilling Magazine*, to which reference is made elsewhere. In the familiar octavo of its class, it is well printed and well illustrated. The first volume contains two full pages by Millais, *Let that be please* (p. 15) and *You will forgive me* (p. 221); three illustrations by E. J. Poynter to *The Painter's Glory* (pp. 124, 131, 136); three by T. Morten (pp. 137, 432, and 531); five by J. D. Watson, *Only Grandmamma* (p. 89), *Christian Martyr* (p. 104), *Sunday Evening*

---

[1] ' J. B.' was Mrs. Blackburn, wife of Hugh Blackburn, Professor of Mathematics in the University of Glasgow. Landseer said that in the drawing of animals he had nothing to teach her.

OTHER ILLUSTRATED PERIODICALS
(p. 191), *The Hermit* (p. 260), and *Mary Magdalene* (p. 346);
three by Charles Green to *How Susy Tried* (pp. 57, 64, 71),
and one each to *Henry II.* (p. 385), and *An Incident in
Canterbury Cathedral* (p. 482), a drawing strangely resembling
a 'John Gilbert.' H. S. Marks is represented by *Home
Longing* (p. 113) and *Age and Youth* (p. 337); H. H.
Armstead by *Fourth Sunday in Lent* (p. 245) and *Angel
Teachers* (p. 539); J. C. Horsley by *Anne Boleyn* (p. 136);
F. R. Pickersgill by *The Still Small Voice* (p. 586); G. H.
Thomas by *Catechising in Church* (p. 225), and R. Barnes
by *Music for the Cottage* (p. 289) and *The Strange Gentle-
man* (p. 293). Besides these the volume contains others by
Rebecca (sister to Simeon) Solomon (p. 571), L. Huard, D. H.
Friston, H. C. Selous, T. Macquoid, W. M'Connell, T.
Sulman, E. K. Johnson (*Spenser*, p. 576), and J. B. Zwecker—
a very fairly representative group of the average illustrator of
the period. The second half of 1863 (vol. ii.) enshrines the
fine Frederick Sandys, *The Waiting Time*, an incident of the
Lancashire cotton famine (p. 91). Another of M. J. Lawless's
most charming designs, *One Dead* (p. 275), (reprinted under
the title of *The Silent Chamber*), will be found here. M. E.
Edwards contributes two, *Ianthe's Grave* (p. 128) and *Child,
I said* (p. 405); G. J. Pinwell is represented once with *By the
Sea* (p. 257); and T. Morten with *The Bell-ringers' Christmas
Story* (p. 513). The other artists include H. C. Selous,
C. W. Cope, F. R. Pickersgill, E. Armitage, A. W. Cooper,
E. H. Wehnert, E. H. Corbould, Marshall Claxton, P. W.
Justyne, P. Skelton, Paulo Priolo, D. H. Friston, H.
Sanderson, Creswick, and T. B. Dalziel. In vol. iii. (1864)
M. J. Lawless has *Harold Massey's Confession* (p. 65); C.
Green, *Thinking and Wishing* (p. 223); G. J. Pinwell, *March
Winds* (p. 232); M. E. Edwards, *At the Casement* (p. 354);
and T. Morten, *The Twilight Hour* (p. 553). Among other
contributors are Florence Caxton, L. Huard, H. M. Vining,
W. M'Connell, Rebecca Solomon, H. Fitzcook, John Absolom,
Percy Justyne, F. W. Keyl, W. J. Allen.

In vol. iv. are J. D. Watson's *Crusaders in Sight of
Jerusalem* (p. 557), T. B. Dalziel's *In the Autumn Twilight*
(p. 441), and A. W. Cooper's *Lesson of the Watermill* (p.
339); Florence Caxton illustrates the serial. And in vol. v.
M. E. Edwards's *Deare Childe* (p. 114), and *The Emblem of*

'ONE DEAD'

THE WAITING TIME

THE CHURCHMAN'S FAMILY MAGAZINE

Life (p. 64), and A. Boyd Houghton's *A Word in Season* (p. 409), are best worth noting. Vol. vi. has a good study of a monk, *Desert Meditations* (p. 493), and a *Gretchen's Lament* (p. 82), by M. E. Edwards. From vol. vii. onwards portraits, chiefly of ecclesiastical dignitaries, take the place of pictures.

THE SHILLING MAGAZINE

This somewhat scarce publication is often referred to as one of the important periodicals of the sixties, but on looking through it, it seems to have established its claim on somewhat slender foundation. True, it contains one of Sandys' most memorable designs—here reproduced in photogravure from an early impression of the block, a peculiarly fine drawing—to Christina Rossetti's poem, *Amor Mundi*. It was reproduced from a photograph of the drawing on wood in the first edition of Mr. Pennell's admirable *Pen Drawing and Pen Draughtsmen*, and in the second edition are reproductions by process, not only of Mr. Sandys' original drawing as preserved in a Hollyer photograph, but of preliminary studies for the figures.

The rest of the illustrations of the magazine, which only lived for a few months, are comparatively few and not above the average in merit. The numbers, May 1865 to May 1866, contain eight drawings by J. D. Watson, illustrating Mrs. Riddell's *Phemie Keller*. Thirteen by Paul Gray illustrate *The White Flower of Ravensworth*, by Miss M. Betham-Edwards. Others noteworthy are : *Gythia*, by T. R. Lamont ; *Dahut*, and *An Incident of* 1809, by J. Lawson ; *Mistrust* and *Love's Pilgrimage*, by Edward Hughes ; a fine composition, *Lost on the Fells*, by W. Small, and a few minor drawings mostly in the text. It was published by T. Bosworth, 215 Regent Street. This is a brief record of a fairly praiseworthy venture, but there is really no more to be said about it.

THE SUNDAY MAGAZINE,

Another sixpenny illustrated monthly more definitely religious in its aim than *Good Words*, of which it was an offspring, was started in 1865. The illustrations from the first were hardly less interesting than those in the other publications under the direction of Mr. Alexander Strahan. Indeed, it would be unjust not to express very clearly and unmistakably the debt which all lovers of black-and-white art owe to the publisher of these magazines. The conditions of oil-painting

OTHER ILLUSTRATED PERIODICALS
demand merely a public ready to buy : whether the artist
negotiates directly with the purchaser, or employs an agent,
is a matter of convenience. But black-and-white illustration
requires a well-circulated, well-printed, well-conducted periodical : not as a middleman whose services can be dispensed
with, but as a vital factor in the enterprise. Therefore
drawings intended for publication imply a publisher, and
one who is not merely a man with pronounced artistic
taste, but also a good administrator and a capable man of
business. These triple qualifications are found but rarely
together, and when they do unite, the influence of such a
personality is of the utmost importance.   Mr. Strahan, who
appears to have combined in no small degree the qualities
which go to make a successful publisher, set on foot two
popular magazines, which, in spite of their having long passed
their first quarter of a century, are still holding their own.   A
third, full of promise, *Good Words for the Young*, was cut off
in its prime, or rather died of a lingering disease, caused by
that terrible microbe *the foreign cliché*.   Others, *The Day of
Rest* and *Saturday Journal*, also affected by the same ailment,
succumbed after more or less effort ; but the magazines that
relied on the best contemporary illustrators still flourish.   The
moral, obvious as it is, deserves to be insisted upon.   To-day
the photograph from life is as popular with many editors as
the *cliché* from German and French originals was in the
seventies ; but a public which tired of foreign electros may
soon grow weary of the inevitable photograph, and so the
warning is worth setting down.
     Like its companion, *Good Words*, it has known fat
years and lean years ; volumes that were full of admirable
drawings, and volumes that barely maintained a respectable
average. From the very first volume of the *Sunday Magazine*
we find among others R. Barnes, A. Boyd Houghton, M. E.
Edwards, Paul Gray, J. Lawson, F. W. Lawson, J. W. North,
G. J. Pinwell, and Marcus Stone well represented.   The
standard of excellence implied by these names was preserved
for a considerable time.   To this Pinwell contributes two
drawings, *The House of God* (p. 144) and *Only a Lost Child*
(p. 592), a typical character-study of town life.   Paul Gray
has a full page, *The Maiden Martyr* (p. 272), engraved by
Swain ; either the drawing is below his level, or it has
66

SUMMER

SWAIN. SC.

'SUNDAY MAGAZINE'
1865, p. 328

THE SUNDAY MAGAZINE
suffered badly at the hands of the engraver. *The Orphan Girl* (p. 296), *Clara Linzell's Commentary* (p. 401), and *Dorcas* (p. 617), by the same artist, are all interesting, but do not represent him at his best. The single contribution by A. Boyd Houghton, *Friar Ives* (p. 384), is not particularly good. In *Winter*, by J. W. North (p. 328), we have a most excellent drawing of a snow-clad farm with a thrashing machine at work in the distance, and two children in the foreground. The delicacy and breadth of the work, and its true tonality deserve appreciation; it was engraved by Swain. *Drowned* (p. 585), by Marcus Stone, is not very typical. *The Watch at the Sepulchre* (p. 940), by J. Lawson, is a spirited group of Roman soldiers. *Caught in a Thunderstorm*, by R. P. Leitch, engraved by W. J. Linton, is interesting to disciples of 'the white line.' Edward Whymper supplies the frontispiece, *The Righi*. M. E. Edwards, in the drawings to *Grandfather's Sunday* (pp. 481, 489), appears to be under the influence of G. H. Thomas. Robert Barnes has twenty illustrations to *Kate the Grandmother*, and one each to *Light in Darkness* (p. 25) and *Our Children*. A series of fourteen to *Joshua Taylor's Passion*, engraved by Dalziel, are unsigned; the style leads one to credit them to F. A. Fraser, who in later volumes occupied a prominent position. F. W. Lawson, in *A Romance of Truth* (pp. 641, 649) and *The Vine and its Branches* (p. 904), has not yet found his individual manner. The rest of the pictures by T. Dalziel, F. J. Slinger, R. T. Pritchett, F. Eltze, W. M'Connell, etc., call for no special comment.

In 1866 J. Mahoney's *Summer*, the frontispiece to the volume, is a notable example of a clever artist, whose work has hardly yet attracted the attention it deserves; *Marie* (p. 753), a study of an old woman knitting, is no less good. Birket Foster's *Autumn* (p. 1) is also a very typical example. Paul Gray's *Among the Flowers* (p. 624), a group of children from the slums in a country lane, is fairly good. W. Small, in *Hebe Dunbar* 'from a photograph' (p. 441), supplies an object-lesson of translation rather than imitation, which deserves to be studied to-day. In it, a really great draughtsman has given you a personal rendering of facts, like those he would have set down had he worked from life, and thereby imparted individual interest to a copy of a photograph. This
67

OTHER ILLUSTRATED PERIODICALS
one block, if photographers would but study it, should convince
them that a good drawing is in every way preferable to a
'half-tone' block from a photograph of the subject; it might
also teach a useful lesson to certain draughtsmen, who employ
photographs so clumsily that the result is good neither as
photography nor as drawing, but partakes of the faults of
both. Three designs to the *Annals of a Quiet Neighbour-
hood*, by Dr. George Mac Donald, (pp. 641, 713, 785), the
first quite in the mood of the hour, a capital piece of
work, and *A Sunday Afternoon in a London Court*, complete Mr. Small's share in this volume. Robert Barnes
supplies the other eight drawings to Dr. Mac Donald's
story, and another, *The Pitman and his Wife* (p. 17), an
excellent specimen of his 'British Workman' manner. F. J.
Shields, a very infrequent contributor to these magazines, has
a biblical group, '*Even as thou wilt*' (p. 33). Edward
Hughes (who must not be confounded with Arthur Hughes,
nor with the present member of the Old Water-Colour
Society, E. R. Hughes) is responsible for *Under a Cottage
Roof* (p. 192), *The Bitter and Sweet* (p. 249), *The First
Tooth* (p. 337), and *The Poor Seamstress* (p. 409); although a
somewhat fecund illustrator not devoid of style and invention, his work fails to interest one much to-day. J. Gordon
Thomson, so many years the cartoonist of *Fun*, is represented
by *On the Rock* (p. 544). F. W. Lawson's *Hope* (p. 120) and
A. W. Bayes's *Saul and David* (p. 703), with a drawing of
wild animals drinking, by Wolf, complete the list of original
work, the rest being engraved from photographs.
    In 1867 A. Boyd Houghton is well to the fore with twelve
illustrations to the serial story by Sarah Tytler, *The Huguenot
Family in the English Village*, besides full-page drawings,
some in his best manner, to *A Proverb Illustrated* (p. 33),
Heroes (p. 129), *Luther the Singer* (p. 256), *The Martyr* (p.
348), *The Last of the Family* (p. 393), and *A Lesson to a King*
(p. 817). W. Small is only represented twice, with *Wind me
a Summer Crown* (p. 65) and *Philip's Mission* (p. 752). J. W.
North has three admirable drawings, *Foundered at Sea* (p.
280), *Peace* (p. 560), *Anita's Prayer* (p. 609), the first and last
of these, both studies of shipwrecks, deserve to be remembered for the truth of movement of the drawing of the waves,
and one doubts if any sea-pieces up to the date of their appear-
68

'SUNDAY MAGAZINE'
1867, p. 817

A LESSON
TO A KING

LUTHER THE
SINGER

JOHN BAPTIST

YESTERDAY
AND TO-DAY

J. W. NORTH

'SUNDAY MAGAZINE'
1867, p 609

ANITA'S PRAYER

G. J. PINWELL

MADAME DE
KRUDENER

'SUNDAY MAGAZINE'
1868, p. 704

ance had approached them for fact and beauty combined.
Both are engraved by Dalziels in an admirably intelligent
fashion. F. W. Lawson's *The Chained Book* (p. 104) and *The
Revocation of the Edict of Nantes* (p. 496), and *In the Times
of the Lollards* (p. 529), all deal with acrimonious memories of
the past. After the scenes of cruelty, persecution, and martyr-
dom which unfortunately are too often the chief dishes in the
menu of a religious periodical, it is a relief to turn to the
Cottar's Farewell (p. 417), by J. D. Watson, or to the ' Norths'
before quoted. This most straightforward and accomplished
study of a dying peasant and his family shows the dignified
and simple treatment which the artist at his happiest moments
employed with complete mastery.

In 1868 A. Boyd Houghton is again the most frequent
contributor of full-page designs; a bare list must suffice.
Sunday at Hippo (p. 57), *Three Feasts of Israel* (p. 67), *Paul's
Judge* (p. 88), *Sunday Songs, Sweden* (p. 112), *The Charcoal
Burners* (p. 118), a drawing which looks like an intentional
'exercise in the manner of Gustave Doré,' who, despite
his enormous popularity in England, seems to have had
singularly little influence on English artists, so that this stands
out as a unique exception. Houghton has also *The Feast
of the Passover* (p. 185), *The Poor Man's Shuttle* (p. 273),
Feast of Pentecost (p. 296), *Samuel the Ruler* (p. 357),
George Herbert's Last Sunday (p. 424), *Baden-Baden* (p. 520),
The Good Samaritan (p. 552), *Church of the Basilicas* (p. 561),
Joseph's Coat (p. 616), *St. Paul Preaching* (p. 681), and *The
Parable of the Sower* (p. 777). G. J. Pinwell is seen in
three examples, *A Westphalian Parsonage* (p. 192), *Madame
de Krudener* (pp. 704, 785); S. L. Fildes is here for the first
time with *The Farmer's Daughter* (p. 656); J. Pettie has a
small drawing, *My Sister* (p. 176); J. Wolf, a clever 'lamb'
study (p. 529); and W. Small a most typical, almost
mannered, *Sunday Morning* (p. 182). J. Mahoney supplies twenty-eight illustrations to *The Occupations of a
Retired Life*, by Edward Garrett, besides separate plates,
Sunday Songs from Denmark (p. 16), *Love Days* (p. 137),
and *Just Suppose* (p. 649). J. Gordon Thomson contributes eighteen drawings for Dr. George Macdonald's *The
Seaboard Parish*, and others of no particular interest are
attributed to Shield, F. A. Fraser, C. Morgan, Miles,

OTHER ILLUSTRATED PERIODICALS

Lamont, and Pasquier. Here, as in many other volumes, are vignettes and tail-pieces by T. Dalziel, some of them most admirably drawn and all charmingly expressed in the engraving. In 1869 A. Boyd Houghton still maintains his position. This year his drawings are *Wisdom of Solomon* (p. 16), *The Jews in the Ghetto* (p. 44), *Martha and Mary* (p. 65), *Rehoboam* (p. 85), *Jewish Patriotism* (p. 125), *Sunday in the Bush* (p. 161), *Miss Bertha* (pp. 384, 513), *Babylonian Captivity* (p. 633), *John Baptist* (p. 641), and *Samson* (p. 760). G. J. Pinwell illustrates Edward Garrett's *The Crust and the Cake* with thirty-four cuts. In one of these (p. 529), as in two other designs by the same artist, you find that in drawing the lines of a harpsichord, or grand piano, he has forgotten that the reversal required by engraving would represent the instrument with its curve on the bass, instead of the treble side—a sheer impossibility, which any pianist cannot help noticing at a glance. His one other contribution this year is *The Gang Children* (p. 25). Represented by a solitary example in each case are J. M'Whirter, *Sunday Songs* (p. 12) ; J. Pettie, *Philip Clayton's First-born* (p. 69) ; Edward Hughes, *Mother Mahoney* (p. 196); Towneley Green, *Village Doctor's Wife* (p. 505) ; Robert Barnes, *A Missionary in the East* (p. 57) ; and Arthur Hughes, *Blessings in Disguise* (p. 156). J. Mahoney has *The Centurion's Faith* (p. 60), *Building of the Minster* (p. 352), *Hoppety Bob* (p. 417), *Roger Rolf* (p. 608), and *Christmas Eighteenth Century* (p. 252). Francis Walker, with his *Sunday Songs* (p. 93), *Bird Fair, Shoreditch* (p. 409), *Feast of Tabernacles* (p. 600), *Widow Mullins* (p. 673), and *A Little Heroine* (p. 736) ; H. French, with *'It is more blessed'* (p. 229), and *A Narrative Sermon* (p. 632); and F. A. Fraser with *Jesuit Missions* (p. 101), *Wesley* (p. 152), *The Year* (p. 217), *A Queer Charity* (p. 576), and *A Schwingfest* (p. 665) ; the three latter belong by rights to the men of the seventies rather than to the group with which this volume is concerned.

In 1870 A. Boyd Houghton, one of the heroes of the sixties, reappears with five contributions, one, quite out of his ordinary manner, being a design for a group of statues, *St. Paul's Companions* (p. 33) ; the others are *My Mother's Knee* (p. 16), *Sunday at Aix-les-bains* (p. 88), *Achsah's Wedding Gifts* (p. 104), and *Sister Edith's Probation* (p. 600). J. Mahoney signs but two : *A Sun-dial in a Churchyard* (p. 704)

70

A. BOYD HOUGHTON

'SUNDAY MAGAZINE'
1868, p. 777

THE PARABLE
OF THE SOWER

MY HEART

BLESSINGS IN
DISGUISE

J. LEIGHTON

'SUNDAY MAGAZINE'
1871, p. 408

A PARABLE

THE SUNDAY MAGAZINE

and *Passover Observances* (p. 736). F. A. Fraser and Towneley Green supply the illustrations to the serials. W. J. Wiegand contributes decorative head-pieces, and Hubert Herkomer has two drawings, *Diana's Portrait* and *Diana Coverdale's Diary*.

In 1871 Houghton has but two : *A Woman that was a Sinner* (p. 104) and *The Withered Flower* (p. 512). Arthur Hughes, in three delightful designs, *My Heart* (p. 10), *The First Sunrise* (p. 302), and *Tares and Wheat* (p. 353) ; J. Mahoney with *Diet of Augsburg* (p. 417) and *Our Milkmen* (p. 217) ; and W. Small with *The Sea-Side Well* (p. 249), *One of Many* (p. 446), and fourteen illustrations to *The Story of the Mine*, are about the only remnants of the old army. John Leighton, a frequent contributor of decorative borders and head-pieces, has a typical full-page, *A Parable* (p. 408). The 'seventies' are represented by R. Macbeth's *Tom Joiner's Good Angel* (p. 313) ; and C. Green (who, like Small, belongs to both periods) with his designs to *The Great Journey* (p. 119) and *Mills of Clough* (pp. 560, 728).

CASSELL'S MAGAZINE,

A popular monthly periodical that is still in full vigour under a slightly altered title, started in the decade immediately before the date that this book attempts to cover. As *Cassell's Family Paper*, a large folio weekly, beyond the fact that the ubiquitous Sir John Gilbert did innumerable good things for its pages, one is not greatly interested in it. But in 1865 it was changed to a quarto shape, and although L. Huard supplied the front page pictures to vol. i., and so the artistic position of the paper was not improved, yet soon after the change we find a great illustrator contributing the weekly drawing for its chief serial. For despite the indifferent engraving accorded to many of the blocks and the absence of any signature, the autograph of William Small is legible in every line of the illustrations to *Bound to the Wheel* which started with vol. ii. in August 26, 1866, and has sixteen half-page illustrations. This was followed by *The Secret Sign*, with the same artist for a few chapters. Then another hand appears, and soon after the monogram F. G. shows that the second Gilbert (a brother, I believe, of the more famous artist) has replaced W. Small. To one drawing

OTHER ILLUSTRATED PERIODICALS

of another serial, *The Lion in the Path*, the signature of T. Morten is appended.

In April 1867 its title is changed to *Cassell's Family Magazine*, and it is printed on toned paper. The serial, *Anne Judge, Spinster*, by F. W. Robinson, has thirty illustrations by Charles Green. No doubt the originals were worthy of that admirable draughtsman; indeed, despite their very ordinary engraving, enough remains to show the handling of a most capable artist. The succeeding serial, *Poor Humanity*, is illustrated by B. Bradley. J. D. Watson contributes occasional drawings—*Ethel*, on p. 22, being the first. M. Ellen Edwards also appears, with F. W. Lawson, F. A. Fraser, Henley, C. J. Staniland, R. T. Pritchett, M. W. Ridley, J. Mahoney, and G. H. Thomas. It is noteworthy of the importance attached to the illustrator at this date, that the names of those artists who have contributed to the magazine are printed in bold type upon the title-page to each volume. These, as later, bear no date, so that only in volumes bound with the wrappers in British Museum fashion can you ascertain the year of their publication. In vol. iii. (May 1868 onwards) you discover on p. 9 a drawing, *Cleve Cliff*, by G. J. Pinwell, Its serial, *A Fight for Life*, is illustrated by G. H. Thomas, whose pictures are not signed, nor have I found that the authorship is attributed to the artists within the magazine itself. But in the 'In Memoriam volume, published soon after his death, several are reprinted and duly credited to him. They were all engraved by W. Thomas. The first appearance of S. L. Fildes, *Woodland Voices*, is on p. 137 of this volume. T. Blake Wirgman has also a notable composition, *A Sculptor's Love*, and in this and in volume iv. there are other drawings by Fildes, Pinwell, and many by F. Barnard, F. S. Walker, and other popular draughtsmen of the period.

In 1870 we find another change, this time to a page that may be a quarto technically, but instead of the square proportions we usually connect with that shape, it seems more akin to an octavo. The illustrations are smaller, but far better engraved and better printed. W. Small illustrates Wilkie Collins's cleverly-constructed story, *Man and Wife*, with thirty-seven pictures. His character-drawing appears at its best in 'Bishopriggs,' the old Scotch waiter, his love of beauty of line in two

72

'IF'

CASSELL'S MAGAZINE

or three sketches of the athlete, ' Geoffrey Delamayne,' the working villain of the story. The dramatic force of the group on p. 305, the mystery of the scene on p. 529, or the finely-contrasted emotions of Anne Silvester and Sir Patrick on p. 481, could hardly be beaten. The other contributors to this vol. i. of the new series, include R. Barnes, Basil Bradley, H. K. Browne, W. R. Duckman, E. H. Corbould, M. E. Edwards, E. Ellis, S. L. Fildes, F. A. Fraser, E. Hughes, F. W. Lawson, H. Paterson, and others, most of whom it were kindness to ignore. For side by side with Mr. Small's masterly designs appear the weakest and most commonplace full pages. Hardly one, except S. L. Fildes's *A Sonnet* (p. 9), tempts you to linger a moment. In vol. ii. the serial story, *Checkmate*, is illustrated by Towneley Green. The drawings throughout are mainly by those who contributed to the first volume. In the third volume, Charles Reade's *A Terrible Temptation* is illustrated by Edward Hughes; a somewhat powerful composition by J. D. L[inton], p. 377; one by W. Small (p. 9), and others by J. Lawson, F. W. Lawson, M. E. Edwards, are all that can claim to be noted.

BELGRAVIA

This illustrated shilling monthly, the same size and shape as most of its predecessors, was not started until 1866, and its earlier volumes have nothing in them sufficiently important to be noticed. In the seventies better things are to be found.

THE ARGOSY

This monthly periodical, as we know it of late years, suggests a magazine devoted to fiction and light literature, with a frontispiece by some well-known artist, and small engravings in the text mostly from photographs, or belonging to the diagram and the record rather than to fine art. I am not speaking of the present shilling series, but of the long array of volumes from 1868 until a few years ago. Nor does this opinion belittle the admirable illustrations by Walter Crane, M. Ellen Edwards, and other artists who supplied its monthly frontispiece. But the first four half-yearly volumes were planned on quite different lines, and these deserve the attention of all interested in the subject of this book, to a degree hardly below that of the better-known magazines;

better known, that is to say, as storehouses of fine illustrations.
As these volumes seem to be somewhat scarce, a brief
résumé of their contents will not be out of place. In the
year 1866 we have William Small at his best in twelve
illustrations to Charles Reade's dramatic novel, *Griffith Gaunt*.
Whether because the ink has sunk into the paper and given
a rich tone to the prints, or because of their intrinsic merit,
it is not quite easy to say, but the fact remains that these
drawings have peculiar richness, and deserve to be placed
among the best works of a great artist not yet fully recognised.
One design by F. Sandys to Christina Rossetti's poem, *If*,
is especially noticeable, the model biting a strand of hair
embodies the same idea as that of *Proud Maisie*, one of the
best-known works of this master. A. Boyd Houghton has a
typical Eastern figure-subject, *The Vision of Sheik Hamil*;
Edward Hughes one, *Hermione*; Paul Gray, a singularly
good drawing to a poem *The Lead-Melting*, by Robert
Buchanan. Another to a poem by George Macdonald, *The
Sighing of the Shell*, is unsigned, whether by Morten or Paul
Gray I cannot say, but it is worthy of either artist ; J. Lawson
has one to *The Earl of Quarterdeck*, M. Ellen Edwards
one to *Cuckoo* and one to *Cape Ushant*, a ballad by William
Allingham ; a group, with Napoleon as the central figure, is
by G. J. Pinwell, and J. Mahoney contributes three : *Autumn
Tourists*, *Bell from the North*, a girl singing by a Trafalgar
Square fountain, and *The Love of Years*. The next year,
1867, is illustrated more sparsely. *Robert Falconer*, by
George Macdonald, has one unsigned drawing, and nine by
William Small ; these, with *A Knight-Errant* by Boyd
Houghton, make up the eleven it contains. In the next year
Walter Crane illustrates the serial, *Anne Hereford*, by Mrs.
Henry Wood, and also a poem, *Margaret*, by his sister.

THE QUIVER

This semi-religious monthly magazine, published by Messrs.
Cassell and Co., was not illustrated at first. It is almost
unnecessary to describe it volume by volume, as a reprint of
its principal illustrations was made in 1867, when fifty-two
pictures were sandwiched between poems, and published in
a small quarto volume entitled '*Idyllic Pictures*, drawn by
Barnes, Miss Ellen Edwards, Paul Gray, Houghton, R. P.

A. BOYD HOUGHTON

THE VISION OF
SHEIK HAMIL

THE SAILOR'S VALENTINE

THE QUIVER

Leitch, Pinwell, Sandys, Small, G. Thomas, etc.' The curiously colloquial nomenclature of the artists on the title-page is the only direct reference to their share in the book, which is well printed, and includes some admirable illustrations. The book is now exceptionally scarce, and like its companion, *Pictures of Society*, selected from *London Society*, must be searched for long and patiently. Personal inquiries at all the accessible shops in London, Bath, and Edinburgh failed to find one bookseller who had ever heard of either book. Yet, in spite of it, single copies of both turned up alternately on the shelves of men who were at the moment of its discovery glibly doubting its existence. The ignorance of booksellers concerning this period is at once the terror and the joy of the collector. For when they do know, he will have to pay for their knowledge.

Yet it would be unfair to the reputation of a periodical which issued so many designs by representative artists of the sixties to dismiss it without a little more detail. Started as a non-illustrated paper on October 6, 1864, it entered the ranks with a very capable staff. In 1866 a third series on toned paper still further established its claim to be considered seriously, and the fact that these few years supplied the matter for the volume just mentioned shows that it fulfilled its purpose well. In volume i. third series (1866), pictures by A. Boyd Houghton will be found on pages 532, 585, 664, 728, 737, 776, and 868 ; and in vol. ii. 1867, he appears upon pages 88 and 456. Those by William Small (pp. 90, 232), G. J. Pinwell (pp. 60, 641), and J. D. Watson (p. 596) also deserve looking up. M. W. Ridley, an illustrator of promise, is also represented. In vol. iii. 1868, J. D. Watson's designs on pages 25, 57, 497, 680, 713, and 745 are perhaps his best. Drawings by John Lawson (p. 108), Hubert Herkomer (p. 73), A. Boyd Houghton (pp. 97, 705, 721, 737), S. L. Fildes (pp. 327, 417, 433), G. J. Pinwell (pp. 121, 193, 449, 481, 585 and 753), C. Green (p. 241), J. Mahoney (p. 328), and T. B. Wirgman (p. 649) all merit notice. In vol. iv. many of the above artists are represented—S. L. Fildes (p. 396), J. D. Watson (p. 407), W. Small (p. 696), and the designs by S. L. Fildes and J. D. Watson in the Christmas number being perhaps the most noticeable. Other frequent contributors include R. Barnes, C J. Staniland, M. E. Edwards, J. A. Pasquier, G. H.

OTHER ILLUSTRATED PERIODICALS

Thomas, F. W. Lawson, and Edith Dunn. Although not to be compared artistically with its rivals, *Good Words* and the *Sunday Magazine*, it is nevertheless a storehouse of good, if not of exceptionally fine, work.

THE CHURCHMAN'S SHILLING MAGAZINE,

A periodical of the conventional octavo size, affected by the illustrated shilling periodicals of the sixties, was commenced in 1867. The first two volumes contain little of note, and are illustrated by R. Huttula, John Leigh, E. F. C. Clarke; the third volume has M. E. Edwards, and in the fifth volume Walter Crane supplies two full pages (pp. 267, 339). Despite the fact that it credited its artists duly in the index, and seemed to have been most favourably noticed at the time, it may be dismissed here without further notice.

TINSLEY'S MAGAZINE

This shilling monthly was started in August 1867 with illustrations by ' Phiz,' W. Brunton, D. H. Friston, and A. W. Cooper. A. Boyd Houghton's contributions include *The Story of a Chignon* (i. p. 544), *For the King* (ii. p. 149), and *The Return from Court* (ii. p. 377). J. D. Watson appears in vol. iii. pp. 87, 399, 665, and a drawing, signed A. T. (possibly Alfred Thompson), is on p. 207. But the magazine, although published at a shilling, and therefore apparently intended as a rival to the *Cornhill* and the rest, is not important so far as its illustrations are concerned.

THE BROADWAY

This international magazine, heralded with much flourish in 1867 by Messrs. Routledge, is of no great importance, yet as it was illustrated from its first number in September 1867 to July 1874, it must needs be mentioned. Examples of the following artists will be found therein :—F. Barnard, G. A. Barnes, W. Brunton, M. E. Edwards, Paul Gray, E. Griset, A. B. Houghton, R. C. Huttula, F. W. Lawson, Matt Morgan, Thomas Nash, J. A. Pasquier, Alfred Thompson, and J. Gordon Thomson.

SAINT PAUL'S,

Yet another shilling magazine which was started in October 1867, and published by Messrs. Virtue and Co., is

ST. PAUL'S

memorable for its twenty-two drawings by Millais. These appeared regularly to illustrate Trollope's *Phineas Finn the Irish Member*. A few illustrations by F. A. Fraser were issued to *Ralph the Heir*, the next story, and to *The Three Brothers*, but from 1871 it appears without pictures. By way of working off the long serial by Trollope, *Ralph the Heir*, independent supplements as thick as an ordinary number, but entirely filled with chapters of the story in question, were issued in April and October 1870. So curious a departure from ordinary routine is worth noting.

GOOD WORDS FOR THE YOUNG,

A most delightful children's magazine, which began as a sixpenny monthly under the editorship of Dr. Norman Macleod in 1869, bids fair to become one of those books peculiarly dear (in all senses) to collectors. There are many reasons why it deserves to be treasured. Its literature includes several books for children that in volume-form afterwards became classics; its illustrations, especially those by Arthur Hughes, appeal forcibly to the student of that art, which is called pre-Raphaelite, Æsthetic, or Decorative, according to the mood of the hour. Like all books intended for children, a large proportion of its edition found speedy oblivion in the nursery; and those that survive are apt to show examples of the amateur artist in his most infantile experiments with a penny paint-box. From the very first it surrounded itself with that atmosphere of distinction, which is well-nigh as fatal to a magazine's longevity as saintliness of disposition to a Sunday-school hero. After a career that may be called truthfully— brilliant, it suddenly changed to a periodical of no importance, illustrated chiefly by foreign *clichés*. How long it lingered in this state does not concern us. Indeed, it is only by a liberal interpretation of the title of this book that a magazine which was not started until 1869 can be included in *the sixties* at all; but it seems to have continued the tradition of the sixties, and until the first half of 1874, although it changed its editor and its title (to *Good Things*), it kept the spirit of the first volume unimpaired; but after that date it joined the majority of uninteresting periodicals for children, and did not survive its recantation for many years.

OTHER ILLUSTRATED PERIODICALS

In 1869 Arthur Hughes has twenty-four drawings to George Macdonald's *At the Back of the North Wind,* and ten to the earlier chapters of Henry Kingsley's *Boy in Grey.* The art of A. Boyd Houghton is seen in three instances : *Cocky Locky's Journey* (p. 49), *Lessons from Russia* (p. 101), and *The Boys of Axleford* (p. 145). J. Mahoney has about a dozen; H. Herkomer one to *Lonely Jane* (p. 28) ; and G. J. Pinwell one to *Black Rock* (p. 255). Although, following the example set by its parent *Good Words,* it credits the illustrations most faithfully to their artists in a separate index, yet it developed a curious habit of illustrating its serials with a fresh artist for each instalment; and, as their names are bracketed, it is not an easy task to attribute each block to its rightful author. The list which I have made is by my side, but it is hardly of sufficient general interest to print here ; as many of the sketches, despite the notable signatures upon them, are trivial and non-representative. Other illustrations in the first volume include one hundred and fifty-five grotesque thumb-nail sketches by W. S. Gilbert to his *King George's Middy,* and many by F. Barnard, B. Rivière, E. F. Brewtnall, E. Dalziel, F. A. Fraser, H. French, S. P. Hall, J. Mahoney, J. Pettie, T. Sulman, F. S. Walker, W. J. Wiegand, J. B. Zwecker, etc.

In 1870 Arthur Hughes contributes thirty-six illustrations to *Ranald Bannerman's Boyhood,* by George Mac Donald (who succeeded Dr. Macleod as editor), forty-eight to the continuation of the other serial by the same author, *At the Back of the North Wind,* four to the concluding chapters of Henry Kingsley's *Boy in Grey,* and one to *The White Princess.* A. Boyd Houghton has but two : *Two Nests* (p. 13), *Keeping the Cornucopia* (p. 33); *Miss Jane* 'wandering in the wood' (p. 44) is by H. Herkomer, while most of the artists who contributed to the first volume reappear ; we find also E. G. and T. Dalziel, Charles Green, Towneley Green, and Ernest Griset.

In 1871, Arthur Hughes, the chief illustrator of this magazine, to whose presence it owes most of its interest (since other artists are well represented elsewhere, but he is rarely met with outside its pages), contributes thirty pictures to Dr. George Mac Donald's *Princess and the Goblin,* and fourteen others, some of which have been republished in *Lilliput*

78

PAUL GRAY

'THE QUIVER'

COUSIN LUCY

H. HERKOMER

'GOOD WORDS FOR THE YOUNG'
1870, p. 44

WANDERING IN
THE WOOD

DON JOSE'S
MULE

ARTHUR HUGHES

'GOOD WORDS FOR THE YOUNG'
1871, p. 100

BARBARA'S
PET LAMB

'GOOD WORDS FOR THE YOUNG'
1871, p. 145

MERCY

'THE QUIVER'

BETWEEN THE
CLIFFS

GOOD WORDS FOR THE YOUNG

Lectures and elsewhere,—one, *Mercy* (p. 195), reappearing in that work, and again as the theme of a large painting in oils, which was exhibited at the Royal Academy 1893, and reproduced in *The Illustrated London News,* May 3rd of that year. A. Boyd Houghton, in *Don José's Mule* (p. 28), has a most delightfully grotesque illustration, and in two drawings for *The Merry Little Cobbler of Bagdad* (pp. 337-338), both in his 'Arabian Nights' vein, is typically representative. For the rest, W. Small in *My Little Gypsy Cousin* (p. 95), a good full page, and Ernest Griset with ten of his humorous animal pictures, combine with most of the artists already named to maintain the well-deserved reputation of the magazine. In 1872 Arthur Hughes supplies nine delightful designs for *Gutta-Percha Willie,* by the Editor; twenty-four to *Innocent's Island,* a long-rhymed chronicle by the author of *Lilliput Levée,* and a curiously fantastic drawing to George MacDonald's well-known poem, *The Wind and the Moon.* Some one, with the initials F. E. F. (not F. A. F.), illustrates *On the High Meadows* in nineteen sketches; with the exception of two by J. Mahoney, the rest of the pictures are chiefly by F. A. Fraser, T. Green, F. S. Walker, W. J. Wiegand, and J. B. Zwecker.

In 1873 the magazine changed its name to *Good Things.* The most attractive illustrations are by Arthur Hughes : ten to *Sindbad in England* (pp. 25, 89, 129, 193, 236, 432, 481, 594, 641), two to *Henry and Amy* (pp. 72, 73), and one each to *A Poor Hunchback* (p. 17), *The Wonderful Organ* (p. 24), and *My Daughter* (p. 136). J. Mahoney has a small design, *The Old Mill* (p. 600). The rest are by Ernest Griset, W. J. Wiegand, and Francis Walker. On and after 1874 the *cliché* enters, and all interest ceases. At this time the business of trading in *clichés* had begun to assume large proportions. You find sometimes, in the course of a single month, that an English periodical hitherto exclusively British becomes merely a vehicle for foreign *clichés.* In this instance the change is so sudden that, excepting a few English blocks which we may presume had been prepared before, the foreigner is supreme. That, in at least three cases, the demise of the publication was merely a question of months is a sequel not to be regretted. But we need not assume too hastily that the *cliché* killed it—possibly it had ceased to be

79

OTHER ILLUSTRATED PERIODICALS

profitable before, and the false economy of spending less has tempted the proprietor to employ foreign illustrations.

BRITANNIA,

Another shilling illustrated magazine, was started in 1869. The British Museum, it seems, possesses no set, and my own copy has disappeared, excepting the first volume, but so far as that proves, and my memory can be trusted, it was illustrated solely by Matt Morgan, a brilliant but ephemeral genius who shortly after migrated to New York. The peculiarity of this magazine is that, like *The Tomahawk*, a satirical journal illustrated by the same artist, its pictures were all printed in two colours, after the fashion of the old Venetian wood-blocks. The one colour was used as a ground with the high lights cut away ; the other block, for the ordinary convention of line-drawing. Some of the pictures are effective, but none are worthy of very serious consideration.

DARK BLUE

Although *Dark Blue*, a shilling monthly magazine, did not begin until March 1871, and ran its brief career until March 1873 only, it deserves mention here, because quite apart from its literary contributions which were notable, including as they did Swinburne's *End of a Month*, Rossetti's *Down Stream*, its earlier volumes contain at least two drawings that will be prized when these things are collected seriously. Besides, it has a certain *cachet* of its own that will always entitle it to a place. Its wrapper in colours, with three classically-attired maidens by a doorway, is singularly unlike that of any other publication ; possibly F. W. L. would not be anxious to claim the responsibility of its design, yet it was new in its day, and not a bad specimen of the good effect of three simple colours on a white ground. Its serial, *Lost*, a Romance by J. C. Freund, was illustrated by F. W. Lawson, T. W. Perry, T. Robinson, and D. T. White ; and its second serial, *Take care whom you trust*, by M. E. Freere and T. W. Ridley. A full-page drawing (they are all separately printed plates in this magazine), by Cecil Lawson, *Spring*, is far more interesting. *Musaeus*, by A. W. Cooper, a somewhat jejune representation of the Hero and Leander motive, and other illustrations by E. F. Clarke, W.

80

DARK BLUE

J. Hennessey, M. Fitzgerald, D. H. Friston, S. P. Hall, J. A. H. Bird, are commonplace designs engraved by C. M. Jenkin; but *The End of a Month*, a study of two heads, by Simeon Solomon, and *Down Stream*, by Ford Madox Brown, (here reproduced from the original drawing on wood by kind permission of Mr. Frederick Hollyer), represent the work of two artists who very rarely appeared as magazine illustrators. The literature includes many names that have since become widely known, but the project failed, one imagines, to secure popular support, and so it must be numbered with the long list of similar good intentions.

THE BRITISH WORKMAN

It would be unjust to ignore a very popular penny magazine because of its purely philanthropic purpose. For from the first it recognised the importance of good illustrations as its great attraction, and enlisted some of the best draughtsmen to fulfil its didactic aim. We cannot help admiring its pluck, and congratulating the cause it championed (and still supports), and its fortune in securing coadjutors. The first number, issued in February 1855, has a design, the *Loaf Lecture*, by George Cruikshank on its first page ; for some time H. Anelay and L. Huard were the most frequent contributors ; then came John Gilbert and Harrison Weir, the earliest important Gilbert being *The Last Moments of Thomas Paine* (January 1862). As a sample of white-line engraving, a block after a medallion of the *Prince Consort*, by L. C. Wyon, and another of *H.M. The Queen*, would be hard to beat. Among these more frequent contributors, we find drawings by J. D. Watson, *My account with Her Majesty* (August 1864) and *Parley and Flatterwell* (December 1865) being the most notable ; and others by A. W. Cooper, and lastly many by R. Barnes, whose studies of humble life yet await the full appreciation they deserve. These large and vigorous engravings maintain a singularly high level of excellence, and, if not impeccable, are yet distinctly of art, and far above the ephemeral padding of more pretentious magazines.

THE BAND OF HOPE REVIEW

Of all unlikely publications to interest artist or collector a halfpenny monthly devoted to teetotalism might take first

OTHER ILLUSTRATED PERIODICALS

place. Not because of its price, nor because it was a monthly with a mission, for many cheap serials have attracted the support of artists who gave liberally of their best for the sake of the cause the publications championed. *The Band of Hope Review* is no esoteric pamphlet, but a perfect instance of a popular venture unconcerned, one would think, with art. It would be easy to claim too much for it; still the good work in its pages merits attention. It was started in 1861 as a folio sheet about the size of *The Sketch*, its front page being always filled by a large wood-engraving. The first full page, by H. Anelay, a draughtsman whose speciality was the good little boy and girl of the most commonplace religious periodicals, promises little enough. A series of really fine drawings of animals and birds by Harrison Weir commenced in No. 2. The third issue included a page by L. Huard, whose work occasionally found its way to the shilling magazines, although the bulk of it appeared in the mass of journals of the type of the *London Journal, Bow Bells*, etc. In the fifth number John Gilbert (not then knighted) appears with a fine drawing, *The Golden Star*; J. Wolf, honourably distinguished as an illustrator of animals, is also represented. For December 1862 John Gilbert provided a decorative composition of *The Ten Virgins*, that is somewhat unlike his usual type. In August 1865 Robert Barnes appears for the first time with admirably drawn boys and girls full of health and characteristically British. Afterwards one finds many of his full pages all vigorous and delightfully true to the type he represents. In August 1866 a group, *Young Cadets*, may be selected as a typical example of his strength and perhaps also of his limitations. In 1870 the falling off apparent everywhere is as noticeable in this unimportant publication as in those of far higher pretensions. Here, as elsewhere, the foreign *cliché* appears, or possibly the subjects were engraved specially, and were not, as was so often the case, merely replicas of German and French engravings. But all the same they are from oil-paintings, not from drawings made for illustration.

THE LEISURE HOUR

The publications of the Religious Tract Society have employed an enormous mass of illustrations, but as the artist's name rarely appears at the period with which we are concerned,

ENOCH ARDEN

THE FEAST OF
TABERNACLES

THE DA·
ATONEM

either in the index of illustrations or below the engravings, the task of tracing each to its source would be onerous and the result probably not worth the labour.

Yet, in the volumes of the *Leisure Hour* for the sixties, there are a few noteworthy pictures which may later on attract collectors to a periodical which so far appealed more, one had thought, to parish workers than to art students.

The 1861 volume starts with the 471st number of the magazine, illustrated by 'Gilbert' (probably Sir John). In 1863 coloured plates are given monthly, three being after originals by the same artist, but, although attributed duly in the advertising pages of its wrapper, the name of the design does not appear in the index. With 1864 a surprise faces you in the illustrations to *Hurlock Chase*, which are vigorous, dramatic, and excellently composed, full of colour and breadth. That they are by G. Du Maurier internal evidence proves clearly, but there is no formal recognition of the fact. Robert Barnes has a full page, *Granny's Portrait* (p. 825). *Enoch Arden* is by 'an amateur whose name the publishers are not able to trace.'[1] In 1865 the illustrations to *The Awdries*, also unsigned, are distinctly interesting; later the well-known monogram of J. Mahoney is met with frequently. In 1866 a series of ten illustrations of the ceremonies of modern Jewish ritual, domestic and ecclesiastical (pp. 72, 167, 216, 328, 376-475, 540, 603, 653, 823) appear. Contrary to the rule usually observed here, they are entitled, 'by S. Solomon.' These are, so far as I know (with four exceptions), the only contributions to periodical literature by Simeon Solomon, an artist who at this date bade fair to be one of the greatest pre-Raphaelite painters. They are distinctly original both in their technical handling and composition, and excellently engraved by Butterworth and Heath. For their sake no collector of the sixties should overlook a book which is to be picked up anywhere at present. The illustrations to *The Great Van Bruch property*, unsigned, are most probably by J. Mahoney. Others include *George III. and Mr. Adams*, a full page by C. J. Staniland (p. 494); a series of *Pen and Pencil Sketches among the Outer Hebrides*, R. T. Pritchett; *Finding the body of William Rufus*, J. M. In 1867 J. Mahoney illustrates the serial, *The Heiress of Cheevely Dale*, and contributes a full page, *The Blue-Coat Boy's*

[1] Possibly A. R. Fairfield.

OTHER ILLUSTRATED PERIODICALS

Mother (p. 812); Whymper has two series, *On the Nile* and *A trip through the Tyrol*, both oddly enough attributed to him in the index. Silent, with scarce an exception, as regards other artists, the sentence, 'engraved by Whymper,' finds a place each time. In 1868 are more Mahoneys; in 1869 Charles Green illustrates the serial.

THE SUNDAY AT HOME

This magazine, uniform with the *Leisure Hour* in style and general arrangement, is hardly of sufficient artistic interest to need detailed comment here. Started in 1852 it relied, like its companion, on Gilbert and other less important draughtsmen. In the sixties it was affected a little by the movement. In 1863 there is one design by G. J. Pinwell, *The German Band* (p. 753), several by C. Green, and one probably by Du Maurier (p. 513), who has also six most excellent drawings to *The Artist's Son* in the number for January, and one each to short stories, *John Henderson* and *Siller and Gowd*, later in the year. A serial in 1865 and one in 1866 are both illustrated by J. Mahoney; and, in the latter year, W. Small supplies drawings to another story. Beyond a full page, obviously by R. Barnes, there is nothing else peculiarly interesting in 1866; in the 1867 volume F. W. Lawson and Charles Green contribute a good many designs. In 1868 S. L. Fildes has one full page, *St. Bartholomew* (p. 329), and F. A. F. appears; in 1869 Charles Green is frequently encountered, but the magazine is not a very happy hunting-ground for our purpose.

OTHER SERIAL PUBLICATIONS

Serial issues of Cassell's *History of England*, the *Family Bible*, and other profusely illustrated works might also repay a close search, but, as a rule, the standard is too ordinary to attract any but an omnivorous collector. Still, men of considerable talent are among the contributors, (Sir) John Gilbert for instance, and others like H. C. Selous, Paolo Priolo, who never fell below a certain level of respectability.

Golden Hours, a semi-religious monthly, started in 1864 as a penny magazine. In 1868 its price was raised to sixpence, and among its artist-contributors we find M. E. Edwards, R. Barnes, and A. Boyd Houghton (represented once only)

OTHER SERIAL PUBLICATIONS

with *An Eastern Wedding* (p. 849). In 1869 Towneley Green, C. O. Murray, and others appear, but the magazine can hardly be ranked as one representative of the period. Nor is it essential to record in detail the mass of illustrations in the penny weeklies and monthlies—to do so were at once impossible and unnecessary; nor the mass of semi-religious periodicals such as *Our Own Fireside* and *The Parish Magazine*, which rarely contain work that rises above the dull average.

THE BOYS' OWN MAGAZINE

The art of this once popular magazine may be dismissed very briefly. J. G. Thomson made a lot of designs to *Silas the Conjuror* and other serials. R. Dudley, a conscientious draughtsman whose speciality was mediæval subjects, illustrated its historical romances with spirit and no little knowledge of archæological details. A. W. Bayes, J. A. Pasquier, and others adorned its pages; but from 1863 to its death it contains nothing interesting except to a very rabid collector.

EVERY BOY'S MAGAZINE

This well-intentioned periodical (Routledge, 1863, etc.), except for certain early works by Walter Crane, would scarce need mention here. Its wrapper for 1865 onwards was from a capital design by Walter Crane, who contributed coloured frontispieces and titles to the 1864 and 1865 volumes. C. H. Bennett illustrated his own romance of *The Young Munchausen*. In 1867 it called itself *The Young Gentleman's Magazine*; an heraldic design by J. Forbes Nixon, with the shields of the four great public schools, replaced the Crane cover. T. Morten, M. W. Ridley, and others contributed. A. Boyd Houghton illustrated *Barford Bridge*, its serial for 1866, and Walter Crane performed the same offices to Mrs. Henry Wood's *Orville College* in 1867. These few facts seem to comprise all of any interest.

AUNT JUDY'S MAGAZINE

The sixpenny magazine for children, edited by Mrs. Alfred Gatty, issued its first number, May 1866. The artists who contributed include F. Gilbert, J. A. Pasquier, T. Morten,

OTHER ILLUSTRATED PERIODICALS

M. E. Edwards, E. Griset, F. W. Lawson, E. H. Wehnert, A. W. Bayes, A. W. Cooper, and others. There are two drawings by George Cruikshank, and later on Randolph Caldecott will be found. In both cases the illustrations were for Mrs. Ewing's popular stories, which had so large a sale, reprinted in volume-form. Neither in the drawings nor in their engraving do you find anything else which is above the average of its class.

Two other magazines remain to be noticed out of their chronological order, both of little intrinsic importance, but of peculiar value to collectors.

EVERYBODY'S JOURNAL,

A weekly periodical the size of the *London Journal*, and not more attractive in its appearance, nor better printed, began with No. 1, October 1, 1859, and ceased to exist early in the following year; probably before the end of January, since the British Museum copy in monthly parts is inscribed 'discontinued' on the part containing the December issues. That a complete set is not in our great reference library is a matter for regret; for the first published illustration by Fred Walker, which was issued in *Everybody's Journal*, January 14, must needs have been in the missing numbers. Those which are accessible include drawings by (Sir) John Gilbert, T. Morten, and Harrison Weir, none of peculiar interest. Among the names of the contributors will be found several that have since become widely known.

ENTERTAINING THINGS

This twopenny monthly magazine, which is probably as unfamiliar to those who read this notice as it was to me until a short time since, was published by Virtue and Co., the first number appearing in January 1861. It contains many designs by J. Portch, F. J. Skill, M. S. Morgan, E. Weedar, W. M'Connell, P. Justyne, and W. J. Linton, none being particularly well engraved. But it contains also Walter Crane's first published drawing—a man in the coils of a serpent (p. 327), illustrating one of a series of articles, *Among the Mahogany Cutters*, which is not very important; another a few pages further on in the volume is even less so. Collectors will also prize *A Nocturne* by G. Du Maurier,

ENTERTAINING THINGS

and some designs by T. Morton (*sic*). The Christmas number contains a delightful design by A. Boyd Houghton, *The Maid of the Wool-pack*, and another drawing by Du Maurier. The publication ceased, according to a note in the British Museum copy, in May 1862. Among rarities of the sixties this magazine may easily take a high place, for one doubts if there are many copies in existence. Should the mania for collecting grow, it is quite possible this volume, of such slight intrinsic value, will command record prices.

BEETON'S ANNUALS

These were of two sorts, a badly printed shilling annual, which appealed to children of all ages, and a six-shilling variety, which appealed to those of a smaller growth. In the higher-priced volumes for 1866 T. Morten, J. G. Thomson, and J. A. Pasquier appear. In the shilling issue, an independent publication, are more or less execrably engraved blocks, after C. H. Bennett, G. Cruikshank, Jun., and others who would probably dislike to have their misdeeds chronicled. These publications added to the gaiety of nations, but when they ceased no eclipse was reported. Yet a patient collation of their pages renewed a certain boyish, if faded, memory of their pristine charm, which the most cautious prophet may assert can never be imparted anew to any reader. *Kingston's Annuals* and *Peter Parley's Annuals*, also revisited, left impressions too sad to be expressed here. Nor need *Routledge's Christmas Annuals* be noticed in detail. *Tom Hood's Comic Annuals*, which contained much work typical of the seventies, although it began its long career in 1869, includes so little work by heroes of the 'sixties' that it need not be mentioned.

The mass of penny magazines for children do not repay a close search. Here and there you will find a design by a notable hand, but it is almost invariably ruined by poor engraving; so that it were kinder not to attempt to dispel the obscurity which envelops the juvenile 'goody-goody' literature of thirty years ago.

CHAPTER VI: SOME ILLUSTRATED WEEKLY PAPERS IN THE SIXTIES

PUNCH.—It is impossible to overlook the famous weekly that from its own pages could offer a fairly representative group of the work of any decade since it was established; a paper which, if it has not attracted every great illustrator, could nevertheless select a hundred drawings from its pages that might be fairly entered in competition with any other hundred outside them. But, at the same time, to give a summary of its record during the sixties, even as compressed as those of *The Cornhill Magazine, Once a Week,* etc., would occupy more pages than all the rest put together. Fortunately the labour has been accomplished quite recently. Mr. M. H. Spielmann's *History of Punch* supplies a full and admirably digested chronicle of its artistic achievements. So that here (excluding the staff-artists, Sir John Tenniel, Mr. Du Maurier, Mr. Linley Sambourne, and the rest, and the greatest *Punch* artist, Charles Keene, who was never actually upon its staff) it will be sufficient to indicate where admirers of the men of the sixties may find examples of their work for *Punch*; Sir John Millais appears twice upon p. 115 of vol. xliv. (1863) with a design to *Mokeanna,* Mr. F. C. Burnand's laughable parody, and again with *Mr. Vandyke Brown's sons thrashing the lay figure,* in the *Almanac* for 1865, a drawing that faces, oddly enough, one of Fred Walker's two contributions, *The New Bathing Company, Limited, Specimens of Costumes to be worn by the Shareholders.* The other Fred Walker, *Captain Jinks of the 'Selfish,'* is on p. 74 of vol. lvii. 1869; George J. Pinwell is an infrequent contributor from 1863 to 1869; Walter Crane appears but once, p. 33 (vol. li. 1866); Frederick Shields's three initials, which appeared in 1870, were drawn in 1867; M. J. Lawless is represented by six drawings, which appeared between May 1860 and January 1861; F. W. Lawson has some initials and one vignette in the volume for 1867; Ernest Griset appears in the *Almanac* for 1867; J. G. Thomson, for twenty years cartoonist of *Fun,* is an occasional contributor between 1861 and 1864; H. S. Marks appears in 1861, and Paul Gray, also with a few initials and 'socials,' up to 1865; Charles Keene's first drawing for

'PUNCH,' MARCH 3, 1866

A LEGEND OF CAMELOT, PART IV

PUNCH

Punch is in 1852, he was 'called to the table' in 1860, and on a few occasions supplied the political cartoon. The mass of his work within the classic pages is too familiar to need more than passing reference. The first drawing by 'George Louis Palmella Busson Du Maurier' appears in 1860, the *Legend of Camelot*, with five drawings, which are already historic, in 1866. These delicious parodies (here reproduced) of the pre-Raphaelite manner are as fascinating to-day as when they first appeared.

FUN

This popular humorous penny weekly, which is still running, would be forever memorable as the birthplace of the famous *Bab* ballads, with W. S. Gilbert's own thumb-nail sketches : yet it would be foolish to rank him as an illustrator, despite the grotesque humour of these inimitable little figures. The periodical, not (I believe) at first under the editorship of Tom Hood, the younger, began in September 21, 1861. The mass of illustrations must be the only excuse for failing to include an orderly summary ; yet there is not, and there is certainly no necessity for, an elaborate chronicle of the paper, like Mr. Spielmann's admirable monograph in *Punch*. But those who are curious to discover the work of less-known men of the sixties will find plenty to reward their search. A clever parody of Millais' pre-Raphaelite manner is given as a tail-piece to the preface of vol. i. A. Eoyd Houghton supplied the cartoons for a short period, November 1866 to April 6, 1867. At least those signed A. H. are attributed to him, and the first would almost suffice by itself to decide it, did any doubt exist. Another cartoonist, who signed his work with the device of a hen, is very freely represented. F. Barnard was also cartoonist for a long time—1869 onwards —and J. G. Thomson, for a score of years, did excellent work in the same department. The authorship of many of the drawings scattered through its pages is easily recognised by their style—others, as for instance one on page five of the *Almanac* for 1866, puzzle the student. It looks like a Paul Gray, but the monogram with which it is signed, although it is indecipherable, is certainly not 'P. G.' W. J. Wiegand, W. Brunton, H. Sanderson, Matt Stretch, Lieut. Seccombe, L. C. Henley, F. S. Walker, and F. W. Lawson (see

for instance, *Almanac* for 1865, p. 11) contributed a great
many of the ' socials' to the early volumes.

Then, as now, you find unconscious or deliberate imita-
tions of other artists' mannerisms. A rash observer might
attribute drawings here to C. Keene (*Almanac* for 1865, vi.),
and credit Tenniel with the title-page to vol. iv. N.S.

Still, as a field to discover the work of young artists who
afterwards become approximately great, *Fun* is not a very
happy hunting-ground. Despite some notable exceptions,
its illustrators cannot be placed even upon the average of the
period that concerns us; the presence of a half a dozen or so
of first-rate men hardly makes a set of the comic paper
essential to a representative collection. After renewed
intimacy with its pages there is a distinct feeling of disappointment. That its drawings pleased you mightily, and
seemed fine stuff at the time, may be true; but it only
proves that the enjoyment of a schoolboy cannot be re-
captured in after-life if the quality of the drawing be too
poor to sustain the weight of old-fashioned dress and jokes
whose first sparkle has dimmed beyond restoration.

JUDY,

The twopenny rival to *Punch*, began life on May 1,
1867. Although Matt Morgan supplied many of the
early cartoons and 'socials,' the really admirable level it
reached in the eighties is not foreshadowed even dimly by
its first volumes. With vol. ii. J. Proctor, an admirable
draughtsman, despite his fondness for the decisive, unsympathetic line which Sir John Tenniel has accustomed us to
consider part and parcel of a political cartoon, is distinctly
one of the best men who have worked this particular form
of satire. Afterwards ' W. B.' contributed many. The mass
of work, in the volumes which can be considered as belonging to the period covered by this book, contains hardly a
single drawing to repay the weary hunt through their pages.
Yet the issues of a later decade are as certain to be prized by
students of the ' eighties' as the best periodicals of the sixties
are by devotees of that period.

PUNCH AND JUDY,

Beginning in October 1869, yet another paper on similar
lines, ran a short but interesting career of twelve weeks, and

PUNCH AND JUDY

continued, in a commonplace way, for a year or two longer. The reason the first dozen issues are worth notice here is that the illustrations are all by 'graphotype process' (which must not be confused with the far earlier 'glyptography'), and so appeal to students of the technique of illustration. The principle of the graphotype process, it is said, was discovered accidentally. The inventor was removing, with a wet camel-hair brush, the white enamel from the face of a visiting-card, when he noticed that the printing on it was left in distinct relief. After many experiments the idea was developed, and a surface of metal was covered with a powdered chalky sub-stance, upon which the drawing was made with a silicate ink which hardened the substance wherever it was applied. The chalk was then brushed away and the drawing left in low but distinct relief on the metal-plate, from which electrotypes could be taken in the usual way. The experiment gained some commercial success, and quite a notable group of artists experimented with it for designs to an edition of Dr. Isaac Watts's *Divine and Moral Songs*, a most curious libretto for an artistic venture. In *Punch and Judy* the blocks are by no means bad as regards their reproduction. Despite the very mediocre drawing of the originals, they are nevertheless pre-ferable to the cheap wood-engravings of their contemporaries. After its change, 'G. O. M.' (if one reads the initials aright), or 'C. O. M.,' contributes some average cartoons. When it first appeared, at least one schoolboy was struck with the curious difference of technique that the illustrations showed, and from that time onwards had his curiosity aroused towards process-work. Therefore, this lapse into anecdotage, in the short record of a venture otherwise artistically unworthy to be noticed here, may be pardoned.

WILL O' THE WISP

This, another periodical of the same class, started on September 12, 1868, but unlike its fellows relied at first solely upon a double-page political cartoon. From the second number these were contributed by J. Proctor until and after April 17, 1869, when other pictures were admitted. With the 31st of July another hand replaces Proctor's vigor-ous work. The volume for 1870 contains many woodcuts (I use the word advisedly),unintentionally primitive, that should

SOME ILLUSTRATED WEEKLY PAPERS
please a certain school to-day. Whether the journal ceased
with its fourth volume, or lasted into the seventies, the
British Museum catalogue does not record, nor is it worth
while to pursue the inquiry further.

THE ILLUSTRATED LONDON NEWS
To notice this important paper in a paragraph is little
better than an insult, and yet between a full monograph
(already anticipated partially in Mr. Mason Jackson's *The
Pictorial Press*) and a bare mention there is no middle course.
As a rule the drawings are unsigned, and not attributed to
the artists in the index.

The Christmas numbers, however, often adopt a different
method, and print the draughtsman's name below each
engraving, which is almost always a full page. In that for
1865 we find Alfred Hunt, George Thomas, S. Read, and
John Gilbert, all regular contributors, well represented. In
the Christmas number of 1866 there is Boyd Houghton's
Child's Christmas Carol, and other drawings by Corbould,
S. Read, J. A. Pasquier, Charles Green, Matt Morgan, and
C. H. Bennett.

OTHER ILLUSTRATED WEEKLIES
The Illustrated Times, first issued in October 1855,
maintained a long and honourable effort to achieve popularity.
A new series was started in 1867, but apparently also failed
to gain a footing. The artists included many men mentioned
frequently in this volume. The non-topical illustrations
occasionally introduced were supplied chiefly by M. E.
Edwards, Adelaide and Florence Claxton, Lieut. Seccombe,
P. Skelton, and T. Sulman. Yet a search through its
pages revealed nothing sufficiently important to notice in
detail.

The Illustrated Weekly News and *The Penny Illustrated
Weekly News* are other lost causes, but the *Penny Illustrated
Paper,* which started in 1861, is still a flourishing concern ;
yet it would be superfluous to give a detailed notice of its
work. *Pan* (date uncertain[1]), a short-lived sixpenny weekly.
Its cover was from a design by Jules Chéret. Facsimiles of

<hr>

[1] The British Museum has no copy, and my own has been mislaid.

A Head by Lord Leighton, and *Proud Maisie* by Frederick Sandys, appeared among its supplements.

THE GRAPHIC

That this admirably conducted illustrated weekly revolutionised English illustration is granted on all sides. Its influence for good or ill was enormous. With its first number, published on December 4, 1869, we find a definite, official date to close the record of the 'sixties'; one by mere chance, chronologically as well as technically, appropriate. Of course the break was not so sudden as this arbitrary limit might suggest. The style which distinguished the *Graphic* had been gradually prepared before, and if Mr. William Small is credited with the greatest share in its development, such a statement, incomplete as most generalities must needs be, holds a good part of the truth, if not the whole. The work of Mr. Small introduced new qualities into wood-engraving; which, in his hands and those of the best of his followers, grew to be meritorious, and must needs place him with those who legitimately extended the domain of the art of drawing for the engraver. But to discuss the style which succeeded that of the sixties would be to trespass on new ground, and that while the field itself is all too scantily searched. Mr. Ruskin dubbed the new style 'blottesque,' but, as we have seen, he was hardly more enamoured of the manner that immediately preceded it.

Many of the surviving heroes of the sixties contributed to the *Graphic*. Charles Green appears in vol. i. with *Irish Emigrants*, G. J. Pinwell with *The Lost Child* (January 8, 1870), A. Boyd Houghton has a powerful drawing, *Night Charges*, and later, the marvellous series of pictures recording his very personal visit to America.

William Small, R. W. Macbeth, S. L. Fildes, Hubert Herkomer, and a crowd of names, some already mentioned frequently in this book, bore the weight of the new enterprise. But a cursory sketch of the famous periodical would do injustice to it. The historian of the seventies will find it takes the place of *Once a Week* as the happy hunting-ground for the earliest work of many a popular draughtsman and painter —that is to say, the earliest work after his student and experimental efforts. To declare that it still flourishes, and with the *Daily Graphic*, its offspring, keeps still ahead of the, popular average, is at once bare truth and the highest compliment which need be paid.

The illustrated weeklies in the sixties were almost as unimportant, relatively speaking, as are the illustrated dailies to-day. Yet to say that the weeklies did fair to monopolise illustration at the present time is a common truth, and, remembering what the *Daily Graphic* and the *Daily Chronicle* have already accomplished, to infer that the dailies will do likewise before 1900 has attained its majority is a prophecy that is based upon a study of the past.

CHAPTER VII : SOME ILLUSTRATED BOOKS OF THE PERIOD BEFORE 1860

O draw up a complete list, with the barest details of title, artist, author, and publisher of the books in the period with which this volume is concerned would be unnecessary, and well-nigh impossible. The *English Catalogue*, 1863-1872, covering but a part of the time, claims to give some 30,000 entries. Many, possibly a large majority, of these books are not illustrated ; but on the other hand, the current periodicals not included contain thousands of pictures. The following chapters cannot even claim to mention every book worth the collector's notice, and refer hardly at all to many which seemed to the compiler to represent merely the commercial average of their time. Whether this was better or worse than the commercial average to-day is of no moment. Nearly all of the books mentioned have been referred to personally, and the facts reported at first hand. In spite of taxing the inexhaustible courtesy of the officials of the British Museum to the extent of eighty or more volumes during a single afternoon, I cannot pretend to have seen the whole output of the period, for it is not easy to learn from the catalogue those particulars that are needed to identify which books are illustrated.

So far as we are concerned here, the interest of the book lies solely in its illustrations, but the catalogue may not even record the fact that it contains any, much less attribute them to their author. Of those in which the artist's share has been recognised by the publisher in his announcements, I have done my best to find the first edition of each. By dint of patient wading through the advertisements, and review columns of literary journals, trade periodicals, and catalogues, a good many have turned up which had otherwise escaped notice ; although for the last twenty years at least I have never missed an opportunity of seeing every illustrated book of the sixties, with a view to this chronicle, which had been shaping itself, if not actually begun, long before any work on modern English illustrators had appeared. When a school-boy I made a collection of examples of the work of each artist whose style I had learned to recognise, and some of that material gathered

95

together so long ago has been of no little use now. These personal reminiscences are not put forward by way of magnifying the result; but rather to show that even with so many years' desultory preparation the digesting and classification of the various facts has proved too onerous. A staff òf qualified assistants under a capable director would be needed to accomplish the work as thoroughly as Mr. Sidney Lee has accomplished a not dissimilar, if infinitely more important, task— *The Dictionary of National Biography.* A certain proportion of errors must needs creep in, and the possible errors of omission are even more to be dreaded than those of commission. A false date, or an incorrect reference to a given book or illustration, is easily corrected by a later worker in the same field ; but an omission may possibly escape another student of the subject as it escaped me. As a rule, in a majority of cases —so large that it is practically ninety-nine per cent., if not more—the notes have been made side by side with the publication to which they refer. But in transcribing hasty jottings errors are apt to creep in, and despite the collation of these pages when in proof by other hands, I cannot flatter myself that they are impeccable. For experience shows that you never open the final printed text of any work under your control as editor or author, but errors, hitherto overlooked, instantly jump from the page and force themselves on your notice. An editor of one of the most widely circulated of all our magazines confesses that he has made it a rule never to glance at any number after it was published. He had too often suffered the misery of being confronted with obvious errors of fact and taste which no amount of patient care on his part (and he is a most conscientious workman) had discovered, until it was too late to rectify them. In the matter of dates alone a difficulty meets one at first sight. Many books dated one year were issued several months before the previous Christmas, and are consequently advertised and reviewed in the year before the date which appears upon their title-page. Again, many books, and some volumes of magazines (Messrs. Cassell and Co.'s publications to wit), bear no date. 'Women and books should never be dated' is a proverb as foolish as it is widely known. Yet all the same, inaccuracy of a few months is of little importance in this context ; a book or a picture does not cease to exist as soon as it is born, like the performance of an actor or a musician. Consequently, beyond its relative place as evidence of the development or decline of the author's talent, it is not of great moment whether a book was issued in 1869 or 1870, whether a drawing was published in January or February. But for those who wish to refer to the subjects noted, the information has been made as exact as circumstances permitted. When, however, a book has been reissued in a second, or later edition, with no reference to earlier issues, it is tempting to accept the date on its title-page without question. One such volume I traced back from 1868 to 1849, and for all I know the original may have been issued some years earlier; for the British Museum library is not complete; every collector can point with pride to a few books on his shelves which he has failed to discover in its voluminous catalogue.

To select a definite moment to start from is not easy, nor to keep rigidly within the time covered by the dates upon the cover of this book. It is necessary to glance briefly at some work issued before 1855, and yet it would be superfluous to re-traverse ground already well covered in *The History of Wood Engraving*, by Chatto and Jackson, with its supplementary chapter by H. G. Bohn (in the 1861 edition), in Mr. W. J. Linton's *Masterpieces of Engraving*, in Mr. Joseph Pennell's two sumptuous editions of *Pen Drawing and Pen Draughtsmen* (Macmillan), and the same author's *Modern Illustrations* (Bell), not to mention the many admirable papers read before learned societies by Messrs. W. J. Linton, Comyns Carr, Henry Blackburn, Walter Crane, William Morris, and others. Still less is it necessary to attempt to indorse their arguments in favour of wood-engraving against process, or to repeat those which support the opposite view. So that here, in the majority of cases, the question of the engraver's share has not been considered. Mr. Pennell, for one, has done this most thoroughly, and has put the case for process so strongly, that if any people yet believe a wood-engraving is always something sacred, while a good process block of line work is a mere feeble substitute, there is little hope of convincing them. Here the result has been the chief concern. The object of these notes is not to prove what wood-engraving ruined, or what might or ought to have been, but merely to record what it achieved, without too frequent expression of regret, which nevertheless will intrude as the dominant feeling when you study many of the works executed by even the better class wood-engravers.

One must not overlook the very obvious fact that, in the earlier years, an illustration was a much more serious affair for all concerned than it is to-day. In Jackson's *Pictorial Press* we find the author says : ' Illustration was so seldom used that the preparation of even a small woodcut was of much moment to all concerned. I have heard William Harvey relate that when Whittingham, the well-known printer, wanted a new cut for his Chiswick Press Series, he would write to Harvey and John Thompson, the engraver, appointing a meeting at Chiswick, when printer, designer, and engraver talked over the matter with as much delibera- tion as if about to produce a costly national monument. And after they had settled all points over a snug supper, the result of their labours was the production a month afterwards of a woodcut measuring perhaps two inches by three. At that time perhaps only a dozen persons besides Bewick were practising the art of wood-engraving in England.'

But this preamble does not seek to excuse the meagre record it prefaces. A complete bibliography of such a fecund illustrator as Sir John Gilbert would need a volume to itself. To draw up detailed lists of all the various drawings in *The Illustrated London News, Punch,* and other prominent weeklies, would be a task needing almost as much co-operation as Dr. Murray's great Dictionary. The subject, if it proves to be sufficiently attractive, will doubtless be done piece by piece by future workers. I envy each his easy pleasure of pointing out the shortcomings of this work, for no keener joy awaits the maker of a handbook than gibbeting his pre- decessors, and showing by implication how much more trustworthy is his record than theirs.

Few artistic movements are so sharply defined that their origin can be traced to a particular moment, although some can be attributed more or less to the influence of one man. Even the pre-Raphaelite movement, clearly distinct as its origin appears at first glance, should not be dated from the formal draft of the little coterie, January 13th, 1851, for, as Mr. W. M. Rossetti writes, ' The rules show or suggest not only what we intended to do, but what had been

D. G. ROSSETTI

THE MAIDS OF
ELFENMERE

occupying our attention since 1848. The day when we codified proved also to be the day when no code was really in requisition.' Nor has the autumn 1848 any better claim to be taken as the exact moment, for one cannot overlook the fact that there was Ford Madox Brown, a pre-Raphaelite, long before the pre-Raphaelites, and that Ruskin had published the first volume of *Modern Painters*. There can be little doubt that it was the influence of the so-called pre-Raphaelites and those in closest sympathy with them, which awakened a new interest in illustration, and so prepared the ground for the men of the sixties ; but to confine our notice from 1857 to 1867—a far more accurate period—would be to start without sufficient reference to the work superseded by or absorbed into the later movement. So we must glance at a few of the books which preceded both the *Music-master* of 1855 and the *Tennyson* of 1857, either volume, the latter especially, being an excellent point whence to reckon more precisely 'the golden decade of British Art,' as Mr. Pennell terms it so happily.

Without going back too far for our purpose, one of the first books that contains illustrations by artists whose work extended into the sixties (and, in the case of Tenniel, far beyond) is *Poems and Pictures*, 'A Collection of Ballads, Songs, and Poems illustrated by English Artists' (Burns, 1846). So often was it reprinted that it came as a surprise to discover the first edition was fourteen years earlier than the date which is upon my own copy. Despite the ornamental borders to each page, and many other details which stamp it as old-fashioned, it does not require a rabid apologist of the past to discuss it appreciatively. From the first design by C. W. Cope, to the last, *A Storm at Sea*, by E. Duncan, both engraved by W. J. Linton, there is no falling off in the quality of the work. The influence of Mulready is discernible, and it seems probable that certain pencil drawings for the *Vicar of Wakefield*, engraved in facsimile—so far as was within the power of the craftsmen at that time—did much to shape the manner of book-illustrations in the fifties.

Nor does it betray want of sympathy with the artists who were thus influenced to regret that they chose to imitate drawings not intended for illustration, and ignored in very many cases the special technique which employs the most direct

99

SOME ILLUSTRATED BOOKS

expression of the material. In *The Mourner*, by J. C. Horsley (p. 22), you feel that the engraver (Thompson) has done his best to imitate the softly defined line of a pencil in place of the clearly accentuated line which is most natural in wood. Yet even in this there is scarcely a trace of that elaborate cross-hatching so easily produced in plate-engraving or pen drawing, so tedious to imitate in wood. Another design, *Time*, by C. W. Cope (p. 88), shows that the same engraver could produce work of quite another class when it was required. Curiously enough, these two, picked at random, reappear in almost the last illustrated anthology mentioned in these chapters, Cassell's *Sacred Poems* (1867).

Several books earlier in date, including De la Motte Fouqué's *Undine*, with eleven drawings by 'J. Tenniel, Junr.' (Burns, 1846), and *Sintram and his Companions*, with designs by H. S. Selous and a frontispiece after Dürer's *The Knight and Death* need only be mentioned. The *Juvenile Verse and Picture Book* (Burns, 1848), with many illustrations by Gilbert, Tenniel, 'R. Cruikskank,' Weigall, and W. B. Scott, which was reissued with altered text as *Gems of National Poetry* (Warne, 1868), and *Æsop's Fables* (Murray, 1848), with 100 illustrations by Tenniel, deserve a bare mention. Nor should The *'Bon Gaultier' Ballads* (Blackwood, 1849) be forgotten. The illustrations by Doyle, Leech, and Crowquill were enormously popular in their day, and although the style of humour which still keeps many of the ballads alive has been frequently imitated since, and rarely excelled, yet its drawings have often been equalled and surpassed, humorous although they are, of their sort.

The Salamandrine, a poem by Charles Mackay, issued in a small quarto (Ingram, Cooke, and Co., 1853), with forty-six designs by John Gilbert, is one of the early volumes by the more fecund illustrators of the century. It is too late in the day to praise the veteran whose paintings are as familiar to frequenters of the Royal Academy now as were his draw-ings when the Great Exhibition entered a formal claim for the recognition of British Art. Honoured here and upon the Continent, it is needless to eulogise an artist whom all agree to admire. The prolific invention which never failed is not more evident in this book than in a hundred others decorated by his facile pencil, yet it reveals—as any one of the rest

100

BEFORE 1860

must equally—the powerful mastery of his art, and its limitations. Thomson's *Seasons*, illustrated by the Etching Club (1852), S. C. Halls *Book of British Ballads* (1852), an edition of *The Arabian Nights*, with 600 illustrations by W. Harvey (1852), and *Uncle Tom's Cabin*, with 100 drawings by George Thomas, can but be named in passing. Gray's *Elegy*, illustrated by 'B. Foster, G. Thomas, and a Lady,' (Sampson Low), *The Book of Celebrated Poems*, with eighty designs by Cope, Kenny Meadows, and others (Sampson Low), *The Vicar of Wakefield*, with drawings by George Thomas, *The Deserted Village*, illustrated by members of the Etching Club—Cope, T. Creswick, J. C. Horsley, F. Tayler, H. J. Townsend, C. Stenhouse, T. Webster, R.A., and R. Redgrave—all published early in the fifties—may also be dismissed without comment. About the same time the great mental sedative of the period—Tupper's *Proverbial Philosophy* (Hatchard, 1854)—was reprinted in a stately quarto, with sixty-two illustrations by C. W. Cope, R.A., E. H. Corbould, Birket Foster, John Gilbert, J. C. Horsley, F. R. Pickersgill and others, engraved for the most part by ' Dalziel Bros.' and H. Vizetelly. The dull, uninspired text seems to have depressed the imagination of the artists. Despite the notable array of names, there is no drawing of more than average interest in the volume, except perhaps *To-morrow* (p. 206), by F. R. Pickersgill, which is capitally engraved by Dalziel and much broader in its style than the rest.

Poems by Henry Wadsworth Longfellow (David Bogue, 1854) appears to be the earliest English illustrated edition of any importance of a volume that has been frequently illustrated since. This book is uniform with the *Poetical Works of John Milton* with 120 engravings by Thompson, Williams, etc., from drawings by W. Harvey, *The Works of William Cowper* with seventy-five illustrations engraved by J. Orrin Smith from drawings by John Gilbert; Thomson's *Seasons* with illustrations 'drawn and engraved by Samuel Williams,' and *Beattie and Collins' Poems* with engravings by the same hand from designs by John Absolon. The title-page of the Longfellow says it is illustrated by ' Jane E. Benham, Birket Foster, etc.' It is odd to find the not very elegant, 'etc.' stands for John Gilbert and E. Wehnert, also to note that the engravers have in each of the above volumes taken precedence of the draughtsman. Except that we miss the pre-Raphaelite group for which we prize the Moxon *Tennyson* to-day, the ideal of these books is very nearly the same as of that volume. This edition of Longfellow must not be confused with another, a quarto, issued the following year (Routledge, 1855), 'with over one hundred designs drawn by John Gilbert and engraved by the brothers Dalziel.' This notable instance of the variety and inventive power of the artist also shows (in the night pieces especially, pp. 13, 360), that the engraver was trying to advance in the direction of 'tone' and atmospheric effect; and endeavouring to give the effect of a 'wash' rather than of a line drawing or the imitation of a steel engraving. This tendency, which was not the chief purpose of the work of the sixties, in the seventies carried the technicalities of the craft to its higher achievements, or, as some enthusiasts prefer to regard it, to its utter ruin, so that the photographic process-block could beat it on its own ground. But these opposite views have been threshed out often enough without bringing the parties concerned nearer together to encourage a new attempt to reconcile the opposing factions. The Longfellow of 1855 was reissued with the addition of *Hiawatha* in 1856. Another edition of *Hiawatha*, illustrated by G. H. Thomas, issued about this time, contains some of his best work.

Allingham's *Music-master* (Routledge, 1855) is so often referred to in this narrative that its mere name must suffice in this context. But, as the book itself is so scarce, a sentence from its preface may be quoted: 'Those excellent painters' (writes Mr. Allingham), 'who on my behalf have submitted their genius to the risks of wood-engraving, will, I hope, pardon me for placing a sincere word of thanks in the book they have honoured with this evidence through art of their varied fancy.' To this year belongs also *The Task*, illustrated by Birket Foster (Nisbet, 1855).

Eliza Cook's Poems (Routledge, 1856) is another sumptuously illustrated quarto gift-book with many designs by John Gilbert, J. Wolf, Harrison Weir, J. D. Watson, and others, all engraved by Dalziel Brothers. A notable drawing by H. H. Armstead, *The Trysting Place* (p. 363), deserves republication. In this year appeared also the famous edition of Adams's *Sacred Allegories* with a number of engravings

BEFORE 1860
from original drawings by C. W. Cope, R.A., J. C. Horsley, A.R.A., Samuel Palmer, Birket Foster, and George C. Hicks. The amazing quality of the landscapes by Samuel Palmer stood even the test of enormous enlargement in lantern slides, when Mr. Pennell showed them at his lectures on the men of the sixties; had W. T. Green engraved no other blocks, he might be ranked as a great craftsman on the evidence of these alone.

In *George Herbert's Poetical Works* (Nisbet, 1856), with designs by Birket Foster, John Clayton, and H. N. Humphreys, notwithstanding the vitality of the text, the drawings are sicklied over with the pale cast of religious sentimentality which has ruined so much religious art in England. A draughtsman engaged on New Testament subjects of that time rarely forgot Overbeck, Raphael, or still more 'pretty' masters. In the religious illustrations of the period many landscapes are included, some of them exquisite transcripts of English scenery, others of the 'Oriental' order dear to the Annuals. The delightful description of one of these imaginary scenes, by Leland, 'Hans Breitmann,' will come to mind, when he says of its artist that

'All his work expanded with expensive fallacies,
Castles, towered walls, pavilions, real-estately palaces.
In the foreground lofty palm-trees, as if full of soaring love,
Bore up cocoa-nuts and monkeys to the smiling heavens above ;
Jet-black Indian chieftains—at their feet, too, lovely girls were
    sighing,
With an elephant beyond them, here and there a casual lion.'

George Herbert the incomparable may be hard to illustrate, but, if the task is attempted, it should be in any way but this delineation of pretty landscapes, with 'here and there a casual lion.' This reflection upon the mildly sacred compositions of 'gift-book' art generally, although provoked by this volume, is applicable to nearly every one of its fellows.

In *Rhymes and Roundelays*, illustrated by Birket Foster (Bogue, 1856), the designs are not without a trace of artificiality, but it contains also some of the earliest and best examples of a most accomplished draughtsman, and in it many popular blocks began a long career of 'starring,' until from guinea volumes some were used ultimately in children's primers and the like.

SOME ILLUSTRATED BOOKS

The Works of William Shakespeare illustrated by John Gilbert (Routledge, 1856-8) will doubtless be remembered always as his masterpiece. At a public dinner lately, an artist who had worked with Sir John Gilbert on the *Illustrated London News*, and in nearly all the books of the period illustrated by the group of draughtsmen with whom both are associated, spoke of his marvellous rapidity—a double-page drawing done in a single night. Yet so sure is his touch that in the mass of these hundreds of designs to Shakespeare you are not conscious of any scamping. Without being archæologically impeccable, they suggest the types and costumes of the periods they deal with, and, above all, represent embodiments of actual human beings. They stand apart from the grotesque caricatures of an earlier school, and the academic inanities of both earlier and later methods. Virile and full of invention, the book is a monument to an artist who has done so much that it is a pleasure to discover some one definite accomplishment that from size alone may be taken as his masterpiece, if merely as evidence that praise, scantily bestowed elsewhere, is limited by space only.

Scott's *Lady of the Lake*, illustrated by John Gilbert, appeared in 1856. The other volumes, *Marmion*, the *Lady of the Lake*, and the *Lay of the Last Minstrel*, appear to have been published previously; but to ascertain their exact date of issue, the three bulky volumes of the British Museum catalogue devoted to 'Scott (Walter)' can hardly be faced with a light heart. This year saw an edition of Bunyan's *Pilgrim's Progress* with outline drawings by J. R. Clayton, who is sometimes styled 'J. R.,' and sometimes 'John.' An illustrated guinea edition of a once popular 'goody' book, *Ministering Children*, with designs by Birket Foster and H. Le Jeune (Nisbet, 1856), an edition of *Edgar Allan Poe's Works*, illustrated by E. H. Wehnert and others (Addey, 1856); Coleridge's *Ancient Mariner*, with pictures by Birket Foster, A. Duncan, and E. H. Wehnert, are also of this year, to which belongs, although it is post-dated, Pollok's *Course of Time* (W. Blackwood, 1857), a book containing fifty fine illustrations by Birket Foster, John Tenniel, and J. R. Clayton, engraved by Edward Evans, Dalziel Brothers, H. N. Woods, and John Green. A block by Dalziel, after Clayton, on page 19, shows a good example of the white line, used horizontally,

FORD MADOX BROWN

WILLMOTT'S 'POETS OF THE
NINETEENTH CENTURY,' 1857

THE PRISONER
OF CHILLON

for the modelling of flesh, somewhat in the way, as Panne-
maker employed it so effectively in many of Gustave Doré's
illustrations years after.   The twenty-seven Birket Fosters
are full of the special charm that his work possesses, and show
once again how a great artist may employ a method, which,
merely 'pretty' in inferior hands, has something of greatness
when he touches it.

In the next year appeared the famous '*Poems by Alfred
Tennyson, D.C.L.*, Poet-Laureate.   London.   Edward Moxon,
Dover St., 1857.'   Not even the bare fact that it was illustrated
appears on the title-page.   As the book has been re-issued lately
in a well-printed edition, a detailed list of its contents is hardly
necessary; nor need any of the illustrations be reproduced
here.   It will suffice to say that Dante Gabriel Rossetti is
represented by five designs to *The Lady of Shallott* (p. 75),
Mariana (p. 82), *Palace of Art* (pp. 113-119), *Sir Galahad*
(p. 305); Millais has eighteen, W. Holman Hunt seven,
W. Mulready four, T. Creswick six, J. C. Horsley six,
C. Stanfield six, and D. Maclise two.   A monograph by Mr.
G. Somes Layard, *Tennyson and his pre-Raphaelite Illustrators*
(Stock, 1894), embodies a quantity of interesting facts, with
many deductions therefrom which are not so valuable.   In the
books about Rossetti and the pre-Raphaelites, and their name
is legion, this volume has rarely escaped more or less notice,
so that one hesitates to add to the mass of criticism already
bestowed.   The whole modern school of decorative illustrators regard it rightly enough as the genesis of the modern
movement; but all the same it is only the accidental presence
of D. G. Rossetti, Holman Hunt, and Millais, which entitles it
to this position.   It satisfies no decorative ideal as a piece of
book-making.   Except for these few drawings, it differs in no
respect from the average 'quarto poets' before and after.   The
same 'toned' paper, the same vignetted pictures, appear; the
proportions of the type-page are merely that in ordinary use;
the size and shape of the illustrations was left apparently to
pure chance.   Therefore, in place of talking of the volume
with bated breath as a masterpiece, it would be wiser to
regard it as one of the excellent publications of the period,
that by the fortuitous inclusion of a few drawings, quite out
of touch with the rest, has acquired a reputation, which, considered as a complete book, it does not deserve.   The

drawings by Rossetti, even as we see them after translation by the engraver had worked his will, must needs be valued as masterpieces, if only for the imagination and thought compressed into their limited space, and from their exquisite manipulation of details. At first sight, some of these—for instance, the soldier munching an apple in the *St. Cecilia*—seem discordant, but afterwards reveal themselves as commentaries upon the text—not elucidating it directly, but embroidering it with subtle meanings and involved symbolism. Such qualities as these, whether you hold them as superfluous or essential, separate these fine designs from the jejune simplicity of the mass of the decorative school to-day. To draw a lady with 'intense' features, doing nothing in particular, and that in an anatomically impossible attitude, is a poor substitute for the fantasy of Rossetti. No amount of poorly drawn confused accessories will atone for the absence of the dominant idea that welded all the disturbing elements to a perfect whole. One artist to-day, or at most two, alone show any real effort to rival these designs on their own ground. The rest appear to believe that a coarse line and eccentric composition provide all that is required, given sufficient ignorance of academic draughtsmanship.

Another book of the same year, *The Poets of the Nineteenth Century*, selected and edited by the Rev. Robert Aris Willmott (Routledge, 1857), is in many respects quite as fine as the Tennyson, always excepting the pre-Raphaelite element, which is not however totally absent. For in this quarto volume Millais' *Love* (p. 137) and *The Dream* (p. 123) are worthy to be placed beside those just noticed. Ford Madox Brown's *Prisoner of Chillon* (p. 111) is another masterpiece of its sort. For this we are told the artist spent three days in a dissecting-room (or a mortuary—the accounts differ) to watch the gradual change in a dead body, making most careful studies in colour as well as monochrome all for a foreshortened figure in a block $3\frac{3}{4}$ by 5 inches. This procedure is singularly unlike the rapid inspiration which throws off compositions in black and white to-day. In a recent book received with well-deserved applause, some of the smaller 'decorative designs' were produced at the rate of a dozen in a day. The mere time occupied in production is of little consequence, because we know

JOHN GILBERT

WILLMOTT'S 'POETS OF THE
NINETEENTH CENTURY,' 1857   HOHENLINDEN

F. R. PICKERSGILL

WILLMOTT'S 'POETS OF THE
NINETEENTH CENTURY,' 1857

THE WATER
NYMPH

that the apparently rapid 'sketch' by Phil May may have
taken far more time than a decorative drawing, with elaborately minute detail over every inch of its surface ; but,
other qualities being equal, the one produced with lavish
expenditure of care and thought is likely to outlive the trifle
tossed off in an hour or two. In the *Poets of the Nineteenth
Century* the hundred engravings by the brothers Dalziel
include twenty-one of Birket Foster's exquisite landscapes,
all with figures ; fourteen by W. Harvey, nine by John Gilbert,
six by J. Tenniel, five by J. R. Clayton, eleven by T. Dalziel,
seven by J. Godwin, five by E. H. Corbould, two by D.
Edwards, five by E. Duncan, seven by J. Godwin, and one
each by Arthur Hughes, W. P. Leitch, E. A. Goodall, T. D.
Hardy, F. R. Pickersgill, and Harrison Weir—a century of
designs not unworthy as a whole to represent the art of the
day ; although Rossetti and Holman Hunt, who figure so
strongly in the Tennyson, are not represented. This year
John Gilbert illustrated the *Book of Job* with fifty designs ;
The Proverbs of Solomon (Nisbet, 1858), a companion volume,
contains twenty drawings.

Another noteworthy volume is Barry Cornwall's *Dramatic
Scenes and other Poems* (Chapman and Hall, 1857) illustrated
by many of the artists already mentioned. The fifty-seven
engravings by Dalziel include one block on p. 45, from a
drawing by J. R. Clayton, which is here reprinted—not so
much for its design as for its engraving ; the way the breadth
of the drapery is preserved, despite the elaborate pattern on
its surface, stamps it as a most admirable piece of work.
Thornbury's *Legends of the Cavaliers and Roundheads* (Hurst
and Blackett, 1857), was illustrated by H. S. Marks.

So far the few books of 1857 noticed have considerable
family likeness. The Bunyan's *Pilgrim's Progress* (Nisbet,
1857), illustrated with twenty designs by G. H. Thomas,
more slight in its method, reflects the journalistic style of its
day rather than the elaborate 'book' manner, which in many
an instance gives the effect of an engraving 'after' a painting
or a large and highly-wrought fresco. As one of the many
attempts to illustrate the immortal Protestant romance it
deserves noting. To this year belongs *The Poetical Works
of Edgar Allan Poe*, illustrated with some striking designs
by John Tenniel, and others by F. R. Pickersgill, R.A.,

SOME ILLUSTRATED BOOKS

Birket Foster, Percival Skelton; and besides these, Felix Darley, P. Duggan, Jasper Cropsey, and A. W. Madot— draughtsmen whose names are certainly not household words to-day. In the lists of 'artists' the portrait of the author is attributed to 'daguerreotype'! one of the earliest instances I have encountered of the formal appearance of the ubiquitous camera as an artist. Longfellow's prose romance, *Kavanagh* (Kent, 1857), with exquisite illustrations by Birket Foster, appeared this year; *Hyperion* (Dean), illustrated by the same author, being issued the following Christmas.

Poetry and Pictures from Thomas Moore (Longman, 1857), the *Poems and Songs of Robert Burns* (Bell and Daldy, 1857), both illustrated by Birket Foster and others, and *The Fables of Æsop*, with twenty-five drawings by C. H. Bennett, also deserve a passing word. *Gertrude of Wyoming*, by Thomas Campbell (Routledge, 1857), is only less important from its dimensions, and the fact that it contains only thirty-five illustrations, engraved by the brothers Dalziel, as against the complete hundred of most of its fellows. The drawings by Birket Foster, Thomas Dalziel, Harrison Weir, and William Harvey include some very good work.

Lays of the Holy Land (Nisbet, 1858), clad in binding of a really fine design adapted from Persian sources, is another illustrated quarto, with one drawing at least—*The Finding of Moses*—by J. E. Millais, which makes it worth keeping; a 'decorative' *Song of Bethlehem*, by J. R. Clayton, is ahead of its time in style; the rest by Gilbert, Birket Foster, and others are mostly up to their best average. The title-page says 'from photographs and drawings,' but as every block is attributed to an artist, the former were without doubt re-drawn and the source not acknowledged—a habit of draughtsmen which is not obsolete to-day.

Perhaps the most important illustrated volume of the next year is *The Home Affections [portrayed] by the Poets*, by Charles Mackay (Routledge, 1858), which continues the type of quarto gilt-edged toned paper table-books so frequent at this time. Its illustrations are a hundred in number, all engraved by Dalziels. Its artists include Birket Foster, John Gilbert, J. R. Clayton, Harrison Weir, T. B. Dalziel, S. Read, John Abner, F. R. Pickersgill, R.A., John Tenniel, with many others, 'and' (as play-bills have it) J. Everett

BARRY CORNWALL'S
'DRAMATIC SCENES'
1857

OLYMPIA AND
BIANCA

J. E. MILLAIS

'HOME AFFECTIONS FROM
THE POETS,' 1858

THERE'S NAE LUCK
ABOUT THE HOUSE

J. E. MILLAIS

'HOME AFFECTIONS FROM
THE POETS,' 1858

THE BORDER
WIDOW

BEFORE 1860

Millais, A.R.A. *There's nae Luck about the House* (p. 245) and *The Border Widow* (p. 359) are curiously unlike in motive as well as handling; the one, with all its charm, is of the Mulready school, the other intense and passionate, highly wrought in the pre-Raphaelite manner. Yet after the Millais' all the other illustrations in the book seem poor. A landscape by Harrison Weir (p. 193), *Lenore*, by A. Madot (p. 159), a very typical Tenniel, *Fair Ines* (p. 135), *Oriana* (p. 115), *Hero and Leander* (p. 91), *The Hermit* (p. 67), and *Good-night in the Porch* (p. 195), by Pickersgill, claim a word of appreciation as one turns over its pages anew. Whether too many copies were printed, or those issued were better pre-served by their owners than usual, no book is more common in good condition to-day than this.

Another book of the same size, with contents less varied, it is true, but of almost the same level of excellence, is *Wordsworth's Selected Poems* (Routledge, 1859), illustrated by Birket Foster, J. Wolf, and John Gilbert. This contains the hundred finely engraved blocks by the brothers Dalziel, some of them of the first rank, which was the conventional equipment of a gift-book at that time.

Other noteworthy volumes of 1858-9 are *Merrie Days of England, Sketches of Olden Times*, illustrated by twenty drawings by Birket Foster, G. Thomas, E. Corbould, and others; *The Scouring of the White Horse*, with designs by Richard Doyle (Macmillan), his Foreign Tour of *Brown, Jones, and Robinson*, and the same artist's *Manners and Customs of the English*, all then placed in the first rank by most excellent critics; *Favourite English Poems of the last two Centuries*, illustrated by Birket Foster, Cope, Creswick, and the rest; Wordsworth's *White Doe of Rylstone* (Long-mans), also illustrated by Birket Foster and H. N. Hum-phreys; *Childe Harold*, with many designs by Percival Skelton and others; Blair's *Grave*, illustrated by Tenniel (A. and C. Black); Milton's *Comus* (Routledge, 1858), with illustrations by Pickersgill, B. Foster, H. Weir, etc.; and C. H. Bennett's *Proverbs with Pictures* (Chapman and Hall). *Thomas Moore's Poems* (Longmans, 1858); *Child's Play*, by E. V. B., appeared also about this time. Krummacher's *Parables*, with forty illustrations by J. R. Clayton (Bohn's Library, 1858), is another unfamiliar book likely to be over-

109

looked, although it contains good work of its sort; inspired a little by German design possibly, but including some admirable drawings, those for instance on pages 147 and 347. *The Shipwreck*, by Robert Falconer, illustrated by Birket Foster (Edinburgh, Black, 1858), contains thirty drawings, some of them charmingly engraved by W. T. Green, Dalziel Brothers, and Edward Evans in 'the Turner vignette' manner; they are delightful of their kind.

In 1859 there seems to be a falling off, which can hardly be traced to the starting of *Once a Week* in July, for Christmas books—and nearly all the best illustrated volumes fall into that category—are prepared long before midsummer. C. H. Bennett's illustrated Bunyan's *Pilgrim Progress* (Longmans) is one of the best of the year's output. A survival of an older type is *A Book of Favourite Modern Ballads*, illustrated by C. W. Cope, J. C. Horsley, A. Solomon, S. Palmer, and others (Kent), which, but for the publisher's announcement, might well be regarded as a reprint of a book at least ten years earlier; but its peculiar method was unique at that time, and rarely employed since, although but lately revived now for half-tone blocks. It consists in a double printing, black upon a previous printing in grey, not solid, but with the 'lights' carefully taken out, so that the whole looks like a drawing on grey paper heightened by white chalk. Whether the effect might be good on ordinary paper, these impressions on a shiny cream surface, set in gold borders, are not captivating.

Odes and Sonnets, illustrated by Birket Foster (Routledge, 1859), has also devices by Henry Sleigh, printed in colours. It is not a happy experiment; despite the exquisite landscapes, the decoration accords so badly that you cannot linger over its pages with pleasure. *Byron's Childe Harold*, with eighty illustrations by Percival Skelton, is another popular book of 1859.

Hiawatha, with twenty-four drawings by G. H. Thomas, and *The Merchant of Venice* (Sampson Low, 1860), illustrated by G. H. Thomas, Birket Foster, and H. Brandling, with ornaments by Harry Rogers, are two others a trifle belated in style. Of different sort is *The Voyage of the Constance*, a tale of the Arctic Seas (Edinburgh, Constable), with twenty-four drawings by Charles Keene, a singularly interesting and apparently scarce volume which reveals powers of imagining landscape which he had never seen in a very realistic manner. I once heard him declare that he had never in his life been near either an Irish bog or a Scotch moor, both subjects being very frequent in his work.

The Seasons, by James Thomson (Nisbet, 1859), illustrated by Birket Foster, F. R. Pickersgill, R.A., J. Wolf, G. Thomas, and Noel Humphreys, is another small quarto gift-book with the merits and defects of its class. Yet, after making all due allowance, one feels that even these average volumes of the fifties, if they do not interest us as much as those of the sixties, are yet ahead, in many important qualities, of the average Christmas gift-book to-day. The academic scholarship and fine craft of this era would equip a whole school of 'decorative students,' and leave still much to spare. Yet if we prefer, in our heart of hearts, the Birmingham books to-day, this is merely to confess that modernity, whether it be frankly actual, or pose as mediæval, attracts us more than a far worthier thing out of fashion for the moment. But such preference, if it exists, is hardly likely to outlast a serious study of the books of ' the sixties.'

CHAPTER VIII : SOME ILLUSTRATED BOOKS OF THE PERIOD 1860-1864

MONG the books dated 1860, or issued in the autumn of that year, are more elaborately illustrated editions of popular poets— all, as a rule, in the conventional quarto, or in what a layman might be forgiven for describing as 'quarto,' even if an expert preferred to call it octavo. Of these Tennyson's *The Princess*, with twenty-six drawings by Maclise, may be placed first, on account of the position held by author and artist. All the same, it belongs essentially to the fifties or earlier, both in spirit and in style. A more ample quarto, *Poems* by James Montgomery (Routledge, 1860), (not the Montgomery castigated by Lord Macaulay), 'selected and edited by Robert Aris Wilmott (Routledge), with one hundred designs by John Gilbert, Birket Foster, F. R. Pickersgill, R.A., J. Wolf, Harrison Weir, E. Duncan, and W. Harvey, is perhaps slightly more in touch with the newer school. Its engravings by the brothers Dalziel are admirable. *The Clouds athwart the Sky* (p. 23), by John Gilbert, and other landscapes by the same hand, may hold their own even by the side of those in the Moxon *Tennyson*, or in Wilmott's earlier anthology. Of quite different calibre is Moore's *Lalla Rookh*, with its sixty-nine drawings by Tenniel, engraved by the Dalziels (Longmans, 1861). If to-day you hardly feel inclined to indorse the verdict of the *Times* critic, who declared it to be 'the greatest illustrative achievement by any single hand,' it shows nevertheless not a few of those qualities which have won well-merited fame for our oldest cartoonist, even if it shows also the limitations which just alienate one's complete sympathy. Yet those who saw an exhibition of Sir John Tenniel's drawings at the Fine Art Society's galleries will be less ready to blame the published designs for a certain hardness of style, due in great part (one fancies) to their engraver.

In Bunyan's *Pilgrim's Progress* (Routledge), with a hundred and ten designs by J. D. Watson, engraved by the Dalziels, we are confronted with a book that is distinctly of the 'sixties,' or perhaps it would be more accurate to say that most of its illustrations are distinguished by the broader

WILLMOTT'S 'ENGLISH SACRED
POETRY' 1862, p. 49

A DREAM

FREDERICK WALKER

WILLMOTT'S 'SACRED
POETRY,' 1862

THE NURSERY
FRIEND

WILLMOTT'S 'SACRED
POETRY,' 1862

S

A CHILD IN
PRAYER

treatment of the new school. It is strange that the ample and admirable achievements of this artist have not received more general recognition. When you meet with one of his designs set amid the work of the greatest illustrators, it rarely fails to maintain a dignified equality. If it lack the supreme artistry of one or the fine invention of another, it is always sober and at times masterly, in a restrained matter-of-fact way. Some sketches reproduced in the *British Architect* (January 22, 1878) display more freedom than his finished works suggest.

Quarles' Emblems (Nisbet), illustrated by C. H. Bennett, a caricaturist whose style seems to have lost touch with modern taste, with decorative adornments by W. H. Rogers, must not be overlooked; nor Tennyson's *May Queen* (Sampson Low), with designs by E. V. B., a gifted amateur, whose work in this book, in *Child's Play*, and elsewhere, has a distinct charm, despite many technical shortcomings.

Lyra Germanica (Longmans, 1861), an anthology of hymns translated from the German by Catherine Winkworth, produced under the superintendence of John Leighton, F.S.A., must not be confused with a second series, with the same title, the same anthologist and art editor, issued in 1868. This book contains much decorative work by John Leighton, who has scarcely received the recognition he deserves as a pioneer of better things. At a time when lawless naturalistic detail was supreme everywhere he strove to popularise conventional methods, and deserves full appreciation for his energetic and successful labours. The illustrations include one fine Charles Keene (p. 182), three by M. J. Lawless (pp. 47, 90, 190), four by H. S. Marks (pp. 1, 19, 57, 100), and five by E. Armitage (pp. 29, 62, 111, 160, 197). The engraving by T. Bolton, after a Flaxman bas-relief, is apparently the same block Bohn includes in his supplementary chapter to the 1861 edition of Chatto and Jackson's *History of Wood-Engraving*, as a specimen of the first experiment in Mr. Bolton's 'new process for photographing on the wood.' As this change was literally epoch-making, this really beautiful block, with its companion p. 111, is of historic interest.

Shakespeare: His Birthplace, edited by J. R. Wise, with twenty-three pictures drawn and engraved by W. J. Linton (Longmans); *The Poetry of Nature*, with thirty-six drawings by Harrison Weir (Low), and *Household Song* (Kent, 1861),

SOME ILLUSTRATED BOOKS

illustrated by Birket Foster, Samuel Palmer, G. H. Thomas, A. Solomon, J. Andrews, and others, including two rather powerful blocks, *To Mary in Heaven* especially, by J. Archer, R.S.A.; *Chambers's Household Shakespeare*, illustrated by Keeley Halswelle, must not be forgotten; nor *A Boy's Book of Ballads* (Bell and Daldy), illustrated by Sir John Gilbert; but *The Adventures of Baron Munchausen*, with designs by A. Crowquill (Trübner), is not very important.

An illustrated edition of Mrs. Gatty's *Parables from Nature* (Bell and Daldy) would be remarkable if only for the *Nativity* by 'E. Burne-Jones.' It is instructive to compare the engraving with the half-tone reproduction of the original drawing which appears in Mr. Pennell's *Modern Illustrations* (Bell). But there are also good things in the book by John Tenniel, Holman Hunt, M. E. Edwards, and drawings of average interest by W. (not J. E.) Millais, Otto Speckter, F. Keyl, L. Frolich, Harrison Weir, and others. In the respective editions of 1861 and 1867 the illustrations vary considerably.

Another book that happened to be published in 1860 would at any time occupy a place by itself. Founded on Blake, David Scott developed a distinctly personal manner, that has provoked praise and censure, in each case beyond its merit. Yet without joining either detractors or eulogists, one must own that the Bunyan's *Pilgrim's Progress* (Edinburgh, 1860), illustrated by David and W. B. Scott, if a most ugly piece of book-making, contains many very noteworthy designs. It is possible, despite the monograph of J. M. Gray (one of the earliest critics who devoted special study to the works of Frederick Sandys) and a certain esoteric cult of a limited number of disciples, that David Scott still remains practically unknown to the younger generation. Yet this book, and Coleridge's *Ancient Mariner*, which he also illustrated, contain a great many weird ideas, more or less adequately portrayed, which should endear themselves to the symbolist to-day.

Goldsmith's Poems, with coloured illustrations by Birket Foster, appeared this year, which saw also many volumes (issued by Day and Son), resplendent with chromo-lithography and 'illuminations' in gold and colours. So that the Christmas harvest, that might seem somewhat meagre in the

H. S. MARKS, R.A.

WILLMOTT'S 'SACRED POETRY'
1862

A QUIET MIND

WILLMOTT'S 'SACRED
POETRY,' 1862

IN A HERMITAGE

WILLMOTT'S 'SACRED
POETRY,' 1862

LIFE'S JOURNEY

FREDERICK SANDYS

WILLMOTT'S 'SACRED
POETRY,' 1862

A LITTLE
MOURNER

short list above, really contained as many high-priced volumes appealing to Art, 'as she was understood in 1860,' as the list of 1897 is likely to include. But the books we deem memorable had not yet appeared, and the signs of 1860 hardly point to the rapid advance which the next few years were destined to reveal. In passing it may be noted that this was the great magenta period for cloth bindings. 'Surely the most exquisite colour that ever left the chemist's laboratory,' exclaims a contemporary critic, after a rapturous eulogy.

The 'wicked fratricidal war in America,' we find by references in the trade periodicals of the time, was held responsible for the scarcity of costly volumes at this date. Perhaps the most important book of 1862 is Willmott's *Sacred Poetry of the 16th, 17th, and 18th centuries* (like many others issued the previous Christmas). It contains two drawings by Sandys, which are referred to elsewhere, three by Fred Walker, seven by H. S. Marks, two by Charles Keene, twenty-eight by J. D. Watson, one by Holman Hunt, eight by John Gilbert, and others by G. H. Andrews, H. H. Armstead, W. P. Burton, F. R. Pickersgill, S. Read, F. Smallfield, J. Sleigh, Harrison Weir, and J. Wolf. Although the absence of Millais and Rossetti would suffice to place it just below the Tennyson, it may be considered otherwise as about of equal interest with that and the earlier anthology of *Poets of the Nineteenth Century*, gathered together by the same editor. It is distinctly a typical book of the earlier sixties, and one which no collector can afford to miss.

Poetry of the Elizabethan Age, with thirty illustrations by Birket Foster, John Gilbert, Julian Portch, and E. M. Wimperis, is not quite representative of the sixties, but of a transitional period which might be claimed by either decade. *The Songs and Sonnets of Shakespeare*, with ten coloured and thirty black-and-white drawings by John Gilbert, to whatever period it may be ascribed, is one of his most superb achievements in book-illustration. *Christmas with the Poets*, 'embellished with fifty-three tinted illustrations by Birket Foster' (Bell and Daldy), can hardly be mentioned with approval, despite the masterly drawings of a great illustrator. As a piece of book-making, its gold borders and weak 'tinted' blocks, printed in feeble blues and browns, render it peculiarly unattractive. Yet in all honesty one must own that its art is far more thorough and its taste possibly no worse essentially than many of the deckle-edged superfluities with neo-primitive designs which are popular at the present time. The work of this artist is perhaps somewhat out of favour at the moment, but its neglect may be attributed to the inevitable reaction which follows undue popularity. There are legends of the palmy days of the Old Water-Colour Society, when the competition of dealers to secure drawings by ' Birket Foster' was so great that they crowded round the doors before they opened on the first day, and one enterprising trader, crushing in, went straight to the secretary and said, ' I will buy the screen,' thereby forestalling his rivals who were hastily jotting down the works by this artist hung with others upon it. But even popular applause is not always misdirected; and the master of English landscape, despite a certain prettiness and pettiness, despite a little sentimentality, is surely a master. There are 'bests' and bests so many; and if Birket Foster is easily best of his kind, and the fact would hardly be challenged, then as a master we may leave his final place to the future, sure that it is always with the great who have succeeded, and not with the merely promising who just escape success. Among the minor volumes of this year, now especially scarce, are Dr. George Mac Donald's *Dealings with the Fairies*, with illustrations by Arthur Hughes; and several of Strahan's children's books : *The Gold Thread*, by Dr. Norman Macleod, with illustrations by J. D. Watson, J. M'Whirter, and others; and *The Postman's Bag*, illustrated by J. Pettie and others. A curious volume, *Spiritual Conceits*, 'illustrated by Harry Rogers,' is printed throughout in black letter, and, despite the title, would be described more correctly to-day as 'decorated' by the artists, for the engravings are 'emblematical devices' more or less directly inspired by the emblem books of the sixteenth and the seventeenth centuries. As one of the few examples of conventional design of the period, it is interesting. New copies are by no means scarce, so it would seem to have been printed in excess of the demand, which, judging by the laudatory criticism it received, could not have been meagre.

1862, the year of the second great International Exhibition, might have been expected to yield a full crop of lavishly produced books, but as a matter of fact there are singularly

PICTURES OF ENGLISH
LANDSCAPE,' 1864

THE GREEN LANE

THE OLD CHAIR-MENDER
AT THE COTTAGE DOOR

few. Two important exceptions occur : Christina Rossetti's
Goblin Market, with the title-page and frontispiece by her
brother, and *The New Forest*, by J. R. Wise, with drawings
by Walter Crane, 'a very young artist, whom we shall be glad
to meet with again,' as a contemporary criticism runs. Yet,
on the whole the men of the sixties appear to have exhausted
their efforts on the new magazines which had just attained
full vigour ; hence, as we might expect, publishers refrained
from competing with the annual volumes, which gave
at least twice as much for seven shillings and sixpence as
they had hitherto included in a guinea table-book. Birket
Foster's *Pictures of English Landscape*, with pictures in
words by Tom Taylor (Routledge 1863), contains thirty
singularly fine drawings engraved by Dalziels, of which the
editor says : ' It is still a moot point among the best critics how
far wood-engraving can be profitably carried—whether it can
attempt, with success, such freedom and subtlety of workman-
ship as are employed, for example, on the skies throughout this
series, or should restrict itself to simple effects, with a broader
and plainer manner of execution.' Its companion was styled
Beauties of English Landscape, and appeared much later.

Early *English Poems, Chaucer to Pope* (Sampson Low,
1863), is another book of the autumn of 1862, which like
the rest is a quarto, with an elaborately designed cover
and the usual hundred blocks delightfully engraved, after
John Gilbert, Birket Foster, George Thomas, T. Creswick,
R.A., R. Redgrave, R.A., E. Duncan, and many others.
Although there is no reference to the fact in the book
itself, many of the illustrations had already done duty in
other books, or possibly did duty afterwards, for, without
a tedious collation of first editions, it is difficult to discover
the first appearance of any particular block. Probably this
was the original source of many blocks which afterwards were
issued in all sorts of volumes, so frequently that their charm is
somewhat tarnished by memories of badly printed *clichés* in
children's primers and the like.

The Life of St. Patrick, by H. Formby, is said to be
illustrated by M. J. Lawless, but the labour in tracking it
was lost ; for, whoever made the designs, the wood-engravings
are of the lowest order, and the book no more interesting
than an illustrated religious tract is usually. A sumptuously

117

produced volume, *Moral Emblems* (Longmans), 'from Jacob
Cats and Robert Fairlie,' contains 'illustrations freely rendered
from designs found in their works,' by John Leighton. The
text is by Richard Pigot, whose later career affords us a
moral emblem of another sort ; if indeed he be the hero of the
Parnell incident, as contemporary notices declared. Its two
hundred and forty-seven blocks were engraved by different
hands—Leighton, Dalziel, Green, Harral, De Wilde, Swain,
and others, all duly acknowledged in the contents. It is only
fair to say that the decorators rarely fall to the level of the
platitudes, interspersed with Biblical quotations, which form
the text of the work. Among other volumes worth mention-
ing are : *Papers for Thoughtful Girls*, by Sarah Tytler, illustrated by J. E. Millais ; *Children's Sayings*, with four pictures
by Walter Crane ; *Stories of Old*, two series, each with seven
illustrations by the same artist ; *Stories little Breeches told*,
illustrated by C. H. Bennett ; and volumes of Laurie's *Shilling
Entertainment Library*, including probably (the date of the
first edition is not quite clear) Defoe's *History of the Plague*,
with singularly powerful designs by Frederick Shields,—'Rem-
brandt-like in power,' Mr. Joseph Pennell has rightly called
them ; and *Puck on Pegasus*, a volume of humorous verses
by H. Cholmondeley Pennell, illustrated, and well illustrated,
by Leech, Tenniel, Doyle, Millais, Sir Noel Paton, 'Phiz,'
Portch, and M. Ellen Edwards. The Doyle tailpiece is
the only one formally attributed, but students will have little
difficulty in identifying the work of the various hands represented in its pages. A volume, artless in its art, that has
charmed nevertheless for thirty years, and still amuses—Lear's
Book of Nonsense—appeared this year ; but luckily its influence
has been *nil* so far, except possibly upon modern posters ;
Wordsworth's *Poems for the Young*, with fifty illustrations by
John Pettie and J. M'Whirter ; an illustrated edition of Mrs.
Alexander's *Hymns for Little Children*, mildly exciting as
works of art, *Famous Boys* (Darton), illustrated by T. Morten ;
One Year, with pictures by Clarence Dobell (Macmillan), and
Wood's Natural History, with fine drawings by Zwecker,
Wolf, and others, are also in the sterile crop of the year
1862. *Passages from Modern English Poets* (1862), illustrated
by the Junior Etching Club, an important book of its sort,
is noticed elsewhere.

FREDERICK SHIELDS

DEFOE'S 'HISTORY OF
THE PLAGUE,' 1862

THE PLAGUE-CART

1860-1864

In 1863 Millais' *Parables of our Lord* was issued, although it is dated 1864. Of the masterpieces it contained a reviewer of the period wrote : 'looked at with unfeeling eyes there is little to commend them to the average class of book-buyers.' This, which is no doubt a fairly representative opinion, may be set against the wide appreciation by artists they aroused at the time, and ever since, merely to show that the good taste of the sixties was probably confined to a minority, and that the public in 1867 or 1897, despite its pretence of culture, is rarely moved deeply by great work. It is difficult to write dispassionately of this book. Granted that when you compare it with the drawings of some of the subjects which are still extant, you regret certain shortcomings on the part of the engravers ; yet, when studied apart from that severe test, there is much that is not merely the finest work of a fine period, but that may be placed among the finest of any period. We are told in the preface that 'Mr. Millais made his first drawing to illustrate the *Parables* in August 1857, and the last in October 1863 ; thus he has been able to give that care and consideration to his subjects which the beauty as well as the importance of *The Parables* demanded.' It is not necessary to describe each one of the many illustrations. Those which appeared in *Good Words* are printed with the titles they first bore in the notice of that magazine. The other eight are : *The Tares, The Wicked Husbandman, The Foolish Virgins, The Importunate Friend, The Marriage Feast, The Lost Sheep, The Rich Man and Lazarus*, and *The Good Shepherd*, all engraved by the brothers Dalziel, who (to quote again from the preface), 'have seconded his efforts with all earnestness, desiring, as far as their powers would go, to make the pictures specimens of the art of wood-engraving.' Here it would be superfluous to ask whether the designs could have been better engraved, or even whether photogravure would not have retained more of the exquisite beauty of the originals. As they are, remembering the conditions of their production, we must needs accept them ; and the full admiration they demand need not be dashed by useless regret. In place of blaming Dalziels, let us rather praise lavishly the foresight and sympathy which called into being most of the books we now prize. Indeed, a history of Dalziels' undertakings fully told would be no small part of

119

a history of modern English illustration. If any one who loves art, especially the art of illustration, does not know and prize these *Parables*, then it were foolish to add a line in their praise, for ignorance of such masterpieces is criminal, and lukewarm approval a fatal confession.

It is difficult to place any book of 1863 next in order to *The Parables*; despite many fine publications, there is not one worthy to be classed by its side. Perhaps the most important in one sense, and the least in another, is Long-mans' famous edition of the *New Testament*, upon the preparation of which a fabulous amount of money was spent. Yet, although an epoch-making book to the wood-engraver, it represents rather the end of an old school than the beginning of a new. Its greatly reduced illustrations, wherein a huge wall-painting occupies the space of a postage-stamp, the lack of spontaneity in its formal 'correct' borders, impress us to-day more as curiosities than as living craft. All the same, it was considered a marvellous achievement; but its spirit, if it ever existed, has evaporated with age; indeed, one cannot help thinking that it was out of date when it appeared. Ten years earlier it would have provoked more hearty approval; but, with Millais' treatment of the similar subjects, who could look at this precise, unimaginative work? That it ever exercised any influence on wood-engraving is doubtful, and that it repaid, even in part, its cost and labour is still more problematical. Bound, if memory can be trusted, in sham carved and pierced oak, it may be still encountered among the *rep* and polished walnut of the period, a monument of misapplied endeavour. Its ideal seems to have been to imitate steel-plates by wood-blocks. Just as Crusaders' tombs had been modelled in Parian to do duty as match-boxes, and a thousand other attempts, then and since, with the avowed intention of imitation, have attracted no little common popularity; so its tediously minute handiwork no doubt won the approbation of those whose approval is artistic insult. One has but to turn to the tiny woodcuts of Holbein's *Dance of Death* to find that size is of no importance; a *netsuke* may be as broadly treated as a colossus, but the art of the miniature is too often miniature art. Therefore, side by side with the splendour of Millais, this mildly exciting 'art-book' comes as a typical contrast. No matter how Millais was rewarded, the mere

'THE PARABLES OF OUR
LORD,' ROUTLEDGE, 1864

THE PRODIGAL
SON

J. E. MILLAIS

'THE PARABLES OF OUR
LORD,' 1864

THE TARES

J. E. MILLAIS

'THE PARABLES OF OUR
LORD,' ROUTLEDGE, 1864

THE SOWER

engraver in this case must have been paid more, if contemporary accounts are true ; yet the result is that nobody wants the one, and every artist, lay or professional, who is awake to really fine things, treasures a chance impression of a *Parable*, torn out of *Good Words*, as a thing to reverence.

On turning back to a scrap-book, where a number of them were preserved by the present writer in the late sixties, the old surprise comes back with irresistible force to find that things which he then ranked first still maintain their supremacy. At that time, when the wonders of Japanese Art were a sealed book, the masterpieces of Dürer and Rembrandt, the triumphs of Whistler, and the exquisite engravings of the French wood-engravers, past and present, all unknown to him, he, in common with dozens of others, was conscious that here was something so great that it was almost uncanny, for, obvious and simple as it looked, it yet accomplished what all others seemed only to attempt.   There are very few pictures which after thirty years retain the old glamour ; but while the Longmans' *New Testament* when seen anew raises no thrill of appreciation, the *Parables* appear as astoundingly great to one familiar with modern illustrations as they did to an ignorant boy thirty years ago.   Other *fetishes* have gone unregretted to the lumber-room, but the Millais of 1863 is a still greater master in 1896. They builded better than they knew, these giants of the sixties, and that the approval of another generation indorses the verdict of the best critics of their own may be taken as a promise of abiding homage to be paid in centuries yet to come.

Curiously enough, among some literary notes for Christmas 1863, we find that ' early next year Messrs. Dalziel hoped to issue their Bible pictures,' and the writer goes on to praise several of the drawings—notably the Leightons, which were even then engraved : this note, nearly twenty years before the book actually appeared, is interesting, but it must not be thought that the time was devoted entirely to the engraving or in waiting for the perfection of photographic transfer to wood.

An English edition of Michelet's *The Bird*, illustrated by Giacomelli (Nelson), was issued this year, and the highly wrought naturalistic details of the engravings became extremely popular.   Its ' pretty ' finish, and tame, colourless effect influenced no little work of the period, and, coupled

SOME ILLUSTRATED BOOKS

with the *clichés* of Gustave Doré engravings, so lavishly reprinted here about this date, did much to promote a style of wood-engraving which found its highest expression in the pages of American magazines years afterwards, and its lowest in the 'decorated' poems of cheap 'snippet' weeklies, which to-day are yet imitated unconsciously by those who work in wash for half-tone processes.

The next important volume of the year, after Millais' *Parables*, judged by our standard, is unquestionably Dalziels' edition of *The Arabian Nights* (Ward, Lock, and Tyler)—'illustrated by A. Boyd Houghton,' one feels tempted to add to the title. But although the book is often referred to as the work of one artist, as a matter of fact it is the work of many. Houghton does not even contribute the largest number; his eighty-seven designs are beaten by T. Dalziel's eighty-nine. Nor is he the greatest draughtsman therein, for there are two by Millais. Still, notwithstanding these, and eight by John Tenniel, ten by G. J. Pinwell, one by T. Morten, two by J. D. Watson, and six by E. Dalziel, it is for Houghton's sake that the book has suddenly assumed importance, even in the eyes of those who do not search through the volumes of the sixties for forgotten masterpieces, but are content with *Once a Week*, the *Cornhill Gallery*, and Thornbury's *Legendary Ballads*. One thing is beyond doubt : that with the *Arabian Nights* and the others on this short list you have a National Gallery of the best things—not the best of all possible collections, not even an exhaustive collection of specimens of each, but a good working assortment that suffices to uphold the glory of 'the golden decade,' and can only be supplemented but not surpassed by the addition of all the others.

The book was issued in weekly numbers, as you see on opening a first edition of the volume at the risk of breaking its back. Close to the fold appears the legend, 'Printed by Dalziel Brothers, the Camden Press, N.W.,' etc. It was eventually issued in two volumes in October 1864, but dated '1865.' Mr. Laurence Housman's volume, *Arthur Boyd Houghton* (Kegan Paul, 1896), and his excellent article in *Bibliographica*, are available for those who wish for a fuller appreciation of this fine book.

By the side of the books already mentioned the rest seem

NOUREDDIN ALI ON
HIS JOURNEY

almost commonplace, but another edition of *The Pilgrim's Progress*, with one hundred illustrations by T. Dalziel, must not be overlooked. These show that one of the famous engravers was also an artist of no mean importance, and explain much of the fine taste that distinguished the publications of the firm with which he was associated. Elsewhere the many original designs by other members of the firm go to prove this up to the hilt.

It is curious to find 1864 the date of the 'new' illustrated edition of *The Ingoldsby Legends* (Bentley).[1] Those familiar with contemporary volumes would have hazarded a time ten to fifteen years earlier, had the matter been open to doubt. It is profusely illustrated by Leech, Tenniel, and Cruikshank, but in no way a typical book of the sixties. *English Sacred Poetry of the Olden Time* (Religious Tract Society, 1864) was issued this year. It contains F. Walker's *Portrait of a Minister* (p. 184); *The Abbey Walk* (p. 6), and *Sir Walter Raleigh* (p. 60), by G. Du Maurier; ten drawings by J. W. North, three by C. Green, three by J. D. Watson, and many by Tenniel, Percival Skelton, and others, all engraved by Whymper; *Our Life illustrated by Pen and Pencil* (Religious Tract Society, undated), is a similar book with designs by J. D. Watson, Pinwell, C. H. Selous, Du Maurier, Barnes, J. W. North. Aytoun's *Lays of the Scottish Cavaliers* is another book of 1863 that is noticeable for its illustrations, from designs by [Sir] Noel Paton. *Robinson Crusoe*, with one hundred designs by J. D. Watson (Routledge); Wordsworth's *Poetry for the Young*, illustrated by J. Pettie and J. M'Whirter (Strahan, 1863); C. H. Bennett's *London People*, and the same artist's *Mr. Wind and Madam Rain* (Sampson Low); *Hymns in Prose* by Mrs. Barbauld, illustrated by Barnes, Whymper, etc.; Dr. Cumming's *Life and Lessons of our Lord*, with pictures by C. Green, P. Skelton, A. Hunt, and others; yet another *Pilgrim's Progress*, this time with illustrations by H. C. Selous and P. Priolo (Cassell), and another *Robinson Crusoe*, illustrated by G. H. Thomas (Cassell); The *Family Fairy Tales*, illustrated 'by a young lady of eighteen,' signed M. E. E., the first published works of M. Ellen Edwards, who soon became—and deservedly—one of the most popular

---

[1] The first edition, 3 vols., 1841, was illustrated by Cruikshank and Leech only.

illustrators of the day ; *Homes without Hands*, by J. G. Wood, with animal drawings by F. W. Keyl; *Hacco the Dwarf*, with illustrations, interesting, because they are (I believe) the earliest published work by G. J. Pinwell ; and *Golden Light* (Routledge), with eighty drawings by A. W. Bayes, are some of the rest of the books of this year that must be dismissed with a bare record of their titles.

The Lake Country, with illustrations drawn and engraved by W. J. Linton (Smith and Elder, 1864), is of technical rather than general interest. Champions of the ' white line ' will find practical evidence of its masterly use in the engravings. *The Victorian History of England* (Routledge, 1864) has at least one drawing by A. B. Houghton, but, so far as a rapid turn over of its pages revealed, only one—the frontispiece. *The Golden Harp* (Routledge) appears to be a re-issue of blocks by J. D. Watson used elsewhere. *What Men have said about Women* (Routledge) is illustrated by the same artist, who is responsible—indirectly, one hopes—for coloured designs to *Melbourne House*, issued about this time. *The Months illustrated with Pen and Pencil* (Religious Tract Society, undated) contains sixty engravings by Butterworth and Heath, after J. Gilbert, Robert Barnes, J. W. North, and others ; uniform in style with *English Sacred Poetry*, it does not reach the same level of excellence. A book, *Words for the Wise* (Nelson), illustrated by W. Small, I have failed to see ; a critic calls attention to it as ' the work of a promising young artist hitherto unknown to us.' *Pictures of English Life*, with sixteen engravings by J D. Cooper, after drawings by R. Barnes. (Sampson Low), contains blocks of a size unusual in books. The superb drawings by Charles Keene to *Mrs. Caudle's Curtain Lectures* (Bradbury and Evans) enrich this prolific period with more masterpieces.

FREDERICK WALKER

'ENGLISH SACRED POETRY'
R. T. S.

PORTRAIT OF
A MINISTER

KING PIPPIN

AUTUMN.

CHAPTER IX: SOME ILLUSTRATED BOOKS, 1865-1872

ITH 1865 we reach the height of the movement—this and the following year being of all others most fertile in books illustrated by the best representative men. It saw Rossetti's frontispiece and title to *The Prince's Progress* (Macmillan, 1866), these two designs being almost enough to make the year memorable. *A Round of Days* (Routledge), one of the finest of the illustrated gift-books, contains Walker's *Broken Victuals* (p. 3), *One Mouth More* (p. 58), and the well-known *Four Seasons* (pp. 37, 39, 41, 43), for one of which the drawing on wood is at South Kensington Museum. A. Boyd Houghton appears with fourteen examples (pp. 1, 2, 5, 19, 20, 21, 22, 30, 47, 48, 71, 73, 77, 78) J. W. North with three exquisite landscapes (pp. 15, 17, 18), G. J. Pinwell with five subjects, Paul Gray with one (p. 81), J. D. Watson with five (pp. 26, 28, 62, 64, 66), T. Morten with one (p. 79), A. W. Bayes with two, T. Dalziel with seven, and E. Dalziel with two. These complete its contents, excepting two delicately engraved studies of heads after Warwick Brookes. The book itself is distinctly a lineal descendant from the annuals of the earlier half of the century; a typical example of a not very noble ideal—a scrap-book of poems and pictures made important by the work of the artists.

Yet, with full recognition of the greater literalism of reproductive process to-day, one doubts if even *The London Garland* (Macmillan, 1895), which most nearly approaches it, will maintain its interest more fully, after thirty years' interval, than does this sumptuous quarto, and a few of its fellows. That we could get together, at the present time, as varied and capable a list of artists is quite possible; but where is the publisher who would risk paying so much for original work designed for a single book, when examples by the same men are to be obtained in equally good reproductions, and not less well printed in many of the sixpenny weeklies and the monthly magazines? The change of conditions seems to forbid a revival of volumes of this class, although the *Yellow Book*, *The Pageant*, *The Savoy*, and *The Quarto*, are not entirely unrelated to them.

SOME ILLUSTRATED BOOKS

To 1864 belongs formally *The Cornhill Gallery*, a hundred impressions from the original blocks of pictures. Among the early volumes issued for Christmas 1865, this is, perhaps, the most important book, but, as its contents are fully noticed elsewhere, no more need be said here. It is amusing to read that a critic disliked ' Mr. Leighton's unpleasant subjects '— the Romola designs! Dalziels' *Illustrated Goldsmith* (Ward and Lock, 1865), may be considered, upon the whole, the masterpiece of G. J. Pinwell, who designed the hundred illustrations which seemed then to be accepted as the only orthodox number for a book. How charming some of these are every student of the period knows. Pinwell, as certain original drawings that remain prove only too clearly, suffered terribly at the engraver's hands, and, beautiful as many of the designs are, one cannot avoid regret that they were not treated more tenderly. It is quite possible that bold work was needed for the serial issue in large numbers, and that the engravers simplified the drawings of set purpose ; but the delicacy and grace of the originals are ill-replaced by the coarser modelling of the faces and the quality of the 'line' throughout. This year saw also *Home Thoughts and Home Scenes*, a book with thirty-five drawings of children, by A. Boyd Houghton (Routledge, 1865) ; which was afterwards reprinted as *Happy Day Stories*. This book is absolutely essential to any representative collection of the period, but nevertheless its designs can hardly be regarded as among the artist's most masterly works.

Warne's edition of *The Arabian Nights* (1866), with sixteen drawings, eight by A. Boyd Houghton, must not be confused with the other edition to which he contributed quite distinct subjects. This, and *Don Quixote* (Warne) appear in the Christmas lists for 1865. The great Spanish novel hardly seems to have sustained the artist to his finest achievements throughout. It contains 100 most interesting designs ; some that reveal his full accomplishment. At the same time it fails to astound you, as the *Arabian Nights* have a knack of doing again and again, whenever you turn over their pages.

This was a great year for Gustave Doré. So many English editions of his books were issued that a summary of the year's art begins with an apology for calling it 'l'année dorée.' Among these *Don Quixote* gained rapid and firm hold

126

WHAT, BILL! YOU
CHUBBY ROGUE

of popular fancy. Many people who have risen superior to Doré to-day, and speak of him with contempt now, at that time grovelled before the French artist's work. A contemporary critic writes of him as one who, 'by common consent occupies the first place of all book-illustrators of all time.' As he is not in any sense an English illustrator we need not attempt to appraise his work here, but it influenced public taste far more than it influenced draughtsmen ; yet the fact that *Don Quixote*, as Houghton depicted him, even now fails to oust the lean - armoured, grotesque hero (one of Doré's few powerful creations), may be the reason for Houghton's version failing to impress us beyond a certain point.

A book of the year, *Ballads and Songs of Brittany*, from the French of Hersart de la Villemarqué, by Tom Taylor (Macmillan), should be interesting to-day, if only for the two steel plates after Tissot, which show that, in his great Eastern cycle of Biblical drawings, he reverts to an earlier manner, which he had employed before the *mondaine* and the *demi-monde* attracted him. The book contains also four Millais', and a fine Keene, which, with most of the other subjects, had already appeared with the poems in *Once a Week*.

Enoch Arden (E. Moxon & Co., 1866), with twenty-five most dainty drawings by Arthur Hughes, is said, in some contemporaneous announcements of the season, to be the first successful attempts at photographing the designs on wood ; but we have already noticed the fine example of Mr. Bolton's new process for photographing on wood, a bas-relief after Flaxman, in the *Lyra Germanica* (1861). Another table-book, important so far as price is concerned, is *The Life of Man Symbolised* (Longmans, 1866), with many illustrations by John Leighton, F.S.A. *Gems of Literature*, illustrated by Noel Paton (Nimmo); *Pen and Pencil Pictures from the Poets* (Nimmo), with forty illustrations by Keeley Halswelle, Pettie, M'Whirter, W. Small, J. Lawson, and others; and *Scott's Poems*, illustrated by Keeley Halswelle, were also issued at this time. An epoch-making book of this season, *Alice in Wonderland* (Macmillan), with Tenniel's forty-two immortal designs, needs only bare mention, for who does not know it intimately?

A very interesting experiment survives in the illustration to Watts's *Divine and Moral Songs* (Nisbet, 1865). This book, edited by H. Fitzcock, the enthusiastic promoter of graphotype, enlisted the services of notable artists, whose tentative efforts, in the first substitute for wood-engraving that attained any commercial recognition, make the otherwise tedious volume a treasure-trove. The Du Maurier on page 14, the J. D. Watson (p. 22), T. Morten (p. 43), Holman Hunt (p. 49), M. E. Edwards (p. 62), C. Green (p. 9), and W. Cave Thomas (p. 75), are all worth study. A not very important drawing, *The Moon Shines Full*, by Dr. C. Heilbuth (p. 3), is a very successful effort to rival the effect of wood-engraving by mechanical means. The titles of the poems come with most grotesque effect beneath the drawings. An artist in knickerbockers, by Du Maurier, entitled 'The excellency of the Bible,' for instance, is apt to raise a ribald laugh; and some of the Calvinistic rhymes and unpleasant theology of the good old doctor are strangely ill-matched with these experiments in a medium which evidently interested the draughtsman far more than the songs which laid so heavy a burden on the little people of a century ago.

Legends and Lyrics, by A. A. Procter (Bell and Daldy, 1865), is another quarto edition of a popular poet, but here, in place of the usual hundred Birket Fosters, Gilberts, and the rest, we have but nineteen engravings; but they are all full pages. Charles Keene's two subjects are *The Settlers* and *Rest* (a night bivouac of soldiers); John Tenniel with *A Legend of Bregenz*, and Du Maurier with *A Legend of Provence* and *The Requital*, also represent the *Punch* contingent. The others are by W. T. C. Dobson, A.R.A., L. Frolich, T. Morten, G. H. Thomas, Samuel Palmer, J. D. Watson, W. P. Burton, J. M. Carrick, M. E. Edwards, and William H. Millais; all engraved by Horace Harral, who cannot be congratulated upon his rendering of some blocks. A very charming set of drawings by J. E. Millais will be found in Henry Leslie's *Little Songs for me to sing* (Cassell, undated). The subjects, seven in number, are slightly executed studies of childhood by a master-hand at the work. The first volume of Cassell's *Shakespeare*, which contains a large number of drawings by H. C. Selous, was issued this year.

A fine collection of reprinted illustrations is *Pictures of Society* (Sampson Low, 1866); its blocks are taken from Mr. James Hogg's publications, *London Society* and *The*

G. J. PINWELL

THE BIT O'
GARDEN

BOOKS OF 1866-67

Churchman's Family Magazine, and include the fine Sandys, *The Waiting Time*, and M. J. Lawless's *Silent Chamber*, both reproduced here by his permission. It is a scarce but very interesting, if unequal, book.

The minor books at this time are rich in drawings by most of the artists who are our quest in this chronicle. The number, and the difficulty of ascertaining which of them contain worthy designs, must be the excuse for a very incomplete list, which includes *Keats's Poetical Works*, with a hundred and twenty designs by G. Scharf; *The Children's Hour* (Hunter, Edinburgh), W. Small, etc.; *Jingles and Jokes for Little Folks*, Paul Gray, etc.; *The Magic Mirror*, W. S. Gilbert (Strahan); *Dame Dingle's Fairy Tales*, J. Proctor (Cassell); *Ellen Montgomery's Bookshelf*, twelve plates in colour by J. D. Watson (Nisbet); *An Old Fairy Tale*, R. Doyle (Routledge); *What the Moon saw*, eighty illustrations by A. W. Bayes (Routledge); *Ernie Elton the Lazy Boy*, *Patient Henry*, *The Boy Pilgrims*, all illustrated by A. Boyd Houghton and published by Warne; *Sybil and her Snowball*, R. Barnes (Seeley); *Stories told to a Child*, Houghton, etc. (Strahan); *Aunt Sally's Life*, G. Thomas, (Bell); *Mother's Last Words*, M. E. Edwards, etc. (Jarrold), and *Watts's Divine Songs* (Sampson Low), with some fine Smalls and Birket Fosters.

Although the style of work that prevailed in 1865-66 was so widely popular, it did not find universal approval. Critics deplored the 'sketchy' style of Dalziels' engraving and, comparing it unfavourably with Longmans' *New Testament*, moaned, 'when shall we find again such engraving as in Mulready's drawings by Thompson.' In *Don Quixote* they owned Houghton's designs were clever, but thought, 'on the whole, the worthy knight deserved better treatment.' And so all along the line we find the then present contrasted with the golden past; even as many look back to-day to the golden 'sixties' from the commonplace 'nineties.' This time saw the beginning of the superb toy-books by Walter Crane —which are his masterpieces, and monuments to the skill and taste of Edmund Evans, their engraver and printer. For wood-block printing in colours, no western work has surpassed them even to this date.

Poems by Jean Ingelow (Longmans, 1867) is a very

129

notable and scarce volume, which was published in the autumn of 1866. It contains twenty drawings by G. J. Pinwell, of which the seven to *The High Tide* are singularly fine; but that they suffered terribly at the engraver's hands some originals, in the possession of Mr. Joseph Pennell, prove only too plainly. J. W. North is represented by twenty-four, A. Boyd Houghton by sixteen, J. Wolf by nine, E. J. Poynter by one, W. Small by four, E. Dalziel by three, and T. Dalziel by twenty. The level of this fine book is singularly high, and it must needs be placed among the very best of one of the most fruitful years.

Another book published at this time, *Ballad Stories of the Affections*, by Robert Buchanan (Routledge, undated), contains some singularly fine examples of the work of G. J. Pinwell, W. Small, A. B. Houghton, E. Dalziel, T. Dalziel, J. Lawson, and J. D. Watson, engraved by the Brothers Dalziel; *Signelil* (pp. 7 and 9), *Helga and Hildebrand* (p. 17), *The Two Sisters* (p. 29), and *Signe at the Wake* (*frontispiece*) show Houghton at his best; *Maid Mettelil* (p. 47) exhibits Pinwell in an unusually decorative mood. Indeed, the thirty-four illustrations are all good, and the book is decidedly one of the most interesting volumes of the period, and unfortunately one least frequently met with to-day.

If *Wayside Poesies* (Routledge, 1867) is not the finest illustrated book of the Christmas season of 1866, it is in the very front rank. Its eighteen drawings by G. J. Pinwell are among the best things he did; the five by Fred Walker are also well up to his best manner, and the nineteen by J. W. North include some of the most exquisite landscapes he ever set down in black and white. It was really one of Messrs. Dalziels' projects, and its publishers were only distributors; so that the credit—and it is not slight—of producing this admirable volume belongs to the popular engravers whose names occur in one capacity or another in almost every paragraph of this chronicle. Still more full of good things, but all reprinted, is *Touches of Nature by Eminent Artists* (Strahan, 1866). This folio volume, 'into which is gathered much of the richest fruit of Strahan and Company's magazines,' does not belie its dedication. As almost every one of its ninety-eight subjects is referred to in the record of the various magazines whence they were collected, it will

OM THE ORIGINAL DRAWING

GLEN OONA

J. W. NORTH

'WAYSIDE POESIES'   GLEN OONA

'WAYSIDE POESIES,' 1867

THE NUTTING

AFLOAT

suffice to note that it contains three by Sandys, nine by Fred Walker, four by Millais, five by A. Boyd Houghton, eight by G. J. Pinwell, two by Lawless, and many by J. W. North, W. Small, J. Pettie, G. Du Maurier, J. Tenniel, J. D. Watson, Robert Barnes, with specimens of Charles Keene, J. Mahoney, Marcus Stone, W. Orchardson, F. J. Shields, Paul Gray, H. H. Armstead, and others.

A volume of even greater interest is *Millais's Collected Illustrations* (Strahan, 1866). The eighty drawings on wood include many subjects originally published in *Lays of the Holy Land, Once a Week, Tennyson's Poems, Good Words, Orley Farm*, etc. etc. Copies in good condition are not often in the market; but it should be the blue riband of every collector, for the blocks here receive more careful printing than that allowed by the exigencies of their ordinary publication, and, free from any gold border, set on a large and not too shiny page, they tell out as well as one could hope to find them. As you linger over its pages you miss many favourites, for it is by no means an exhaustive collection even from the sources mentioned; but it is representative and full of superb work, interspersed though it be with the less fine things done while the great draughtsman was still hampered by the conventions of Mulready and Maclise.

Idyllic Pictures (Cassell, 1867) is another reprinted collection, this time selected entirely from one magazine, *The Quiver*. It contains a fine Sandys here called *October*, elsewhere *The Advent of Winter*, whereof the artist complained bitterly of the 'cutting.' In March 1884, the *Art Journal* contained a very excellent paper on 'Frederick Sandys,' by J. M. Gray, where the original drawing for this subject is reproduced by process. The more important things in *Idyllic Pictures* are: G. J. Pinwell's *Faded Flowers* (p. 13), *Sailor's Valentine* (p. 47), *The Angel's Song* (p. 73), *The Organ-man* (p. 121), and *Straight On* (p. 169); A. Boyd Houghton's *Wee Rose Mary* (p. 89), *St. Martin* (p. 181), and *Sowing and Reaping* (p. 189); Paul Gray's *Cousin Lucy* (*Frontispiece*), *A Reverie* (p. 17), *By the Dead* (p. 21), *Mary's Wedding-day* (p. 141), and *The Holy Light* (p. 193); W. Small's *Between the Cliffs* (p. 29), *My Ariel* (p. 43), *A Retrospect* (p. 85), *Babble* (p. 109), and *Church Bells* (p. 173); T. Morten's *Izaak Walton* (p. 69) and *Hassan* (p. 81); M. E. Edwards's *A Lullaby* (p. 49), *Seeing*

SOME ILLUSTRATED

Granny (p. 117), and *Unrequited* (p. 129), with others by the artists already named, and R. Barnes, H. Cameron, R. P. Leitch, C. J. Staniland, and G. H. Thomas.

Two Centuries of Song, selected by Walter Thornbury (Sampson Low, 1867), is a book almost exactly on the lines of those of the earlier sixties, which seems at first sight to be out of place amid the works of the newer school. It has nineteen full-page drawings, set in ornamental borders, which, printed in colours, decorate (? disfigure) every page of the book. The illustrations, engraved by W. J. Linton, Gavin Smith, H. Harral, are by eminent hands : H. S. Marks, T. Morten, W. Small, G. Leslie, and others. The frontispiece, *Paying Labourers, temp. Elizabeth,* by the first named, is very typical ; *Phyllis,* by G. Leslie, a pretty half-mediæval, half-modern 'decorative' subject ; and *Colin and Phœbe,* by W. Small, a delightful example of a broadly-treated landscape, with two figures in the distance—a really notable work. In my own copy, freely annotated with most depreciatory criticisms of text and pictures in pencil by a former owner, the illustration (p. 138) has vanished, but on its fly-leaf the late owner has written—

> 'This verse its picture had,
> A vulgar lass and lout ;
> The *wood-cut* was so bad
> That I *would cut* it out.'

That it is signed G. W. is a coincidence more curious than pleasing to me, and I quote the quatrain chiefly to show that the term 'wood-cut' for 'wood-engraving' has been in common use unofficially, as well as officially, all through this century. Nevertheless it is a distinct gain to differentiate between the diverse methods, by refusing to regard the terms as synonymous.

Foxe's *Book of Martyrs* (Cassell, undated), issued about this time, has a number of notable contributors ; but the one-sided gruesome record of cruelties which, whether true or false, are horribly depressing, has evidently told upon the artists' nerves. The illustrators, according to its title-page, are : 'G. H. Thomas, John Gilbert, G. Du Maurier, J. D. Watson, A. B. Houghton, W. Small, A. Pasquier, R. Barnes, M. E. Edwards, T. Morten, etc.' Some of the pictures have the names of artist and engraver printed below, while others

'SEND THE CULPRIT
FROM THE HOUSE
INSTANTLY'

'STORY OF A FEATHER'
p. 14

'HE FELT THE SURPASS-
ING IMPORTANCE OF
HIS POSITION'

IZAAK WALTON

are not so distinguished. Those most worthy of mention are by A. Boyd Houghton (pp. 389, 480, 508, 572, 596, and 668), S. L. Fildes (p. 493), G. Du Maurier (p. 541), and W. Small (pp. 333, 365, 624). Among artists not mentioned in the title-page are F. J. Skill, J. Lee, J. Henley, and F. W. Lawson. The first volume of Cassell's *History of England* appeared this year with many engravings after W. Small and others.

Another book of the season worth noting is *Heber's Hymns* (Sampson Low, 1867). It contains 100 illustrations by T. D. Scott, W. Small, H. C. Selous, Wilfrid Lawson, Percival Skelton, and others; but they can hardly be styled epoch-making. *Christian Lyrics* (Sampson Low, 1868) (re-issued later in Warne's *Chandos Classics*), contains 250 illustrations by A. B. Houghton, R. Barnes, and others.

The Story of a Feather (Bradbury, Evans, and Co. 1867), illustrated by G. Du Maurier, is a book that deserves more space than can be allowed to it. It holds a large number of drawings, some of which, especially the initial vignettes, display the marvellously fecund and dramatic invention of the artist. *The Spirit of Praise* (Warne, 1867) is an anthology of sacred verse, containing delightful drawings by W. Small (pp. 57, 97, 149, 189,), by Paul Gray (p. 89), by G. J. Pinwell (pp. 19, 157), by A. Boyd Houghton (p. 53), and others by J. W. North and T. Dalziel.

To 1866 belongs most probably *Gulliver's Travels*, illustrated with eighty designs by 'the late T. Morten,' in which the ill-fated artist is seen at his best level; they display a really convincing imagination, and if, technically speaking, he has done better work elsewhere, this is his most successful sustained effort.

Moore's Irish Melodies (Mackenzie) contains many illustrations by Birket Foster, Harrison Weir, Cope, and others. *Art and Song* has thirty original illustrations engraved on *steel*, which naturally looks very out of date among its fellows. *A New Table-Book* by Mark Lemon (Bradbury) is illustrated by F. Eltze. Mackay's 1001 *Gems of Poetry* (Routledge) numbers among its illustrations at least one Millais.

Books containing designs by artists whose names appear after the title, may be noted briefly here. *Little Songs for Little Folks*, J. D. Watson; *Æsop's Fables*, with 114 drawings by Harrison Weir (Routledge); *Washerwoman's Found-*

SOME ILLUSTRATED
ling, W. Small (Strahan); *Lilliput Levée*, J. E. Millais,
G. J. Pinwell, etc. (Strahan); *Roses and Holly* (Nimmo);
Moore's Irish Melodies, Birket Foster, H. Weir, C. W.
Cope, etc. (Mackenzie); *Chandos Poets: Longfellow*, A.
Boyd Houghton, etc. (Warne); *Things for Nests* (Nisbet).
The popularity of the illustrator at this time provoked a critic
to write: 'Book-illustration is a thriving fad. *Jones fecit* is
the pendant of everything he does. The dearth of intellectual
talent among book-illustrators is amazing. The idea is thought
less of than the form. Mental growth has not kept pace
with technical skill'—a passage only worth quoting because
it is echoed to-day, with as little justice, by irresponsible
scribblers.

In another criticism upon this year's books we find: 'For
the pre-Raphaelite draughtsman and the pre-Bewick artist,
who love scratchy lines without colour, blocks which look
like spoilt etchings, and the first "proofs" of artists' work
untouched by the engraver, nothing can be better.' It was
the year of Doré's *Tennyson*, and Doré's *Tupper*, a year
when the fine harvests were nearly at an end, when a new
order of things was close at hand, and the advent of *The
Graphic* should set the final seal to the work of the sixties
and inaugurate a new school.

But, although the Christmas of 1866 saw the ingathering
of the most fertile harvest, the next three years must be
not overlooked. In 1867 *Lucile*, with Du Maurier's designs,
carries on the record; and *North Coast and other Poems*,
by Robert Buchanan (Routledge, 1868), nobly maintains the
tradition of Dalziels. It contains fifty-three drawings: thirteen
by Houghton, six by Pinwell, two by W. Small, one by
J. B. Zwecker, three by J. Wolf, twenty-five by T. and
three by E. Dalziel, and the engraving is at their best
level, the printing unusually good.

Golden Thoughts from Golden Fountains (Warne, 1867)
is another profusely illustrated anthology, on the lines of
those which preceded it. The first edition was printed in
sepia throughout, but the later editions printed in black do
more justice to the blocks. In it we find seventy-three
excellent designs by A. Boyd Houghton, G. J. Pinwell,
W. Small, J. Lawson, W. P. Burton, G. Dalziel, T. Dalziel,
and others; if the book, as a whole, cannot be placed

T. MORTEN

GULLIVER IN LILLIPUT

'GULLIVER'S TRAVELS'
CASSELL

THE LAPUTIANS

among the best of its class, yet all the same it comprises some admirable work. *The Savage Club Papers*, 1867 (Tinsley), has also a galaxy of stars in its list of illustrators, but their sparkle is intermittent and feeble. True that Du Maurier, A. Boyd Houghton, J. D. Watson, and a host of others drew, and Dalziels, Swain, Harral, and the rest engraved their work; but all the same it is but an ephemeral book. *Krilof and His Fables* (Strahan, 1867) enshrines some delightful, if slight, Houghtons, and many spirited animal drawings by Zwecker. Wood's *Bible Animals* is also rich in fine zoological pictures. The *Ode on the Morning of Christ's Nativity* (Nisbet, 1867) would be notable if only for its three designs by Albert Moore, who appears here as an illustrator, probably the only time he ever contributed to any publication. Notwithstanding two or three powerful and fantastic drawings by W. Small, the rest are a very mixed lot, conceived in all sorts of manners. *The Illustrated Book of Sacred Poems* (Cassell, undated) is a big anthology, with a silver-print photograph by way of frontispiece. It contains a rather fine composition, *Side by Side* (p. 17), with no signature or other means of identification. W. Small (p. 21), J. D. Watson (pp. 69, 89, 105, 200, 209), M. E. Edwards, H. C. Selous, J. W. North, and many others are represented; but the engravers, for the most part, cannot be congratulated upon their interpretation of the artists' designs.

Other books worth mention are: *The Mirage of Life*, with twenty-nine characteristic illustrations by John Tenniel (Religious Tract Society); *The Story without an End*, illustrated by E. V. B.; *Cassell's Illustrated Readings*, two volumes with a mass of pictures of unequal merit, but the omnivorous collector will keep them for the sake of designs by F. Barnard, J. D. Watson, J. Mahoney, W. Small, S. L. Fildes, and many another typical artist of the sixties, in spite of the unsatisfactory blocks; *Fairy Tales*, by Mark Lemon, illustrated by C. H. Bennett and Richard Doyle; *Pupils of St. John the Divine*, illustrated by E. Armitage (Macmillan); *Puck on Pegasus* (the new and enlarged edition); *Poetry of Nature*, illustrated by Harrison Weir; and *Original Poems* by J. and E. Taylor (Routledge, 1868), with a large number of designs by R. Barnes, A. W. Bayes, etc.

135

SOME ILLUSTRATED BOOKS

With 1868 the end is near; the few books of real merit which bear its date were almost all issued in the autumn of the previous year. *The Savage Club Papers*, 1868, is a book not worth detailed comment; *Five Days' Entertainment at Wentworth Grange*, by F. T. Palgrave (Macmillan), contains some charming designs by Arthur Hughes; *Stories from Memel*, illustrated by Walter Crane (W. Hunt and Co.), is a pleasant book of the year; and, about this time, other work by the same artist appeared in *The Merrie Heart* (Cassell). *King Gab's Story Bag* (Cassell), *The Magic of Kindness* (Cassell), and other children's books I have been unable to trace, nor the *Poetry of Nature*, edited by J. Cundall.

Lyra Germanica (Longmans), a second anthology of hymns translated from the German, contains three illustrations by Ford Madox Brown, *At the Sepulchre*, *The Sower*, and *Abraham*, six by Edward Armitage, R.A., and many head-pieces and other decorations by John Leighton, which should not be undervalued because the taste of to-day is in favour of a bolder style, and dislikes imitation Gothic detail. Of their sort they are excellent, and may be placed among the earliest modern attempts to decorate a page, with some show of consistency of treatment. Compared with the so-called 'rustic' borders of earlier efforts, they at once assume a certain importance. The binding is similar to that upon the first series.

Tom Brown's School Days, illustrated by Arthur Hughes and S. P. Hall, is one of the most notable books of the year. It is curious that at the close of the period, as at its beginning, this artist is so much to the fore, although examples of his work appear at long intervals during the years' chronicle. Yet, as 1855 shows his work in the van of the movement, so also he supplies a goodly proportion of the interesting work which is the aftermath of the sixties, rather than the premature growth of the seventies. *Tom Brown* is too well known in its cheap editions, where the same illustrations are used, to require any detailed comment here. *Gray's Elegy* (illustrated in colour by R. Barnes, Birket Foster, Wimperis, and others) is of little importance.

In 1869 *The Nobility of Life* (Warne), an anthology, edited by L. Valentine, is attractive, less by reason of its coloured plates after J. D. Watson, C. Green, E. J. Poynter, and others, than from its headpieces, by A. Boyd Houghton

'GOLDEN THOUGHTS FROM
GOLDEN FOUNTAINS'

LOVE

MARK THE GREY-
HAIRED MAN

(pp. 26, 106, 122, 136, 146, 178), Francis Walker (pp. 82, 170), J. Mahoney (p. 98), which, subsidiary as they appear here, are in danger of being overlooked. *Carmina Crucis* (Bell and Daldy, 1860), poems by Dora Greenwell, has two or three decorative pieces, by G. D. L[eslie], which might be attributed to the influence of the *Century Guild Hobby Horse*, if direct evidence did not antedate them by twenty years. *Miss Kilmansegg*, illustrated by Seccombe; *The Water Babies*, Sir Noel Paton and P. Skelton; *In Fairyland*, R. Doyle (Longmans); *Vikram and the Vampire*, E. Griset (Longmans), and *Æsop's Fables* (Cassell), with one hundred clever and humorous designs, by the same artist, are among the few others that are worth naming.

Several series of volumes, illustrated by various hands, may be noticed out of their due order. For the date of the first volume is often far distant from the last, and yet, as the series maintained a certain coherency, it would be confusing to spread its record over a number of years and necessitate continual reiteration of facts.

The *Choice Series* of selections from the poets, published by Messrs. Sampson Low and Co., include several volumes issued some time before they were included as part of this series. The ideal of all is far more akin to that of the early fifties—when the original editions of several of these were first issued—than to that of the sixties. They include Bloomfield's *Farmer's Boy* (1857), Campbell's *Pleasures of Hope* (1855), Coleridge's *Ancient Mariner* (1857), Goldsmith's *Deserted Village* and *Vicar of Wakefield*, Gray's *Elegy* (1853), Keats's *Eve of St. Agnes*, Milton's *L'Allegro*, Warton's *The Hermit*, Wordsworth's *Pastoral Poems*, and Rogers's *Pleasures of Memory* (1864). All the volumes, but the last, have wood-engravings by various hands after drawings by Birket Foster, Harrison Weir, Gilbert and others; but in the *Pleasures of Memory* 'the large illustrations' are produced by a new method without the aid of an engraver, and some little indulgence is asked for them on the plea of the inexperience of the artists in this process. 'The drawing is made' (to continue the quotation) 'with an etching needle, or any suitable point, upon a glass plate spread with collodion. It is then photographed [? printed] upon a prepared surface of wax, and from this an electrotype is formed in relief which is printed with the type.' Samuel Palmer, J. D. Watson, Charles Green, and others are the artists to whom this reference applies, and the result, if not better than the best contemporary engraving, is certainly full of interest to-day.

The *Golden Treasury* Series (Macmillan and Co.) contains, in each volume, a vignette engraved on steel by Jeens, after drawings by J. E. Millais, T. Woolner, W. Holman Hunt, Sir Noel Paton, Arthur Hughes, etc.

Although the 'Household Edition' of Charles Dickens's complete works was issued early in the seventies, it is illustrated almost entirely by men of the sixties, and was possibly in active preparation during that decade. Fred Barnard takes the lion's share, the largest number of drawings to the most important volumes. His fame as a Dickens illustrator might rest secure on these alone, although it is supplemented by many other character-drawings of the types created by the author of *Pickwick*. To *Sketches by Boz* he supplies thirty-four designs, to *Nicholas Nickleby* fifty-nine, to *Barnaby Rudge* forty-six, to *Christmas Books* twenty-eight, to *Dombey and Son* sixty-four, to *David Copperfield* sixty, to *Bleak House* sixty-one, and to the *Tale of Two Cities* twenty-five. 'Phiz' re-illustrates *The Pickwick Papers* with fifty-seven designs, concerning which silence is best. J. Mahoney shows excellent work in twenty-eight drawings to *Oliver Twist* and fifty-eight each to *Little Dorrit* and *Our Mutual Friend*; Charles Green's thirty-nine illustrations to the *Old Curiosity Shop* are also admirable. F. A. Fraser is responsible for thirty to *Great Expectations*, E. G. Dalziel for thirty-four to *Christmas Stories* (from *All the Year Round*), twenty-six to the *Uncommercial Traveller*, and a few to minor pieces, issued with *Edwin Drood*, which contain S. L. Fildes's excellent designs. H. French contributes twenty to *Hard Times*, A. B. Frost illustrates *American Notes*, J. Gordon Thomson *Pictures from Italy*, and J. M'L. Ralston supplies fifteen for *A Child's History of England*. To re-embody characters already stereotyped, for the most part, by the earlier plates of the original editions, was a bold enterprise : that it did not wholly fail is greatly to its credit. It is quite possible that as large a number of readers made their first acquaintance with the *dramatis personæ* of the novels in these popular editions as in the older books, and it would be interesting to discover what they really felt when the much-vaunted copper-plates afterwards fell under their notice. The sentiment of English people has been amply expended on the Hablot K. Browne designs. Cruikshank is still considered a great master by many people; but if one could 'depolarise' their pictures (to use Wendell Holmes's simile), and set them before their admirers free from early associations, free from the glamour of Dickens romance, and then extract a frank outspoken opinion, it would be, probably, quite opposite to that which they are now ready to maintain.

Recognising that the old illustrations are still regarded with a halo of memory and romance, not unlike that which raises Mumbo Jumbo to a fetish among his worshippers, a wish to estimate anew the intrinsic value, considered as works of art, of these old illustrations, is not provoked by merely destructive tendencies. So long as Thackeray's drawing of *Amelia* is accepted as a type of grace and beauty, how can the believer realise the beauty of Millais's *Was it not a lie?* in *Framley Parsonage*. In the earlier and later engravings alike, the costume repels; but in the one there is real flesh and blood, real passion, real art, in the other a merely conventional symbol, which we agree to accept as an interesting heroine, in the way a child of five accepts the scratches on his slate as real pirates and savages. There is little use in trying to appreciate the best, if the distinctly second-best is reverenced equally; and so, at any cost of personal feeling, it is simply the duty of all concerned to rank the heroes of the sale-room, 'Phiz,' Cruikshank, and Leech at their intrinsic value. This is by no means despicable. For certain qualities which are not remotely connected with art belong to them; but the beauty of truth, the knowledge born of academic accomplishment, or literal imitation of nature, were alike absolutely beyond their sympathy. Hence to praise their work as one praises a Dürer, a Whistler, or a Millais, is apt to confuse the minds of the laity, already none too clear as to the moment when art comes in. This protest is not advanced to prove that every drawing mentioned in these pages surpasses the best work of the men in question, but merely to suggest whether it would not be better to recognise that the praise bestowed for so many years was awarded to a conventional treatment now obsolete, and should not be regarded as equivalent to that bestowed upon works of art which owe nothing to parochial conventions, and are based on unalterable facts, whether a Hokousaï or a Menzel chances to be the interpreter.

The *Chandos Poets* (Warne), a series of bulky octavos, with red-line borders, are of unequal merit. Some, *Willmott's Poets of the Nineteenth Century*, *James Montgomery's Poems*, *Christian Lyrics*, and *Heber's Poetical Works*, appear to be merely reprints of earlier volumes with the original illustrations; others have new illustrations by men of the sixties. The *Longfellow* has several by A. Boyd Houghton, who is also represented by a few excellent designs in the *Byron*; *Legendary Ballads* (J. S. Roberts) has three full-page designs, by Walter Crane, to *Thomas of Ercildoune* (p. 357), *The Jolly Harper* (p. 462), and *Robin Hood* (p. 580). Later volumes, with designs by F. A. Fraser and H. French, do not come into our subject.

Other series of the works of 'standard poets,' as they were called, all resplendent in gold and colours, and more or less well illustrated, were issued by Messrs. Routledge, Nimmo, Warne, Cassell, Moxon, and others, beginning in the fifties. Here and there a volume has interest, but one suspects that many of the plates had done duty before, and those which had not are not always of great merit; as, for instance, the drawings by W. B. Scott to the poetical works of L. E. L. (Routledge). In these various books will be found, *inter alia*, examples of Sir John Gilbert, Birket Foster, E. H. Corbould, W. Small, and Keeley Halswelle.

Hurst and Blackett's Standard Library is the title of a series of novels by eminent hands in single volumes, each containing a frontispiece engraved on steel. That to *Christian's Mistake* is by Frederick Sandys, engraved by John Saddler. *John Halifax, Nothing New, The Valley of a Hundred Fires*, and *Les Misérables*, each have a drawing by Millais, also engraved by John Saddler. In *Studies from Life* Holman Hunt is the draughtsman and Joseph Brown the engraver. *No Church, Grandmother's Money*, and *A Noble Life*, contain frontispieces by Tenniel, *Barbara's History*, one by J. D. Watson, and *Adèle*, a fine design by John Gilbert. Others by Leech and Edward Hughes are not particularly interesting. The steel engraving bestowed upon most of these obliterated

THE END, 1870

all character from the designs, and superseded the artist's
touch by hard unsympathetic details; but, all the same, compositions by men of such eminence deserve mention.

   With 1870 the end of our subject is reached; it is the year
of *Edwin Drood*, which established S. L. Fildes's position as an
illustrator of the first rank; it also has a pleasant book of quasi-
mediæval work, *Mores Ridicula*, by J. E. Rogers (Macmillan),
(followed later by *Ridicula Rediviva* and *The Fairy Book*, by
the author of *John Halifax*, with coloured designs by the
same artist), of which an enthusiastic critic wrote: 'Worthy
to be hung in the Royal Academy side by side with Rossetti,
Sandys, Barnes, and Millais'; Whymper's *Scrambles on the
Alps*, a book greatly prized by collectors, with drawings by
Whymper and J. Mahoney; *The Cycle of Life* (S.P.C.K.); and
Episodes of Fiction (Nimmo, 1870) containing twenty-eight
designs by R. Paterson, after C. Green, C. J. Staniland, P.
Skelton, F. Barnard, Harrison Weir, and others. *Novello's
National Nursery Rhymes*, by J. W. Elliott, published in
1871, belongs to the sixties by intrinsic right. It includes
two delightful drawings by A. Boyd Houghton—one of which,
Tom the Piper's Son (owned by Mr. Pennell), has been
reproduced from the original by photogravure in Mr. Laurence
Housman's monograph—and many by H. S. Marks, W. Small,
J. Mahoney, G. J. Pinwell, W. J. Wiegand, Arthur Hughes,
T. and E. Dalziel, and others.

   H. Leslie's Musical Annual (Cassell, 1870) contains a
fine drawing, *The Boatswain's Leap*, by G. J. Pinwell, and a
steel engraving, *A Reverie*, after Millais, which was re-issued
in *The Magazine of Art*, September 1896. *Pictures from
English Literature* (Cassell) is an excuse for publishing
twenty full-page engravings after elaborate drawings by Du
Maurier, S. L. Fildes, W. Small, J. D. Watson, W. Cave
Thomas, etc. etc. This anthology, with a somewhat hetero-
geneous collection of drawings, seems to be the last genuine
survivor of the old Christmas gift-books, which is lineally
connected with the masterpieces of its kind.

   Soon after the inevitable anthology of poems reappeared,
in humbler pamphlet shape, as a birthday souvenir, or a
Christmas card, embellished with chromo-lithographs, as it
had already been allied with photographic silver-prints; but
it is always the accident of the artists chosen which imparts

141

permanent interest to the otherwise feeble object; whether it take the shape of a drawing-room table-book, gaudy, costly, and dull, or of a little booklet, it is a thing of no vital interest, unless by chance its pictures are the work of really powerful artists. The decadence of a vigorous movement is never a pleasant subject to record in detail. Fortunately, although the king died, the king lived almost immediately, and *The Graphic*, with its new ideals and new artists, quickly established a convention of its own, which is no less interesting. If it does not seem, so far as we can estimate, to have numbered among its articles men who are worthy in all respects to be placed by Rossetti, Millais, Sandys, Houghton, Pinwell, Fred Walker, and the rest of the typical heroes of the sixties, yet in its own way it is a worthy beginning of a new epoch.

Before quitting our period, however, a certain aftermath of the rich harvest must not be forgotten; and this, despite the comparatively few items it contains, may be placed in a chapter by itself.

DEATH OF KING
WARWOLF

CHAPTER X: THE AFTERMATH, A FEW BELATED VOLUMES

THAT Thornbury's *Legendary Ballads* (dated 1876) should be regarded as a most important volume in a collection of the 'sixties' is not odd, when you find that its eighty-one illustrations were reprinted from *Once a Week*. Many of the drawings were republished in this book, with the poem they originally illustrated; others, however, were joined to quite different text. If the memories of those living are to be trusted, not a few of the artists concerned were extremely annoyed to find their designs applied to new purposes. To take a single instance, the Sandys design to *King Warwolf* re-accompanied the poem itself, but the drawing by John Lawson, which is herein supposed to illustrate the lines,

> 'And then there came a great red glare
> That seemed to crimson fitfully
> The whole broad Heaven.'

was first published with a poem, *Ariadne*, by W. J. Tate, in August 1866, long after *King Warwolf* first appeared. Its design is obviously based on this passage:

> 'My long hair floating in the boisterous wind,
> My white hands lightly grasping Theseus' knees,
> While he, his wild eyes staring, urged his slaves
> To some last effort of their well-tried skill.'

But it requires a great effort of perverted imagination to drag in the picture, which shows a Greek hero on one ship, watching, you suppose, the dying Norse king on another ship; when the ballad infers, and the dramatic situation implies, that the old monarch put out at once across the bar, and his people from the shore watched his ship burn in the night. To wrench such a picture from its context, and apply it to another, was a too popular device of publishers. As, however, it preserves good impressions of blocks otherwise inaccessible, it would be ungracious to single out this particular instance for blame. Yet all the same, those who regard the artist's objection to the sale of *clichés* for all sorts of purposes, as a merely sentimental grievance, must own that he is justified in being annoyed, when the whole intention of his work is burlesqued thereby.

A contemporary review says that the illustrations had

THE AFTERMATH,

'appeared before in *Once a Week*, *The Cornhill*, and elsewhere.'
It would be a long and ungrateful task to collate them, but,
so far as my own memory can be trusted, they are all from
the first named. In place of including a description of the book
itself, a few extracts, from a review by Mr. Edmund Gosse in
the *Academy* (February 1876, p. 177), will not only give a
vivid appreciation of the work of two of the artists, but show
that twenty years ago the book was prized as highly as we
prize it to-day. He says : 'We have thought the illustrations
sufficiently interesting to demand a separate notice for themselves, the more so as in many cases they are totally uncon-
nected with Mr. Thornbury's poems. . . . We are heartily
glad to have collected for us some of the most typical illustrations of a school that is, above all others, most characteristic of
our latest development in civilisation, and of which the principal members have died in their youth, and have failed to
fulfil the greatness of their promise.

'The artists represented are mainly those who immediately followed the so-called pre-Raphaelites, the young men
who took up many of their principles, and carried them out in
a more modern and a more quiet way than their more ambitious masters. Mr. Sandys, who pinned all his early faith to
Holbein, and Messrs. Walker, Pinwell, Lawless, and Houghton,
who promised to form a group of brother artists unrivalled in
delicacy and originality of sentiment, are here in their earliest
and strongest development. . . . M. J. Lawless contributes
no less than twenty designs to the volume. We have
examined these singular and beautiful drawings, most of them
old favourites, with peculiar emotion. The present writer
[Mr. Edmund Gosse] confesses to quite absurd affection for
all the few relics of this gifted lad, whose early death seems
to have deprived his great genius of all hope of fame. Years
ago these illustrations, by an unknown artist, keenly excited
a curiosity which was not to be satisfied till we learned, with a
sense of actual bereavement, that their author was dead. He
seems to have scarcely lived to develop a final manner ; with
the excessive facility of a boy of high talent we find him
incessantly imitating his elder rivals, but always with a
difference. . . . No doubt, in M. J. Lawless, English art
sustained one of the sharpest losses it ever had to mourn.

'Of Pinwell no need to say so much. He has lived, not

W. HOLMAN HUNT

WILLMOTT'S 'SACRED
POETRY,' 1862

THE LENT
JEWELS

J. LAWSON

ARIADNE

long enough indeed to fulfil the great promise of his youth, but
to ensure his head a lasting laurel. There have been stronger
intellects, purer colourists, surer draughtsmen among his contemporaries, but where shall we seek a spirit of poetry more
pathetic, more subtle, more absolutely modern than his ? The
critics are for ever urging poets and painters to cultivate the
materials that lie about them in the common household-life
of to-day. It is not so easy to do so ; it is not to be done
by writing "idylls of the gutter and the gibbet" ; it is not to
be done by painting the working-man asleep by his baby's
cradle. Perhaps no one has done it with so deep and thorough
a sympathy as Pinwell ; and it is sympathy that is needed,
not curiosity or pity.' But it would be hardly fair to quote
further from Mr. Gosse's appreciation twenty years ago of artists
still living. The volume contains eight designs by Sandys,
namely, *Labours of Thor* (*Harold Harfagr*), *King Warwolf*,
The Apparitor of the Secret Tribunal (*Jacques de Caumont*),
Tintoretto (*Yet once more on the organ play*), *The Avatar
of Zeus* (*The King at the Gate*), *The search of Ceres for
Proserpine* (*Helen and Cassandra*), *The Boy Martyr*, *The
Three Statues of Egina*, and *The Miller's Meadow* (*The Old
Chartist*) ; the alternative title given in brackets is that of the
original as it first appeared in *Once a Week*. To show how
carelessly the author treated the artists, to whom, in a flowery
preface, he says he owes so much, 'for they have given to his
airy nothings a local habitation and a name, and have caught
and fixed down on paper, like butterflies in an entomologist's
cabinet, many a fleeting Cynthia of his brain,' it will suffice
to quote his profuse acknowledgments to 'Mr. Poynter, an old
schoolfellow of the author's, and now Professor in the London
University, [who] has expended all his learning, taste, and
thought in the *The Three Statues.* The drapery might be
copied by a sculptor, it is arrayed with such fine artistic
feeling, and over the whole the artist has thrown the solem-
nity of the subject, and has shown, in Pluto's overshadowing
arm, the vanity of all things under the sun — even the
pure ambition of a great artist.' This charming eulogy, be
it noted, is bestowed on a drawing that is by Frederick
Sandys!!! not by Poynter, who is unrepresented in the book.
The four Whistlers of *Once a Week* are all here, absurdly
renamed. There are twenty by M. J. Lawless, seven by

THE AFTERMATH,

T. Morten, ten by J. Lawson, one by A. Boyd Houghton, two by Fred Walker, eight by G. J. Pinwell, six by W. Small, three by J. Tenniel, three by F. Eltze, and one each by J. D. Watson, C. Keene, G. Du Maurier, Towneley Green, C. Green, T. R. Macquoid, P. Skelton, A. Fairfield, E. H. Corbould, and A. Rich. The book is well printed, and a treasure-house of good things, which appear to more advantage upon its 'toned paper' than in the pages of the periodical where they first saw daylight.

The preface to *Dalziels' Bible Gallery* is dated October 1880, so that the volume was probably issued for the season of 1880-81. As we have seen, the work was in active preparation in the early sixties. It contained sixty-nine blocks excellently printed upon an India tint. These include nine by the late Lord Leighton, P.R.A., three by G. F. Watts, R.A., five by F. R. Pickersgill, R.A., twelve by E. J. Poynter, R.A., three by E. Armitage, R.A., two by H. H. Armstead, R.A., one by Sir E. Burne-Jones, one by Holman Hunt, three by Ford Madox Brown, six by Simeon Solomon, two by A. Boyd Houghton, two by W. Small, one by E. F. Brewtnall, fourteen by T. Dalziel, one by E. Dalziel, two by A. Murch, and one by F. S. Walker, and one by Frederick Sandys. The praise lavished on these designs is amply justified if you regard them as a whole; but, turning over the pages critically after a long interval, there is a distinct sense of disillusion. At the time they seemed all masterpieces; sixteen years after they stand confessed as a very mixed group, some conscientious pot-boilers, others absolutely powerful and intensely individual. The book is monumental, both in its ambitious intention and in the fact that it commemorates a dead cause. It is easy to disparage the work of the engravers, but when we see what fine things owe their very existence to Messrs. Dalziels' enterprise, it is but just to pay due tribute to the firm, and to regret that so powerful an agency is no longer actively engaged in similar enterprises.

As copies are both scarce and costly, it may be well to call attention to a volume entitled *Art Pictures from the Old Testament* (Society for Promoting Christian Knowledge, 1897), wherein the whole sixty-nine reappear supplemented by twenty-seven others, which would seem to have prepared for the *Bible Gallery*, but not previously issued :

ALZIELS' 'BIBLE
ALLERY,' 1880

THE PARABLE OF THE
BOILING POT

DALZIELS' 'BIBLE GALLERY,' 1883

CAIN AND ABEL

DALZIELS' 'BIBLE
GALLERY,' 1880

MOSES VIEWING THE
PROMISED LAND

SIR FREDERICK LEIGHTON, P.R.A.

DALZIELS' 'BIBLE
GALLERY,' 1880

ABRAM AND
THE ANGEL

A FEW BELATED VOLUMES
thirteen of these added designs are by Simeon Solomon, two
by H. H. Armstead, R.A., three by E. Armitage, R.A., three
by F. R. Pickersgill, R.A., three by T. Dalziel, and one each
by F. S. Waltges (*sic*), G. J. Pinwell, and E. G. Dalziel.

As impressions of the famous blocks are obtainable at a
low cost, it would be foolish to waste space upon detailed
descriptions. Of course the popular reprint ought not to be
compared with the fine proofs of the great *édition-de-luxe*,
which cost about twenty times as much. But for many
purposes it is adequate, and gives an idea of the superb
qualities of the Leighton designs, and the vigour and strongly
dramatic force of the Poynters. It is interesting to compare
Sir Edward Burne-Jones's original design for *The Boiling Pot*,
reproduced in *Pen-Drawing and Pen-Draughtsmen by Joseph
Pennell* (Macmillan, 1894), with the engraving, which is from
an entirely different version of the subject. Other drawings
on wood obviously intended for this work, but never used,
can be seen at South Kensington Museum.

A few belated volumes still remain to be noticed—they
are picked almost at random, and doubtless the list might be
supplemented almost indefinitely: *The Trial of Sir Jasper*,
by S. C. Hall (Virtue, undated), with illustrations by Gilbert,
Cruikshank, Tenniel, Birket Foster, Noel Paton, and others,
including W. Eden Thomson and G. H. Boughton. The
latter, a drawing quite in the mood of the sixties, seems to
be the earliest illustration by its author. Another design by
H. R. Robertson, of a dead body covered by a cloth in a
large empty room, is too good to pass without comment.
Beauties of English Landscape, drawn by Birket Foster, is a
reprint, in collected form, of the works of this justly popular
artist; it is interesting, but not comparable to the earlier
volume with a similar title. In *Nature Pictures*, thirty
original illustrations by J. H. Dell, engraved by R. Paterson
(Warne), the preface, dated October 1878, refers to 'years of
patient painstaking labour on the part of artist and engraver';
so that it is really a posthumous child of the sixties, and one
not unworthy to a place among the best.

Songs of Many Seasons, by Jemmett Brown (Pewtress
and Co., 1876), contains two little-known designs by Walter
Crane, two by G. Du Maurier and one by C. M. (C. W.
Morgan). *Pegasus Re-saddled* (H. S. King, 1877), with ten

147

THE AFTERMATH,
illustrations by G. Du Maurier is, as its title implies, a companion volume to the earlier *Puck on Pegasus*, by H. Cholmondeley Pennell. *The Children's Garland* (Macmillan, 1873), contains fourteen capital things by John Lawson—no relative of 'Cecil' or 'F. W. Lawson.'

The Lord's Prayer, illustrated by F. R. Pickersgill, R.A., and Henry Alford, D.D. (Longmans, 1870), has a curiously old-fashioned air. One fancies, and the preface supports the theory, that its nine designs should be considered not as an aftermath to the sixties, but as a presage of the time, near the date of *The Music-master*. Their vigorous attempt to employ modern costume in dignified compositions deserves more than patronising approval. Any art-student to-day would discover a hundred faults, but their one virtue might prove beyond his grasp. Although engraved on wood by Dalziel, printed as they are upon a deep yellow tint, the pictures at first sight suggest lithographs, rather than wood-engravings. *Rural England*, by L. Seguin (Strahan, 1885) has many delightful designs by Millais and Pinwell, but all, apparently, reprints of blocks used in *Good Words* and elsewhere.

Possibly the whole series of Mr. Walter Crane's toy-books, which began to be issued in the mid-sixties, should be noticed here ; but they deserve a separate and complete iconography. In fact, any attempt to go beyond the arbitrary date is a mistake, and this chapter were best cut short, with full consciousness of its being a mere fragment which may find place in some future volume, upon 'the seventies,' that I hope may find its historian before long.

A book of this sort, which aimed to be complete, should contain a critical summary of the period it attempts to record. But to extract from the mass of material a clearly-defined purpose, and build up a plausible theory to show that all the diverse tendencies could be traced to a common purpose, would surely be at best merely an academic argument. All that the sixties prove, to a very sincere if incapable student, seems to be that the artist, if he be indeed an artist, can make the meanest material serve his purpose. The men of the sixties tried obviously to do their best. They took their art seriously, if not themselves. It is tempting to affirm that the tendency now is for no one to take himself seriously, and even at times

EDWARD J. POYNTER, R.A.

ZIELS' 'BIBLE
LERY,' 1880

JOSEPH BEFORE
PHARAOH

EDWARD J. POYNTER, R.A.

DALZIELS' 'BIBLE
GALLERY,' 1880

PHARAOH HONOURS
JOSEPH

to look upon his art, whatever it may be, as merely a useful medium to exploit for his own ends. Yet such an opinion would be probably too sweeping; and one is driven back to the primal fact, that the energy and knowledge which results in masterly achievement is, and must always be, beyond rules, beyond schools, as it is beyond fashion or mood. A man who tries to do his best, if he be endowed with ripe knowledge and has the opportunity, will make a fine thing; which, whether intended for a penny paper, or a guinea gift-book, will possess both vitality and permanent value.

But the men of the sixties took themselves quite seriously; and this is surely evident from their drawings. Not a few committed suicide, or died from over-work; neither catastrophe being evidence of flippant content with the popularity they had achieved. Whether inspired by pure zeal for art, by rivalry, or by money-making, they felt the game well worth the candle, and did all they could do to play it fairly. Those of us to-day who try to do our best may be inept, ignorant, and attain only failure; yet the best is not achieved by accident, and the only moral of the sixties is the moral of the nineties: 'Whatsoever thy hand findeth to do, do it with all thy might.'

Whether it be the triumph of a master or a pot-boiling illustrator, the real artist never takes his art lightly. Life, even reputation, he may play with, but his craft is a serious thing. In short, the study of the thousands of designs— some obviously burlesqued by the engraver, others admirably rendered—will not leave an unprejudiced spectator with a cut and dried opinion. That, as it happened, a number of really distinguished men enlisted themselves as illustrators may be granted, but each one did his own work in his own way; and to summarise the complex record in a sentence to prove that any method, or any manner, is a royal road to greatness is impossible. Yet no one familiar with the period can avoid a certain pride in the permanent evidence it has left, that English art in illustration, (no less than English music in the part-songs of the Elizabethan period), has produced work worthy to be entered on the cosmopolitan roll of fame. This is unquestionable; and being granted, no more need be said, for an attempt to appraise the relative value of totally distinct things is always a foolish effort.

CHAPTER XI: CERTAIN INFLUENCES UPON THE ARTISTS OF THE SIXTIES

LTHOUGH it would be retraversing beaten paths to trace the illustrator of the sixties back to Bewick, or to still earlier progenitors in Dürer or the Florentines, there can be little doubt that the pre-Raphaelites gave the first direct impulse to the newer school. That their work, scanty as it is, so far as book-illustration is concerned, set going the impulse which in Kelmscott Press Editions, the Birmingham School, the Vale Press, Beardsley, Bradley, and a host of others on both sides of the Atlantic, is 'the movement' of the moment is too obvious to need stating. But for 'the sixties' proper, the paramount influence was Millais—the Millais after the pre-Raphaelite Brotherhood had disbanded. Despite a very ingenious attempt to trace the influence of Menzel upon the earlier men, many still doubt whether the true pre-Raphaelites were not quite ignorant of the great German. Later men—Fred Walker especially, and Charles Keene many years after—knew their Menzel, and appreciated him as a few artists do to-day, and the man in the street may at no distant future. But some of the survivors of the pre-Raphaelites, both formal and associated, deny all knowledge of Menzel at this date; others, however, have told Mr. Joseph Pennell that they did know his work, and that it had a distinct influence. Some who did not know him then regret keenly that they were unaware of his very existence until they had abandoned illustration for painting. All agree, of course, in recognising the enormous personality of one who might be called, without exaggeration, the greatest illustrator of the century; so that, having stated the evidence as it stands, no more need be added, except a suggestion that the theory of Menzel's influence, even upon those who declare they knew not the man, may be sound. An edition of *Frederick the Great*, by Kügler, with five hundred illustrations by Menzel, was published in England (according to the British Museum Catalogue, the book itself is undated) in 1844.[1] It is quite possible that any one of the men of the time might have seen it by chance, and turned over its pages ignorant of its artist's name. A

[1] Virtues issued another edition in 1845.

DALZIELS' 'BIBLE
GALLERY,' 1880

ELIJAH AND THE
WIDOW'S SON

few minutes is enough to influence a young artist, and the one who in all honesty declares he never heard of Menzel may have been thus unconsciously influenced. But, if a foreign source must be found, so far as the pre-Raphaelites are concerned, Rethel seems a far more possible agent. His famous prints, *Death the Friend* and *Death the Avenger*, had they met his eye, would doubtless have influenced Mr. Sandys, and many others who worked on similar lines.

Whether Lasinio's 'execrable engravings,' as Ruskin calls them, or others, will be found to have exerted any influence, I have no evidence to bring forward. In fact the theory is advanced only as a working hypothesis, not as an argument capable of proof. It is possible that France at that time was an important factor as regards technique, as it has been since, and is still. But, without leaving our own shores, the logical sequence of development from Bewick, through Harvey, Mulready and others, does not leave very many terrible gaps. It is true that this development is always erratic — now towards the good, now to meretricious qualities.

The more one studies the matter, the more one fancies that certain drawings not intended for engraving by Mulready, and others by Maclise, must have had a large share in the movement which culminated about 1865 and died out entirely about 1870. But whatever the influence which set it going, the ultimate result was British; and, for good or evil, one cannot avoid a feeling of pride that in the sixties there was art in England, not where it was officially expected perhaps, but in popular journals.

It is quite possible that the revival of etching as a fine art, which took place early in the second half of this century, had no little direct influence on the illustration of the period. Many artists, who are foremost as draughtsmen upon wood, experimented with the etcher's needle. *The Germ*, 1850, was illustrated by etchings; but, with every desire to develop this suggestion, it would be folly to regard the much discussed periodical as the true ancestor of *Once a Week* and the rest; even the etching which Millais prepared for it, but never issued, would not suffice to establish such claim. Two societies, the Etching Club and the Junior Etching Club, are responsible for the illustration of several volumes, wherein the etched line is used in a way almost identical with the same artists' manner when drawing for the engraver. Indeed, the majority of these etchings would suffer little if reproduced by direct process to-day, as the finesse of *rebroussage* and the more subtle qualities of biting and printing are not present conspicuously in the majority of the plates.

The *Poems by Tom Hood*, illustrated by the Junior Etching Club, include two delightful Millais', *The Bridge of Sighs* and *Ruth*, a *Lee Shore* by Charles Keene, and two illustrations to the *Ode to the Moon*, and *The Elm-tree* by Henry Moore.

Passages from Modern English Poets, illustrated by the Junior Etching Club, was issued (undated), by Day and Son, in 1862, in a large octavo. In 1876 another edition in larger quarto, with the etchings transferred to stone, and printed as lithographs, was published by William Tegg. In this notable volume Millais is represented by *Summer Indolence* (p. 10), a most graceful study of a girl lying on her back in a meadow with a small child, who is wearing a daisy chain, seated at her side. Mr. J. McNeill Whistler contributes two delightful landscapes, *The Angler* (p. 7) and *A River Scene* (p. 45). In these the master-hand is recognisable at a glance, although the authorship of many of the rest can only be discovered by the index. They would alone suffice to make the book a treasure to light upon. To praise them would be absurd, for one can conceive no more unnecessary verbiage than a eulogy of Mr. Whistler's etchings—one might as well praise the beauty of June sunshine. There are many other good things in the book—a Tenniel, *War and Glory* (p. 3), four capital studies by Henry Moore (pp. 1, 16, 27, 28), which come as a revelation to those who only know him as a sea-painter. Four others by M. J. Lawless, an artist who has been neglected too long, *The Drummer* (p. 2), *Sisters of Mercy* (p. 12), *The Bivouac* (p. 30), and *The Little Shipwrights* (p. 36), are all interesting, if not quite so fascinating, as his drawings upon wood. H. S. Marks has a *genre* subject, *A Study in the Egyptian Antiquity Department of the British Museum*. This portentous title describes an etching of a country lad in smock-frock, who, with dazed surprise, is staring into vacancy amid the gigantic scarabs, the great goddess Pasht, and other familiar objects of the corridor leading to the Refreshment-room in the great Bloomsbury building, which people of Grub

Street hurry through daily, with downcast eyes, to enjoy the frugal dainties that a beneficent institution permits them to take by way of sustenance during the intervals of study in the Reading-room. Another plate, *Scene of the Plague in London*, 1665, by Charles Keene, would hardly tempt one to linger before it, but for its signature. It is a powerful bit of work, but does not show the hand of the great *Punch* artist at its best. The rest of the contributions to this volume are by C. Rossiter, F. Smallfield, Viscount Bury, Lord G. Fitzgerald, J. W. Oakes, A. J. Lewis, F. Powell, J. Sleigh, H. C. Whaite, Walter Severn, and W. Gale. Two by J. Clark deserve mention. To find the painter of cottage-life, with all his Dutch realistic detail, in company with Mr. Whistler, is a curious instance of extremes meeting.

Without wishing to press the argument unduly, it is evident that etching which afterwards developed so bravely, and left so many fine examples, exerted also a secondary influence on the illustration of the sixties. Hence the some-what extended reference to the few books which employed it largely for illustrations.

Those who would have you believe that the great English masters of illustration failed to obtain contemporary appreciation should note the three editions of this work as one fact, among a score of others, which fails to support their theory. Whether from a desire to extol the past or not, it is certain that those publishers who have been established more than a quarter of a century claim to have sold far larger editions of their high-priced illustrated volumes then than any moderately truthful publisher or editor would dare to claim for similar ventures to-day. Of course there were fewer books of the sort issued, and the rivalry of illustrated journalism was infinitely less; still the people of the fifties, sixties, and seventies paid their tribute in gold freely and lavishly, and if they offered the last insult of the populace—popularity—to these undoubted works of art, it prevents one placing artists of the period among the noble army of martyrs. Their payment was quite equal to that which is the average to-day, as a file-copy of one of the important magazines shows. They were reproduced as well as the means available permitted; the printing and the general 'get-up' of the books, allowing for the different ideals which obtained then, was not inferior to the average to-day, and, as a rule, the authorship of the drawings was duly acknowledged in the table of contents, and the artists 'starred' in contemporary advertisements. It is painful to own that even the new appreciation is not absolutely without precedent. One notable instance of depreciation cannot be forgotten. Mr. Ruskin, who never expressed admiration of the illustrations of the sixties, in *Ariadne Florentina*, chose the current number of the *Cornhill Magazine* for the text of a diatribe in which the following passages occur :—

'The cheap popular art cannot draw for you beauty, sense, or honesty ; but every species of distorted folly and vice—the idiot, the blackguard, the coxcomb, the paltry fool, the degraded woman—are pictured for your honourable pleasure in every page, with clumsy caricature, struggling to render its dulness tolerable by insisting on defect—if, perchance, a penny or two may be coined out of the cockneys' itch for loathsomeness. . . . These . . . are favourably representative of the entire art industry of the modern press—industry enslaved to the ghastly service of catching the last gleams in the glued eyes of the daily more bestial English mob—railroad born and bred, which drags itself about the black world it has withered under its breath. In the miserable competitive labour of finding new stimulus for the appetite—daily more gross, of this tyrannous mob, we may count as lost beyond any hope, the artists who are dull, docile, or distressed enough to submit to its demands. And for total result of our English engraving industry for the last hundred and fifty years, I find that practically at this moment [1876] I cannot get a *single* piece of true, sweet, and comprehensible art to place for instruction in any children's school.'

But ignoring Mr. Ruskin—if it be possible to ignore the absolute leader of taste in the sixties—we find little but praise. Yet the popularity of 1860-1870 naturally incurred the inevitable law of reaction, and was at its lowest ebb in the eighties; but now late in the nineties our revived applause is but an echo of that which was awarded to the work when it appealed not only by all its art, but with novelty and an air of being 'up to date' that cannot, in the course of things, be ever again its portion. We are not so much better than our fathers, after all, in recognising the good things of the sixties, or in trying to do our best in our way. Which is just what they tried to do in theirs.

CHAPTER XII: SOME ILLUSTRATORS OF THE SIXTIES

ALTHOUGH space forbids biographical notice, even in the briefest form, of all the artists mentioned in the preceding pages, and it would be folly to summarise in a few hasty sentences the complete life-work of Sir J. E. Millais, P.R.A., Sir John Gilbert, R.A., Mr. Birket Foster, or Mr. G. Du Maurier, to take but a few instances; yet in the case of Mr. Arthur Hughes, the late M. J. Lawless, and others, to give more exact references to their published illustrations is perhaps easier in this way than any other, especially as a complete iconography of all the chief artists in the movement had perforce to be abandoned for want of space. Many illustrators—Ford Madox Brown, Charles Keene, A. Boyd Houghton, Dante Gabriel Rossetti, W. B. Scott, Fred Walker, and J. Wolf—have already been commemorated in monographs; not confined, it is true, in every instance to the subject of this book, but naturally taking it as part of the life-work of the hero, even when, as in Rossetti's case, the illustrations form but an infinitesimally small percentage of the works he produced. The artists hereafter noticed have been chosen entirely from the collector's standpoint, and with the intention of assisting those who wish to make representative or complete collections of the work of each particular man.

GEORGE HOUSMAN THOMAS (1824-1868) was born in London, December 4, 1824. When only fourteen he became apprenticed to G. Bonner, a wood-engraver, and at fifteen obtained the prize of a silver palette from the Society of Arts, for an original drawing, *Please to remember the Grotto*. After he had served his apprenticeship, in conjunction with Henry Harrison he set up in Paris as a wood-engraver. The firm became so successful that they employed six or seven assistants. He was then tempted to go to New York to establish an illustrated paper, which was also a success, although losses on other ventures forced the proprietors to give it up. This led the artist to turn his attention to another field of engraving for bank notes, which are estimated among the most beautiful of their kind. A few years later he returned to England, and became attached to the *Illustrated London News.* In 1848 a special expedition to Italy, which resulted in a long series of illustrations of Garibaldi's defence of Rome against the French, not merely established his lasting reputation, but incidentally extended his taste and knowledge by the opportunity it gave him for studying the works of the old masters. In 1854 a sketch of sailors belonging to the Baltic Fleet, which was published in the *Illustrated London News*, attracted the attention of the Queen, who caused inquiries to be made, which led to the artist being employed by Her Majesty to paint for her the principal events of her reign. Besides a series of important paintings in oil, he executed a large number of drawings and sketches which form an album of great interest.

'As an illustrator of books he was remarkable,' says his anonymous biographer,[1] 'for facility of execution and aptness of character.' His illustrations of *Hiawatha* (Kent and Co.), *Armadale* (Wilkie Collins), and *The Last Chronicle of Barset* (Anthony Trollope), are perhaps the most important; but *London Society*, Mrs. Gatty's *Parables*, *Cassell's Magazine*, *The Quiver*, *Illustrated Readings*, and many other volumes of the period, contain numerous examples of his work in this department. In the person of his brother, Mr. W. Luson Thomas, the managing director of the *Graphic* and the *Daily Graphic*, and his nephew, Carmichael Thomas, Art Director of the *Graphic*, the family name is still associated with the most notable movement in illustration during the period which immediately followed that to which this book is devoted.

Sir John Everett Millais, Bart., P.R.A. (born June 8, 1829, died August 13, 1896).—As these proofs were being sent to press, the greatest illustrator of all (having regard to his place as the pioneer of the school which immediately succeeded the pre-Raphaelites, the number of his designs, and their superlative excellence), has joined the majority of his fellow-workers in the sixties. It would be impossible in a few lines to summarise his contributions to the 'black-and-white' of English art; that task will doubtless be undertaken adequately. But, if all the rest of the work of the period were

[1] *In Memoriam*, *George H. Thomas* (Cassell, undated), a folio volume with about one hundred illustrations.

DALZIELS' 'BIBLE
GALLERY' 1880

JOSEPH'S COAT

lost, his contributions alone might justly support every word that has been or will be said in praise of 'the golden decade.' From the 1857 *Tennyson* to his latest illustration he added masterpiece to masterpiece, and, were his triumphant career as a painter completely ignored, might yet be ranked as a great master on the strength of these alone.

PAUL GRAY (1848-1868).—A most promising young illustrator, whose early death was most keenly regretted by those who knew him best, Paul Gray, was born in Dublin, May 17, 1848. He died November 14, 1868. In the progress of this work mention has been made of all illustrations which it has been possible to identify; many of the cartoons for *Fun*, being unsigned, could not be attributed to him with certainty. *The Savage Club Papers*, First Series (Tinsley, 1863), contain his last drawing, *Sweethearting*. In the preface we read : 'When this work was undertaken, that clever young artist [Paul Gray] was foremost in offering his co-operation ; for he whom we mourned, and whose legacy of sorrow one had accepted, was his dear friend. The shock which his system, already weakened by the saddest of all maladies, received by the sudden death of that friend was more than his gentle spirit could sustain. He lived just long enough to finish his drawing, and then he left us to join his friend.' In the record of the periodicals of the sixties will be found many references to his work, which is, perhaps, most familiar in connection with Charles Kingsley's *Hereward the Wake*.

DANTE GABRIEL ROSSETTI (*b.* 1828, *d.* 1882). The comparatively few illustrations by Rossetti have been described and reproduced so often, that it would seem superfluous to add a word more here. Yet, recognising their influence to-day, we must also remember that many people who are attracted by this side of Rossetti's art may not be familiar with the oft-told story of his career. He, more than any modern painter, would seem to be responsible for the present decorative school of illustrators, whose work has attracted unusual interest from many continental critics of late, and is recognised by them as peculiarly 'English.' While the man in the street would no doubt choose 'Phiz,' Cruikshank, Leech, Tenniel, Gilbert, Fred Walker, or Pinwell as typically 'English,' the foreigner prefers to regard the illustrations by

Rossetti, his immediate followers, and his later disciples as representing that English movement, which the native is apt to look upon as something exotic and bizarre.

Yet it is not necessary to discuss Rossetti's position as founder of the pre-Raphaelite school, nor to weigh his claims to the leadership against those of Ford Madox Brown and Holman Hunt. But, without ignoring the black-and-white work of the two last named, there can be no doubt that it is Rossetti who has most influenced subsequent draughtsmen.

Nor at the time was his position as an illustrator misunderstood. When we find that he received £30 each for the small Tennyson drawings on wood, the fact proves at the outset that the market value of his work was not ignored by his publishers. At the present day when any writer on men of the sixties is accused of an attempt to 'discover' them, and the appreciation he bestows is regarded as an attempt to glorify the appreciator at the expense of the appreciated, it is well to insist upon the fact that hardly one of the men in favour to-day failed to meet with substantial recognition at the time. It was not their fate to do drawings for love, or to publish engravings at their own cost, or sell as cheap curios works which now realise a thousand times their first cost.

Drawings paid for at the highest market rate, or, to speak more accurately, at 'star' prices, published in popular volumes that ran through large editions, received favourably by contemporary critics, and frequently alluded to as masterpieces by writers in current periodicals, cannot be said to have been neglected, nor have they even been out of favour with artists.

That work, which has afforded so much lasting pleasure, was not achieved without an undue amount of pain, is easily proved in the case of Rossetti. So pertinent is a description by his brother, published lately, that it may be quoted in full, to remind the illustrators of to-day, who draw on paper and card-board at their ease to any scale that pleases them, how much less exacting are the conditions under which they work than those encountered by the artists who were forced to draw upon an unpleasant surface of white pigment spread upon a shining wooden block :—

'The Tennyson designs, which were engraved on wood and published in the *Illustrated Tennyson*, in which Millais, Hunt, Mulready, and others co-operated,' says Mr. William Michael Rossetti, 'have in

SOME ILLUSTRATORS OF THE SIXTIES

the long run done not a little to sustain my brother's reputation with the public. At the time they gave him endless trouble and small satisfaction. Not indeed that the invention or the mere designing of these works was troublesome to him. He took great pains with them, but, as what he wrought at was always something which informed and glowed in his mind, he was not more tribulated by these than by other drawings. It must be said, also, that himself only, and not Tennyson, was his guide. He drew just what he chose, taking from his author's text nothing more than a hint and an opportunity. The trouble came in with the engraver and the publisher. With some of the doings of the engraver, Dalziel (not Linton, whom he found much more conformable to his notion), he was grievously disappointed. He probably exasperated Dalziel, and Dalziel certainly exasperated him. Blocks were re-worked upon and proofs sent back with vigour. The publisher, Mr. Moxon, was a still severer affliction. He called and he wrote. Rossetti was not always up to time, though he tried his best to be so. In other instances he was up to time, but his engraver was not up to his mark. I believe that poor Moxon suffered much, and that soon afterwards he died; but I do not lay any real blame on my brother, who worked strenuously and well. As to our great poet Tennyson, who also ought to have counted for something in the whole affair, I gather that he really liked Rossetti's designs when he saw them, and he was not without a perceptible liking and regard for Rossetti himself, so far as he knew him (they had first met at Mr. Patmore's house in December 1849); but the illustration to *St. Cecilia* puzzled him not a little, and he had to give up the problem of what it had to do with his work.'[1]

Later on, in the same volume, we find an extract from a letter dated February 1857, which Dante Gabriel Rossetti wrote to W. Bell Scott :—

'I have designed five blocks for Tennyson, save seven which are still cutting and maiming. It is a thankless task. After a fortnight's work my block goes to the engraver, like Agag delicately, and is hewn in pieces before the Lord Harry.

'ADDRESS TO DALZIEL BROTHERS

' O woodman spare that block,
O gash not anyhow !
It took ten days by clock,
I'd fain protect it now.

Chorus—Wild laughter from Dalziels' Workshop.'

Several versions of this incident are current, but Mr. Arthur Hughes's account has not, I think, been published. It

[1] *Dante Gabriel Rossetti : Letters and Memories*, by William Michael Rossetti. Ellis and Elvey, 1895, vol. i. p. 189.

chanced that one day, during the time he was working in Rossetti's studio, the engraver called, and finding Rossetti was out, poured forth his trouble and stated his own view of the matter with spirit. For his defence, as he put it, much sympathy may be awarded to him. The curious drawings executed in pencil, ink, and red chalk, crammed with highly-wrought detail, that were to be translated into clean black and white, were, he declared, beyond the power of any engraver to translate successfully. How Mr. Hughes pacified him is a matter of no importance; but it is but fair to recollect that, even had the elaborate designs been executed with perfection of technique, any engraver must have needs encountered a task of no ordinary difficulty. When, however, the white coating had been rubbed away in parts, and all sorts of strokes in pen, pencil, and pigment added, it is not surprising that the paraphrase failed to please the designer. Although the drawings naturally perished in the cutting, and cannot be brought forward as decisive evidence, we may believe that the engraver spoilt them, and yet also believe that no crafts-man who ever lived would have been absolutely successful.

The number of Rossetti's book-illustrations is but ten in all, according to the list given in Mr. William Sharp's admirable monograph. To these one might perhaps add the frontispiece to that volume; as although the pen-drawing, *A sonnet is a moment's monument*, was never intended for reproduction, it forms a most decorative page. There is also a design for a frontispiece to the *Early Italian Poets*, which was first reproduced in the *English Illustrated Magazine*, No. 1. The actual frontispiece was etched but never used, and the exquisitely dainty version survives only in two impressions from the plate, both owned by Mr. Fairfax Murray. Another frontispiece, to *The Risen Life*,[1] a poem by R. C. Jackson, in a cover designed by D. G. R. (R. Elkins and Co., 10 Castle St., East Oxford St., W., 1884), belongs to the same category, in which may be placed *The Queen's Page*, drawn in 1854, and reproduced in *Flower Pieces* by Allingham (Reeves & Turner, 1888). The ten which were all (I believe) drawn upon the wood include: *Elfen-mere*, published first in William Allingham's *The Music-master*, 1855, and afterwards reprinted in a later volume, *Life and Phantasy*, and again in *Flower*

---

[1] A silver-print photograph only.

SOME ILLUSTRATORS OF THE SIXTIES

Pieces (1888), by the same author. This design 'revealed to young Burne-Jones' (so his biographer, Mr. Malcolm Bell, has recorded) that there existed a strange enchanting world beyond the hum-drum of this daily life—a world of radiant, many-coloured lights, of dim mysterious shadows, of harmonies of form and line, wherein to enter is to walk among the blest—that far-off world of Art into which many a time since he has made his way and brought back visions of delight to show his fellow-men. The first suspicion of that land of faëry came to him when, in a small volume of poems by William Allingham, he found a little wood-cut, 'Elfenmere,' signed with a curious entwinement of the initials D. G. R. The slumbering spirit of fancy awoke to life within him and cast her spells upon him never to be shaken off.'

In the *Oxford and Cambridge Magazine*, 1856, Mr. Burne-Jones wrote of this very design : 'There is one more I cannot help noticing, a drawing of higher finish and pretension than the last, from the pencil of Rossetti, in Allingham's *Day and Night Songs*, just published. It is, I think, the most beautiful drawing for an illustration I have ever seen : the weird faces of the maids of Elfen-mere, the musical, timed movement of their arms together as they sing, the face of the man, above all, are such as only a great artist could conceive.'

This picture, 'three damsels clothed in white,' who came

'With their spindles every night ;
Two and one, and three fair maidens,
Spinning to a pulsing cadence,
Singing songs of Elfen-mere,'

reproduced here, is still issued in William Allingham's volume of poems entitled *Flower Pieces* (Reeves and Turner, 1888).

Five illustrations to Moxon's edition of *Tennyson's Poems*, 1857, two in Christina Rossetti's *The Goblin Market and other Poems*, 1862, and two in *The Prince's Progress and other Poems*, 1866, by the same author, complete the ten in question. As the *Tennyson* has been republished lately, and a monograph, *Tennyson and his pre-Raphaelite Illustrators*, by G. Somes Layard (Elliot Stock, 1894), has brought together every available scrap of material connected with the famous quintette of designs, it would be superfluous to describe them here in detail. Any distinctly recognised 'movement' is very rarely a *crescendo*, but nearly always a waning

161

force that owes what energy it retains to the original impetus of its founder.   Should this statement be true of any fashion in art, it might be most easily supported, if applied to Rossetti's ten drawings on wood, set side by side with the whole mass of modern 'decorative' illustration.   Even a great artist like Howard Pyle has hardly added a new motive to those crowded into these wood-engravings.   The lady by the casement, '*The long hours come and go*,' upon the title-page of *The Prince's Progress*, is an epitome of a thousand later attempts. Mr. Fairfax Murray has collected over a dozen studies and preliminary drawings for this little block, that would appal some of the younger men as evidence of the intense care with which a masterpiece was wrought of old.   Highly-finished drawings were done over and over again until their author was satisfied. The frontispieces to *Goblin Market* and to *The Prince's Progress*, no less than the Tennyson designs, form, obviously enough, the treasure-trove whence later men have borrowed; too often exchanging the gold for very inferior currency. Without attempting to give undue credit to Rossetti, or denying that collateral influences—notably that of Walter Crane—had their share in the revival of the nineties, there can be no doubt that the strongest of the younger 'decorative' artists to-day are still fascinated by Rossetti—no less irresistibly than 'the young Burne-Jones' was influenced in 1855.

Therefore the importance of these ten designs cannot be exaggerated.   Whether you regard their influence as unwholesome, and regret the morbidity of the school that founded itself on them, or prefer to see in them the germ of a style entirely English in its renaissance, which has already spread over that Continent which one had deemed inoculated against any British epidemic, the fact remains that Rossetti is the golden milestone wherefrom all later work must needs be measured.   No doubt the superb work of Frederick Sandys, had it been more accessible to the younger artists when the new impetus to decorative black-and-white began to attract a popular audience, would have found hardly as ardent disciples.

M. J. LAWLESS (born 1837, died 1864).—This artist, faithful to the best tradition of the pre-Raphaelite illustrators, seems to have left few personal memories.   Born in 1837, a son of Barry Lawless, a Dublin solicitor, he was educated at

You should have wept her yesterday

'THE PRINCE'S PROGRESS'
1866

SOME ILLUSTRATORS OF THE SIXTIES

Prior Park School, Bath, and afterwards attended several drawing schools, and was for a time a pupil of Henry O'Neil, R.A. He died August 6, 1864. Mr. Edward Walford, who contributes a short notice of Matthew James Lawless to the *Dictionary of National Biography*, has only the barest details to record. Nor do others, who knew him intimately, remember anything more than the ordinary routine of a short and uneventful life. But his artistic record is not meagre. In contemporary criticism we find him ranked with Millais and Sandys; not as equal to either, but as a worthy third. A fine picture of his, *The Sick Call* (from the Leathart Collection), was exhibited again in 1895 at the Guildhall.

But it is by his work as an illustrator he will be remembered, and, despite the few years he practised, for his first published drawing was in *Once a Week*, December 15, 1859 (vol. i. p. 505), he has left an honourable and not inconsiderable amount of work behind him. No search has lighted upon any work of his outside the pages of the popular magazines, except a few etchings (in the publications of the Junior Etching Club), three designs of no great importance in *Lyra Germanica* (Longmans, 1861), and a pamphlet, the *Life of St. Patrick*, with some shocking engravings, said by his biographer to be from Lawless's designs. In the chapters upon *Once a Week*, *London Society*, *Good Words*, etc., every drawing I have been able to identify is duly noted. It is not easy to refrain from eulogy upon the work of a draughtsman with no little individuality and distinction, who has so far been almost completely forgotten by artists of the present day. The selection of his work reproduced here by the courtesy of the owners of the copyright will, perhaps, send many fresh admirers to hunt up the rest of it for themselves.

ARTHUR BOYD HOUGHTON (1836-1875) was born in 1836, the fourth son of his father, who was a captain in the Royal Navy. He visited India, according to some of his biographers; others say that he was never in the East, but that it was a brother who supplied him with the oriental details that appear in so many of his drawings. Be that as it may, his fellow-workers on the *Arabian Nights* pretended to be jealous of his Egyptian experience, and declared that it was no good trying to rival from their imaginings the scenes that he knew by heart.

SOME ILLUSTRATORS OF THE SIXTIES

At present, when all men unite to praise him, it would almost lend colour to a belief that he was unappreciated by his fellows to read in a contemporary criticism: 'His designs were often striking in their effects of black and white, but were wanting in tone and gradation—a defect partly due to the loss of one eye.' This is only quoted by way of encouragement to living illustrators, who forget that their hero, despite sympathy and commissions, suffered also much the same misunderstanding that is often their lot. Against this may be set a criticism of yesterday, which runs :—

'As regards "the school of the sixties," now that it has moved away, we can rightly range the heads of that movement, and allowing for side impulses from the technique of Menzel, and still more from the magnetism of Rossetti's personality, we see, broadly speaking, that with Millais it arrived, with Houghton it ceased. Under these two leaders it gathered others, but within ten years its essential work was done. It has all gone now nobly into the past from the hands of men, some still living, some dead but yesterday.

'In Houghton's work, two things strike us especially, when we see it adequately to-day : its mastery of technique and style, and its temperament: the mastery so swift and spontaneous, so lavish of its audacities, so noble in its economies ; the temperament so dramatic, so passionate, so satiric, and so witty. In many of his qualities, in vitality and movement, Houghton tops Millais. What is missing from his temperament, if it be a lack and not a quality, is the power to look at things coolly ; he has not, as Millais, the deep mood of stoical statement, of tragedy grown calm. His tragic note is vindictive, a little shrill : when he sets himself to depict contemporary life, as in the *Graphic America* series, he is sardonic, impatient, at times morose : his humour carries an edge of bitterness. But in whatever mood he looks at things, the mastery of his aim is certain.' [1]

The mass of work accomplished in illustration alone, between his first appearance and his death in 1875, is amazing. There is scarce a periodical of any rank which has not at least one example from his pen. The curt attention given here to the man must be pardoned, as reference to his work is made on almost every page of this book. For an appreciative essay, that is a model of its class, one has but to turn to Mr. Laurence Housman's volume [2] which contains also five original drawings on wood (reproduced in photogravure) and eighty-three others from *Dalziel's Arabian Nights* (Ward, Lock & Co., 1863-

[1] A Catalogue of forty des.gns by A. Boyd Houghton, exhibited at *The Sign of the Dial* 53 Warwick Street, W. [1896].
[2] *Arthur Boyd Houghton*, by Laurence Housman, Kegan Paul & Co., 1896.

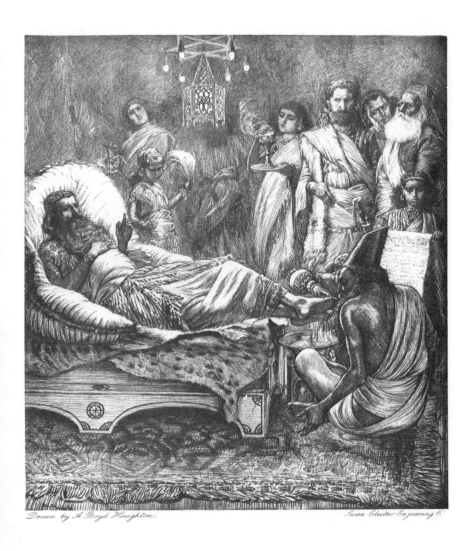

READING THE CHRONICLES

65 and Warne, 1866), *Don Quixote*, the two volumes of Mr. Robert Buchanan's Poems—*Ballad Stories of the Affections* (1866), and *North Coast* (1868), *Home Thoughts* (1865), *National Nursery Rhymes* (1871), and *The Graphic* (1870).

FREDERICK WALKER[1] (1840-1875), who was born in Marylebone on the 26th of May 1840, has been the subject of so many appreciations, and at least one admirable monograph, that a most brief notice of his career as an illustrator will suffice here. His father was a designer of jewelry and his grandfather had some skill in portrait-painting. How he began drawing from the Elgin marbles in the British Museum at the age of sixteen has been told often enough. Many boys of sixteen have done the same, but it is open to doubt if any one of them has absorbed the spirit of their models so completely as Fred Walker did. It would be hardly asserting too much to say for him that they replaced humanity, and that his male figures seem nearly always youths from the Parthenon in peasant costume. At seventeen or eighteen he was working at Leigh's life-class in Newman Street, and at the same time was employed in Mr. Whymper's wood-engraving establishment. His first appearance in *Everybody's Journal* is duly noted elsewhere, also his first drawing in *Once a Week*; but the peculiar affection he had inspired by his work has kept most of his critics from saying that some of his earliest designs, as we know them after engraving, appear distinctly poor. But, from the time he ceased to act as 'ghost' for Thackeray, and signed his work with the familiar F. W., his career shows a distinct and sustained advance until the ill-fated 1875, in which George Mason, G. J. Pinwell, and A. Boyd Houghton also died.

It is unnecessary to recapitulate in brief the various contributions to the *Cornhill Magazine, Good Words, Once a Week*, etc., which have already been noted in detail. Nor would it be in place here to dwell upon the personality of the artist; sufficient matter has been printed already to enable lovers of his works to construct a faithful portrait of their author—lovable and irritable, with innate genius and hereditary disease both provoking him to petulant outbursts that still live in his friends' memories. One anecdote will suffice. A group of

---

[1] *The Portfolio*, June 1894: 'Frederick Walker,' by Claude Phillips.

SOME ILLUSTRATORS OF THE SIXTIES
well-known painters were strolling across a bridge on the
Upper Thames. Walker, who was passionately fond of music,
had been playing on a tin whistle, which one of the party,
half in joke, half weary of the fluting, struck from his mouth,
so that it fell into the stream below. In a moment Walker
had thrown off his clothes, and, 'looking like a statue come
to life, so exquisitely was he built,' plunged from the wall of
the bridge, and, diving, rescued his tin whistle, which he bore
to land in triumph. The trifling incident is an epitome of
the character of the wayward boy, who kept his friends nevertheless. 'He did not seek beauty,' wrote an ardent student
of his work, 'but it came, while Pinwell thought of and strove
for beauty always, yet often failed to secure it.' That he
knew Menzel, and was influenced by him, is an open secret;
but he also owes much to the pre-Raphaelites — Millais
especially. Yet when all he learned from contemporary
artists is fully credited, what is left, and it is by far the largest
portion, is his own absolutely—owing nothing to any pre-
decessor, except possibly to the sculptors of Greece. He
died in Scotland in June 1875, and was buried at the Marlow
he painted so delightfully, leaving behind him the peculiar
immortality that is awarded more readily to a half-fulfilled life
than to one which has accomplished all it set out to do, and
has outlived its own reputation.

GEORGE JOHN PINWELL (1842-1875).—This notable illustrator, whose work bulks so largely in the latter half of the
sixties, was born December 26, 1842, and died September 8,
1875. He studied at the Newman Street Academy, enter-
ing in 1862. At first his illustrations show little promise;
some of the earliest, in *Lilliput Levee*, a book of delightful
rhymes for children, by Matthew Browne, are singularly
devoid of interest. No engraver's name appears on them,
nor is it quite clear by what process they were reproduced.
They are inserted plates, and, under a strong magnifying
glass, the lines suggest lithography. The unfamiliar medium,
supposing they were drawn in lithographic ink, or by graphotype, or some similar process, would account for the entire
absence of the qualities that might have been expected.
Some others, in *Hacco the Dwarf* and in *The Happy Home*,
the latter in crude colours, are hardly more interesting.

MY TREASURE

SOME ILLUSTRATORS OF THE SIXTIES

According to Mr. Harry Quilter,[1] Pinwell began life as a butterman's boy in the City Road, whose duty, among other things, was to 'stand outside the shop on Saturday nights shouting Buy! Buy! Buy!' Later on he seems to have been a 'carpet-planner.' If one might read the words as 'carpet-designer,' the fact of turning up about this time at Leigh's night-school, where he met Fred Walker, would not be quite so surprising.

Between Walker and Pinwell a friendship sprang up, but it seems to have been Thomas White who introduced the former to *Once a Week*, wherein his first contribution, *The Saturnalia*, was published, January 31, 1863. In 1864 he began to work for Messrs. Dalziel on the *Arabian Nights* and the *Illustrated Goldsmith*, which latter is his most important volume. In 1869 he became a member of the Old Water Colour Society, but his work as a colourist does not concern us here. Nor is it necessary to recapitulate the enormous quantity of his designs which in magazines and books are noticed elsewhere in these pages. Some illustrations to *Jean Ingelow's Poems*, notably seven to *The High Tide*, represent his best period. But he suffered terribly by translation at the engravers' hands. The immobility, which characterises so many of his figures, does not appear in the few drawings which survive. Mr. Pennell is the fortunate possessor of several of the designs for *The High Tide*; but the pleasure of studying these originals is changed to pain when one remembers how many others were cut away by the engraver. It is curious that three men, so intimately associated as Walker, Pinwell, and Houghton, should have preserved their individuality so entirely. It is impossible to confuse the work of any of them. Walker infused a grace into the commonplace which, so far as the engravings are concerned, sometimes escaped Pinwell's far more imaginative creations; while Houghton lived in a world of his own, wherein all animate and inanimate objects obeyed the lines, the swirling curves, he delighted in. If, as has been well said, Walker was a Greek—but a dull Greek—then Pinwell may be called a Naturalist with a touch of realism in his technique, while Houghton was romantic to the core in essence and manipulation alike.

[1] Preface to a Catalogue of the *Birmingham Society of Artists*, March 1895.

SOME ILLUSTRATORS OF THE SIXTIES

ARTHUR HUGHES.—In 1855 appeared *The Music-master*, the second enlarged and illustrated edition of *Day and Night Songs*, a book of poems by William Allingham, to which reference has been made several times in this chronicle. Of its ten illustrations, seven and a vignette are from the hand of Arthur Hughes. The artist thus early associated with the leaders of the pre-Raphaelite movement, and still actively at work, was never, technically, a member of the Brotherhood. In 1858, however, we find him one of the enthusiastic young artists Rossetti had gathered round him with a view to the production of the so-called frescoes in the Oxford Union. The oft-told tale of this noble failure need not be repeated here. Those who were responsible for the paintings in question appear more or less relieved to find that the work has ceased to exist. True, the majority of picture-lovers who have never seen them regard them, sentimentally, as the fine flower of pre-Raphaelite art, which faded before it was fully open. Judging from the restored fragments which remain, had they been permanent, they would not have been more than interesting curiosities; examples of the 'prentice efforts' of men who afterwards shaped the course of British art, not merely for their own generation, but, as we can see to-day, for a much longer time. The great difficulties of the task these ardent novices undertook so light-heartedly may or may not have checked the practice of wall-painting in England, if, indeed, one can speak of a check to a movement that never existed. To trace in detail the course of Mr. Hughes's work, from this date to the present, would be a pleasant and somewhat lengthy task. Yet, although greater men are less fully dealt with, a running narrative showing where the illustrations appeared will be more valuable than any attempt to estimate the intrinsic value of the work, or explain its attractive quality. That the work is singularly lovable, and has found staunch and ardent admirers amid varying schools of artists, is unquestionable. Without claiming that it equals the best work of the 'Brotherhood,' it has a charm all its own. The sense of delight in lovely things is present throughout, nor does its elegance often degenerate to mere prettiness. The naïve expression of a child's ideal of lovely forms, with a curiously well-sustained type of beauty, neither Greek nor Gothic, yet having a touch of paganism in its mysticism, is always present in it. With a

168

peculiarly individual manner—so that the signature, which is usually to be found in some unobtrusive corner, is needless,— a student of illustration can 'spot' an Arthur Hughes at the most rapid glance as surely as he could identify a Du Maurier.

There are painters and draughtsmen of all periods, before whose work you are well content to cease from criticism, and to enjoy simply, with all their imperfections, the qualities that attract you. Passionate intensity, the perfection of academic draughtsmanship, dramatic composition as it is usually understood, may, or may not, be always evident. Whether they are or not is in this case of entirely secondary importance. Certain indefinable qualities, lovable and lasting, are sure to be the most noticeable, whether you light on a print that has escaped you hitherto, or turn up one that you have known since the day it was published. Like caters for the like, and this love which the work provokes from those to whom it appeals seems also its chief characteristic. In the whole mass of pictorial art you can hardly find its equal in this particular respect. The care and sorrow of life, its disillusions and injustice, are not so much forgotten, or set aside thoughtlessly, as recognised at their relative unimportance when contrasted with the widespread, yet absolutely indefinable thing, which it is convenient to term Love. Not, be it explained, Love in its carnal sense, but, in an abstract spiritual way, which seeks the quiet happiness in adding to the joy of others, and trusts that somehow, somewhere, good is the final end of ill.

It may be that this attempt to explain the impression of Mr. Hughes's work is a purely personal one, but it is one that intimate study for many years strengthens and raises to the unassailable position of a positive fact. At the risk of appearing mawkishly sentimental, even with the greater risk of reflecting sentimentality upon artistic work which it has not, this impression of Mr. Arthur Hughes's art must be set down unmistakably. Looking upon it from a purely technical aspect, you might find much to praise, and perhaps a little to criticise ; but, taking it as an art addressed often enough to the purpose of forming artistic ideals in the minds of the young, you cannot but regret that the boys and girls of to-day, despite the army of artists of all ranks catering for them, cannot know

SOME ILLUSTRATORS OF THE SIXTIES

the peculiar delight that the children of the sixties and early seventies enjoyed.

Arthur Hughes was born in London in 1832, and became a pupil of Soames of the Royal Academy Schools, exhibiting for the first time at the annual exhibition in 1854. In 1855 appeared, as we have just seen, *The Music-master*. The artist seems to have worked fitfully at illustrations, but his honourable labours in painting dispose of any charge of indolence, and, did but the scope of this work permit it, a still more interesting record of his artistic career could be made by including a list of pictures exhibited at the Royal Academy, the Institute, the Grosvenor, the New Gallery, and elsewhere. Between 1855 and 1861 I have found no illustrations, nor does he himself recall any. In the latter year there are two designs in *The Queen* to poems by George Mac Donald and F Greenwood. The next magazine illustration in order is *At the Sepulchre* in *Good Words*, 1864. In 1866 appeared an edition of Tennyson's 'Enoch Arden, with twenty-five illustrations by Arthur Hughes.' This noteworthy book is one of the essential volumes to those who make ever so small a collection of the books of the sixties. Although the work is unequal, it contains some of his most delightful drawings. In the same year *London Society* contained *The Farewell Salutation*. In 1867 George Mac Donald's *Dealings with the Fairies* was published. This dainty little book, which contains some very typical work, is exceptionally scarce. Another book which was published in 1868 is now very difficult to run across in its first edition, *Five Days' Entertainment at Wentworth Grange*, by F. T. Palgrave, illustrated with seventeen designs, the woodcuts (*sic*) being by J. Cooper, and a vignette engraved on steel by C. H. Jeens.

To 1869 belongs the book with which the artist is most frequently associated, *Tom Brown's School Days*, by Tom Hughes, not a relative of the illustrator as the name might suggest. To descant on the merits of this edition to-day were foolish. When one hears of a new illustrated edition being contemplated, it seems sacrilege, and one realises how distinctly a newly illustrated *Tom Brown* would separate the generation that knew the book through Mr. Arthur Hughes's imagination from those who will make friends with it in company with another artist. Incidents like these bring

THE LETTER

THE DIAL—'SUN COMES,
MOON COMES'

home the inevitable change of taste with passing time more
vividly than far weightier matters enforce it.

Good Words in 1869 contains two drawings to *Carmina
Nuptialia*, and *The Sunday Magazine* the same year has a
very beautiful composition, *Blessings in Disguise.* In 1870
1871 *Good Words for the Young* includes, in the first two
volumes, no less than seventy-six illustrations by Mr. Hughes
to *At the Back of the North Wind*, fourteen to *The Boy in
Grey*, thirty to *Ranald Bannerman's Boyhood*, thirty to *The
Princess and Goblin*, ten to *Lilliput Revels*, six to *Lilliput
Lectures*, and two to *King Arthur*, besides one each to *Fancy*,
The Mariner's Cave, and a notable design to *The Wind and
the Moon.* In 1871 also belongs *My Lady Wind* (p. 38), *Little
Tommy Tucker* (p. 46), in *Novello's National Nursery
Rhymes.*

In 1870 *Good Words* contains four : *The Mother and the
Angel* and three full-page designs, which rank among the
most important of the artist's work in illustration, to
Tennyson's *Loves of the Wrens.* This song-cycle, which the
late Poet Laureate wrote expressly for Sullivan to set to music,
was issued in 1870 in a sumptuous quarto. The publisher,
Strahan, who at that time issued all Tennyson's work, had
intended to include illustrations, and three were finished
before the poet vetoed the project. These were cut down
and issued with the accompanying lyrics in *Good Words.*
Although the artist, vexed no doubt at their curtailment, and
by no means satisfied with their engraving, does not rank
them among his best things, few who collect his work will
share his view. Despite the trespass beyond the limit of
this book, it would be better to continue the list to date,
and it is all too brief. In 1872 *Good Words* contains five of
his designs, and *Good Words for the Young* twenty-four to
Innocent's Island, and eight to *Gutta-Percha Willie.*

1872 saw two remarkably good volumes decorated by
this artist, T. Gordon Hake's *Parables and Tales* (Chapman
and Hall) and *Sing Song*, a book of nursery rhymes by
Christina Rossetti (Routledge).

In 1873 ten to *Sindbad the Sailor*, and six or seven
others appeared in *Good Words for the Young*, now entitled
Good Things. To this year belongs also *Speaking Likenesses*
by Christina Rossetti, with its dozen fanciful and charming

SOME ILLUSTRATORS OF THE SIXTIES

designs; and a frontispiece and full page (p. 331), in Mr. George Mac Donald's *England's Antiphon* (Macmillan). In 1889 or 1890 *The Graphic* Christmas number contained two full-page illustrations by this artist. To 1892 belongs a delightful vignette upon the title-page of Mrs. George Mac Donald's *Chamber Dramas*. With a bare mention of seven drawings, inadequately reproduced in *The London Home Monthly*, 1895, the record of Mr. Arthur Hughes's work must close. Several designs to a poem by Jean Ingelow, *The Shepherd's Lady*, the artist has lost sight of, and the date of the first edition of *Five Old Friends and a Young Prince*, by Miss Thackeray, with a vignette, I have failed to trace at the British Museum or elsewhere. As Mr. Arthur Hughes, in the *Music-master* (1855), heads the list, so it seemed fit to mark his position by a fuller record than could be awarded to other of his contemporaries still living; partly because the comparatively small number of illustrations made a fairly complete record possible.

FREDERICK SANDYS.—This most admirable illustrator 'was born in Norwich in 1832, the son of a painter of the place, from whom he received his earliest art-instruction. Among his first drawings was a series of illustrations of the birds of Norfolk, and another dealing with the antiquities of his native city. Probably he first exhibited in 1851, with a portrait (in crayons) of "Henry, Lord Loftus" which appears as the work of "F. Sands" in the catalogue of the Royal Academy to whose exhibitions he has contributed in all forty-seven pictures and drawings.'[1]

The above, extracted from Mr. J. M. Gray's article, 'Frederick Sandys and the woodcut designers of thirty years ago,' gives the facts which concern us here. A most interesting study of the same artist by the same critic, in the *Art Journal*,[2] supplies more description and analysed appreciation. The eulogy by Mr. Joseph Pennell in *The Quarto*[3] must not be forgotten. Further references to Mr. Sandys appear in a lecture delivered by Professor Herkomer at the Royal Institution, printed in the *Art Journal*, 1883, and in a review of Thornbury's *Ballads* by Mr. Edmund Gosse in *The Academy*.[4]

It is quite possible, although only thirteen of the thirty or

[1] *Century Guild Hobby Horse*, vol. iii. p. 47 (1888).   [2] March 1884.
[3] No. 1, 1896.   [4] 1876, i. 176.

DANAE IN THE
BRAZEN CHAMBER

FREDERICK SANDYS

DALZIELS' 'BIBLE
GALLERY,' 1880

JACOB HEARS THE VOICE
OF THE LORD

so of illustrations by Frederick Sandys appeared in *Once a Week*, that these thirteen have been the most potent factor in giving the magazine its peculiar place in the hearts of artists. The general public may have forgotten its early volumes, but at no time since they were published have painters and pen-draughtsmen failed to prize them. During the years that saw them appear there are frequent laudatory references in contemporary journals, with now and again the spiteful attack which is only awarded to work that is unlike the average. Elsewhere mention is made of articles upon them which have appeared from time to time by Messrs. Edmund Gosse, J. M. Gray, Joseph Pennell, and others. During the 'seventies,' no less than in the 'eighties' or 'nineties,' men cut out the pages and kept them in their portfolios ; so that to-day, in buying volumes of the magazine, a wise person is careful to see that the 'Sandys' are all there before completing the purchase. Therefore, should the larger public admit them formally into the limited group of its acknowledged masterpieces, it will only imitate the attitude which from the first fellow-artists have maintained towards them.

The original drawings, *'If,' Life's Journey, The Little Mourner,* and *Jacques de Caumont,* were exhibited at the 'Arts and Crafts,' 1893. That a companion volume to Millais's *Parables,* with illustrations of *The Story of Joseph,* was actually projected, and the first drawings completed, is true, and one's regret that circumstances — those hideous circumstances, which need not be explained fully, of an artist's ideas rejected by a too prudish publisher—prevented its completion, is perhaps the most depressing item recorded in the pages of this volume.

That some thirty designs all told should have established the lasting reputation of an artist would be somewhat surprising, did not one realise that almost every one is a masterpiece of its kind. Owing to the courtesy of all concerned, so large a number of these are reproduced herewith that a detailed description of each would be superfluous. But, at the risk of repeating a list already printed and reprinted, it is well to condense the scattered references in the foregoing pages in a convenient paragraph, wherein those republished in Thornbury's *Legendary Ballads* (Chatto, 1876) are noted with an asterisk :—

SOME ILLUSTRATORS OF THE SIXTIES

THE CORNHILL MAGAZINE: *The Portent* ('60), *Manoli* ('62), *Cleopatra* ('66); ONCE A WEEK: **Yet once more on the organ play, The Sailor's Bride, From my Window, *Three Statues of Ægina, Rosamund Queen of the Lombards* (all 1861), **The Old Chartist, *The King at the Gate, *Jacques de Caumont, *King Warwolf, *The Boy Martyr, *Harold Harfagr* (all '62), and *Helen and Cassandra* ('66); GOOD WORDS: *Until her Death* ('62), *Sleep* ('63); CHURCHMAN'S FAMILY MAGAZINE: **The Waiting Time* ('63); SHILLING MAGAZINE: *Amor Mundi* ('65); THE QUIVER: *Advent of Winter* ('66); THE ARGOSY: *'If'* ('65); THE CENTURY GUILD HOBBY HORSE: *Danae* ('88); WILMOT'S SACRED POETRY: *Life's Journey, The Little Mourner*; CASSELL'S FAMILY MAGAZINE: *Proud Maisie* ('81); and DALZIELS' BIBLE GALLERY: *Jacob hears the voice of the Lord.*

In addition, it may be interesting to add notes of other drawings:—*The Nightmare* (1857)[1], a parody of *Sir Isumbras at the Ford*, by Millais, which shows a braying ass marked 'J. R.' (for John Ruskin), with Millais, Rossetti, and Holman Hunt on his back; *Morgan le Fay*, reproduced as a double-page supplement in *The British Architect*, October 31, 1879; a frontispiece, engraved on steel by J. Saddler, for Miss Muloch's *Christian's Mistake* (Hurst and Blackett), and another for *The Shaving of Shagpat* (Chapman and Hall, 1865); a portrait of Matthew Arnold, engraved by O. Lacour, published in *The English Illustrated Magazine*, January 1884; another of Professor J. R. Green, engraved by G. J. Stodardt, in *The Conquest of England*, 1883; and one of Robert Browning, published in *The Magazine of Art* shortly after the poet's death; *Miranda*, a drawing reproduced in *The Century Guild Hobby Horse*, vol. iii. p. 41; *Medea*, reproduced (as a silver-print photograph) in Col. Richard's poem of that name (Chapman and Hall, 1869); a reproduction of the original drawing for *Amor Mundi*, and studies for the same, in the two editions of Mr. Pennell's *Pen-Drawing and Pen-Draughtsmen* (Macmillan); a reproduction of an unfinished drawing on wood, *The Spirit of the Storm*, in *The Quarto* (No. 1, 1896); *Proud Maisie* in *Pan* (1881), reissued in *Songs of the North*, and engraved by W. Spielmayer (from the original in possession of Dr. John Todhunter) in the *English Illustrated Magazine*,

---

[1] A large broadsheet reproduced by some lithographic process.

FREDERICK SANDYS

May 1891, and the original drawing for the *Advent of Winter* and one of *Two Heads*, reproduced in J. M. Gray's article in the *Art Journal* (March 1884). Whether the *Judith* here reproduced was originally drawn for engraving I cannot say.

To add another eulogy of these works is hardly necessary at this moment, when their superb quality has provoked a still wider recognition than ever. Concerning the engraving of some Mr. Sandys complained bitterly, but of others, notably the *Danae*, he wrote in October 1880 : ' My drawing was most perfectly cut by Swain, from my point of view, the best piece of wood-cutting of our time—mind I am not speaking of my work, but Swain's.' To see that the artist's complaint was at times not unfounded one has but to compare the *Advent of Winter* as it appears in a reproduction of the drawing (*Art Journal*, March 1884) and in *The Quiver*. ' It was my best drawing entirely spoilt by the cutter,' he said ; but this was perhaps a rather hasty criticism that is hardly proved up to the hilt by the published evidence.

As a few contemporary criticisms quoted elsewhere go to prove, Sandys was never ignored by artists nor by people of taste. To-day there are dozens of men in Europe without popular appreciation at home or abroad, but surely if his fellows recognise the master-hand, it is of little moment whether the cheap periodicals ignore him, or publish more or less adequately illustrated articles on the man and his work. Frederick Sandys is and has been a name to conjure with for the last thirty years. Though still alive, he has gained (I believe) no official recognition. But that is of little consequence. There are laureates uncrowned and presidents unelected still living among us whose lasting fame is more secure than that of many who have worn the empty titles without enjoying the unstinted approval of fellow-craftsmen which alone makes any honour worthy an artist's acceptance.

SIR EDWARD BURNE-JONES.—The illustrations of this artist are so few that it is a matter of regret that they could not all be reproduced here. But the artist, without withholding permission, expressed a strong wish that they should not be reprinted. The two in *Good Words* have been already named. Others to a quite forgotten book must not be mentioned ; but it is safe to say that no human being, who did not know by whom they were produced, would recognise them. A beautiful design[1] for a frontispiece to Mr. William Morris's *Love is Enough* was never engraved. The *Nativity* in Gatty's *Parables from Nature*, and the one design in the *Dalziel Bible* have already been named. Many drawings for *Cupid and Psyche*, the first portion of a proposed illustrated folio edition of *The Earthly Paradise*, were actually engraved, some of the blocks being cut by Mr. Morris himself. Several sets of impressions exist, and rumour for a long time babbled of a future Kelmscott Press edition. Of his more recent designs nothing can be said here; besides being a quarter of a century later than the prescribed limits of the volume, they are as familiar as any modern work could be.

WALTER CRANE.—This popular artist was born in Liverpool, August 15, 1845, his father being sometime secretary and treasurer of the (then) Liverpool Academy. After a boyhood spent mostly at Torquay the family came to London in 1857. In 1859 he became a pupil of Mr. W. J. Linton, the well-known engraver, and remained with him for three years. About 1865 he first saw the work of Burne-Jones at the Society of Painters in Water Colours. These drawings, and some Japanese toy-books which fell in his way, have no doubt strongly influenced his style; but the earlier pre-Raphaelites and the *Once a Week* school had been eagerly studied before. Although Mr. Crane, with his distinctly individual manner, is not a typical artist of the sixties any more than of the seventies, or of to-day, and although his style had hardly found its full expression at that time, except in the toy-books, yet no record of the period could be complete without a notice of one whose loyalty to a particular style has done much to found the modern 'decorative school.'

His first published drawing, *A man in the coils of a serpent*, appears in a quite forgotten magazine called *Entertaining Things*, vol. i. 1861, p. 327 (Virtue); others, immature, and spoilt by the engraver, are in *The Talking Fire-irons* and similar tracts by the Rev. H. B. Power. In many of the magazines, of which the contents are duly noted, —*Good Words, Once a Week, The Argosy, London Society*, etc.—reference has been already made to each of his drawings

---

[1] Owned by Mr. Fairfax Murray.

TREASURE-TROVE

as it appeared therein. A bibliography of his work, to be exhaustive, would take up more room than space permitted here. As it will be the task of the one, whoever he may be, who undertakes to chronicle English illustrations of the seventies, it may be left without further notice. For, with the exception of the *New Forest* (1862), all the other books which may be called masterpieces of their order, *Grimms' Household Stories, The Necklace of Princess Fiorimonde, The Baby's Bouquet, Baby's Opera, Æsop's Fables, Flora's Feast, Queen Summer*, the long series of Mrs. Molesworth's children's books, many 'coloured boards' for novels, and the rest, belong to a later period.

To find that a large paper copy of *Grimms' Household Stories* fetched thirty-six pounds at Lord Leighton's sale is a proof that collectors of 'Cranes' are already in full cry. Two hundred and fifty copies of this book were issued in large paper ; the copy in question, although handsomely bound, did not derive its value solely from that fact. Modern readers rubbed their eyes to find a recent *édition de luxe* fetching a record price ; but, if certain signs are not misleading, the market value of many books of the sixties will show a rapid increase that will surprise the apathetic collector, who now regards them as commonplace. To believe that the worth of anything is just as much as it will bring is a most foolish test of intrinsic value ; but, should the auctioneer's marked catalogue of a few years hence show that 'the sixties' produced works which coax the reluctant guineas out of the pockets of those who a short time before would not expend shillings, it will but reflect the well-seasoned verdict of artists for years past. In matters of science and of commerce the man in the street acts on the opinion of the expert, but in matters of art he usually prefers his own. If, when he wakens to the intrinsic value of objects about which artists know no difference of opinion, he has to pay heavily for his conceited belief in his own judgment, it is at once poetic justice and good common sense.

Space forbids, unfortunately, detailed notices of Fred Barnard, C. H. Bennett, T. Morten, George Du Maurier, John Pettie, R.A., and many other deceased artists whose works have been frequently referred to in previous chapters.

Fairly complete iconographies had been prepared of the

SOME ILLUSTRATORS OF THE SIXTIES

works of Mr. Birket Foster, Sir John Gilbert, and Ernest Griset. These, and other no less important lists, have also been omitted for the same reason.

Nor is it necessary to include here notices of artists whose fame has been established in another realm of art—such as Mr. Whistler, Mr. Luke Fildes, R.A., Professor Herkomer, R.A., Messrs. W. Q. Orchardson, R.A., H. S. Marks, R.A., H. H. Armstead, R.A., Edmund J. Poynter, R.A., G. H. Boughton, J. W. North, R.A., and George Frederick Watts, R.A.

Others, including W. Small, Charles Green, Sir John Tenniel, would each require a volume, instead of a few paragraphs, to do even bare justice to the amazing quantity of notable illustrations they have produced. Fortunately most of them are still alive and active, so that a more worthy excuse remains for omitting to give a complete iconography of each one here, for they belong to a far more extended period than is covered by this book.

DALZIEL BROTHERS

The firm of Dalziel Brothers deserves more notice than it has received in the many incidental references throughout this book. To Mr. Thomas Dalziel (still alive though past fourscore) and to his brother Edward may be awarded the credit of exercising keen critical judgment in the discovery of latent talent among the art students of their day, and of acting as liberal patrons of the art of illustration. In a most courteous letter, written in reply to my request for some details of the establishment of the firm, the youngest brother of the four (Mr. Thomas Dalziel) writes: 'We were constant and untiring workers with our own hands, untiring because it was truly a labour of love. The extension and development of our transactions and the carrying out of many of the fine art works which we published, is unquestionably due to my brother Edward Dalziel, and to this I am at all times ready to bear unhesitating testimony.'

That these talented engravers were draughtsmen of no mean order might be proved in a hundred instances ; one or two blocks here reprinted will suffice to establish their right to an honourable position as illustrators.

Among the young artists to whom they gave commissions,

178

BEDREDDIN HASSAN AND
THE PASTRYCOOK

T. DALZIEL

THE DESTRUCTION OF SODOM

DALZIELS' 'BIBLE GALLERY,' 1880

THE FIRM OF DALZIEL BROTHERS

at the time in a student's career when encouragement of that description is so vital, we find :—Fred Walker, G. J. Pinwell, A. Boyd Houghton, J. D. Watson, John Pettie, R.A., Professor Herkomer, R.A., J. W. North, A.R.A., and Fred Barnard. Artists of eminence, who in all human probability would never have experimented in drawing upon wood but for Messrs. Dalziels' suggestion, include the late Lord Leighton, P.R.A., Mr. G. F. Watts, R.A., and Mr. H. Stacy Marks, R.A. Other illustrators who owe much to the enterprise of this firm, and who in turn helped to make its reputation, include Mr. Birket Foster, Sir John Gilbert, R.A., Mr. George Du Maurier, Sir John Tenniel, and Mr. Harrison Weir.

It has been impossible to credit these engravers with their due share in every work mentioned in our pages, because to do this would have necessitated, in common justice, a complete record of the other engravers also ; in itself enough to double the length of the chronicle already far too verbose. The engravings in *Punch* in its early years, and the *Cornhill* through its finest period, were intrusted to Messrs. Dalziel, while of *Good Words* and *The Sunday Magazine* the choice of pictures and their reproduction alike were entirely under their control.

The Dalziel Brothers were born at Wooler, Northumberland, but spent most of their early days in Newcastle-on-Tyne. Their craft was learned from pupils of Thomas Bewick. In 1835 George Dalziel came to London, followed soon after by Edward, and later by John and Thomas. They were all draughtsmen as well as engravers. Thomas devoted himself entirely to drawing. There was also a sister, 'Margaret' (who died in 1894), who practised the art of wood-engraving for many years, with results distinguished for their minute elaboration and fine feeling.

Soon after settling in London, George was associated with Ebenezer Landells (who died in 1869) ; and the brothers later became intimate with Bewick's favourite pupil, William Harvey, for whom they engraved many of his drawings for Lane's *Arabian Nights*, Charles Knight's *Shakespeare* and *Bunyan*, and many other works. Still later they became acquainted with [Sir] John Gilbert, and were 'the first who endeavoured to render his drawings throughout according to his own style of lining and suggested manipulation.'

THE FIRM OF DALZIEL BROTHERS.

Their effort was to translate the draughtsman's line, not to paraphrase it by tint-cutting. As a former apologist has written : ' This has been called " facsimile work "; but it is not so, strictly speaking. Certainly, whatever it may be called, it required as much artistic knowledge and taste to produce a good result as the so-called tint-work against which they [Dalziel Brothers] have no word to say, having practised that branch of art to a considerable extent, as may be seen in hundreds of instances, but perhaps most notably in the Rev. J. G. Wood's *Natural History* and *The History of Man.*'

The Dalziels had clever pupils to whom they attribute most readily no little of their success ; of these Harry Fenn and C. Kingdon, who both went to America, may be specially mentioned. But a record of so notable an enterprise cannot be adequately treated here ; yet a few authorised facts must needs find place. Did space permit, the eulogies of many artists who were entirely satisfied with Messrs. Dalziels' engraving could be quoted as a set-off to the few, Rossetti included, who were querulous. It would be invidious to pick out their best work, but Millais's *Parables*, Birket Foster's *Beauties of English Landscape*, and the illustrated editions of classics : *Don Quixote, Arabian Nights, Goldsmith's Works, The Bible Gallery*, etc. etc., which bear their imprint, may be numbered among their highest achievements.

The share of Mr. Edmund Evans in many notable volumes that owe at least a moiety of their interest to his engraving, and of Messrs. Swain, must needs be left without comment. Mr. Joseph Swain contributed to *Good Words* in 1888 some very interesting articles on Fred Walker, C. H. Bennett, and G. J. Pinwell. These have since been issued in a volume,[1] with essays, by various hands, on Frederick Shields, [Sir] John Tenniel, and others. It contains ninety illustrations, including the rare early ' Fred Walker ' from *Everybody's Journal*, and specimens of Mr. Shields's illustrations to an edition of *The Pilgrim's Progress*, published (apparently) by the *Manchester Examiner*. But so far as I know, neither Mr. Evans nor Messrs. Swain (in the sixties at all events) projected works as Messrs. Dalziel did ; and the appreciation which they merit, in their own field, would be unfairly recorded in a few hasty lines.

[1] *Toilers in Art*, edited by H. C. Ewart (Isbister and Co.).

INDEX

INDEX

INDEX

CLARKE, E. F. C., 76, 80.
CLAXTON, A., illustrations to *London Society*, 56.
—— other illustrations, 57, 58, 62, 92.
CLAXTON, FLORENCE, 50, 57, 64, 92.
CLAXTON, MARSHALL, 64.
CLAYTON, JOHN, illustrations to:
    Herbert's 'Poetical Works,' 103.
    'Pilgrim's Progress,' 104.
    Pollok's 'Course of Time,' 104.
    'Poets of Nineteenth Century,' 107.
    'Dramatic Scenes,' 107.
    'Lays of the Holy Land,' 108.
    'Home Affections,' 108.
    Krummacher's 'Parables,' 109.
Clichés, beginning of the use of, 79.
—— bad influence on original productions, 79.
'Cloister and the Hearth,' The, 20.
Coleridge's 'Ancient Mariner' (1856), illustrations by:
    B. FOSTER, A. DUNCAN, and WEHNERT, 104.
    (1860), D. SCOTT, 114.
Collecting, cost of, 7.
Collections, how to arrange, 7.
—— methods for preserving, 7.
Collectors, two objects of, 4-5.
—— delights of, 5.
—— objects supplied by the present volume for, x. 5-6.
—— dangers to be avoided by, 6.
Collins's (Wilkie) 'Armadale,' 41, 42.
COLOMB, W., 50.
Cook's (Eliza) 'Poems' (1856), illustrations by ARMSTEAD, J. GILBERT, J. D. WATSON, H. WEIR, J. WOLF, 102.
COPE, C. W., 64, 99, 100, 101, 102; illustrations to:
    'Favourite English Poems,' 109.
    'Book of Favourite Modern Ballads,' 110.
    Moore's 'Irish Melodies,' 133.
COOKE, E. W., 49.
COOPER, A. W., 46, 57, 58, 60, 64, 76, 80, 81, 86.
CORBOULD, E. H., 57, 64, 73, 92, 101, 107, 109, 140, 146.
'Cornhill Gallery': its quality and characteristics, 39, 126.
Cornhill Magazine, 14.
—— aim of its editor, 38.
—— the anonymity of artists in, 44.
—— illustrations and illustrators of, 38-44.
    ALLINGHAM, H., 43.
    BARNES, R., 41, 42.
    BENNETT, C. H., 40.
    DOYLE, R., 40.
    DU MAURIER, G., 41, 42, 43.
    EDWARDS, M. E., 42.
    FILDES, S. L., 42.
    HERKOMER, H., 42.
    HOPKINS, A., 43.

Cornhill Magazine, illustrations and illustrators of—*continued*.
    HUGHES, A., 41.
    KEENE, C., 41.
    LAWSON, F. W., 42.
    LEIGHTON, F., 40.
    LESLIE, C. D., 43.
    MILLAIS, J. E., 40.
    PATERSON, H., 43.
    PATON, NOEL, 41.
    PINWELL, G. J., 41.
    SANDYS, F., 40, 42.
    SMALL, W., 43.
    STONE, MARCUS, 43.
    THACKERAY, W. M., 39, 40.
    WALKER, F., 40, 41, 42.
Cornwall (Barry), 'Dramatic Scenes' (1857), illustrations by DALZIEL, CLAYTON, 107.
Cowper's 'Works,' illustrations by JOHN GILBERT, 101.
—— 'The Task,' illustrations by BIRKET FOSTER, 102.
CRANE, W., illustrations to:
    Once a Week, 33, 176.
    Good Words, 49, 176.
    London Society, 56, 60, 176.
    Argosy, 73, 74, 176.
    Churchman's Shilling Magazine, 76.
    Every Boy's Magazine, 85.
    Punch, 88.
    Entertaining Things, 176.
    'The New Forest,' 117, 176.
    'Children's Sayings,' 118.
    'Stories of Old,' 118.
    Toy-Books, 129, 148.
    'Stories from Memel,' 136.
    'Merry Heart,' 136.
    'King Gab's Story Bag,' 136.
    'Magic of Kindness,' 136.
    'Poetry of Nature,' 136.
    Roberts's 'Legendary Ballads,' 140.
    'Songs of Many Seasons,' 137.
    'The Necklace of Princess Fiorimonde,' 176.
    Grimms' 'Fairy Tales,' 176.
    'The Baby's Bouquet,' 176.
    'Baby's Opera,' 176.
    Æsop's 'Fables,' 176.
    'Flora's Feast,' 176.
    'Queen Summer,' 176.
—— critical and biographical notice of, 175, 176.
—— a pupil of W. J. LINTON, 175.
—— influence of BURNE-JONES and Japanese art, 176.
CRESWICK, T., 64, 101; illustrations to:
    Tennyson's 'Poems,' 105.
    'Favourite English Poems,' 109.
    'Early English Poems,' 117.
CROPSEY, J., 108.
CROWQUILL, A., 60; illustrations to:
    'Bon Gaultier Ballads,' 100.
    'Munchausen,' 114

185

ENGLISH ILLUSTRATION

INDEX

ENGLISH ILLUSTRATION

INDEX

INDEX

ENGLISH ILLUSTRATION

'IDYLLIC PICTURES' (1867), illustrations by R. BARNES, BOYD HOUGHTON, H. CAMERON, M. E. EDWARDS, P. GRAY, R. P. LEITCH, G. J. PINWELL, F. SANDYS, W. SMALL, C. J. STANILAND, and G. H. THOMAS, 131, 132.

ILLINGWORTH, S. E., 60.

'Illustrated Book of Sacred Poems' (1867?), illustrations by M. E. EDWARDS, J. W. NORTH, H. C. SELOUS, W. SMALL, and J. D. WATSON, 138.

Illustrated Chronicle of the Great Exhibition, 14.

Illustrated Family Journal, 14.

Illustrated London News, 14; illustrations of the 'seventies,' 92.
  BENNETT, C. H., 92.
  BOYD-HOUGHTON, A., 92.
  CORBOULD, E. H., 92.
  GILBERT, J., 92.
  GREEN, C., 92.
  HUNT, ALFRED, 92.
  MORGAN, MATT, 92.
  PASQUIER, J. A., 92.
  READ, S., 92.
  THOMAS, GEORGE, 92.

Illustrated Times, illustrations in, by A. CLAXTON, F. CLAXTON, M. E. EDWARDS, Lieutenant SECCOMBE, P. SKELTON, T. SULMAN.

Illustrated Weekly News, 92.

Illustration, reasons for serial issue of,
—— demand for, 10.
—— importance of, 10.
—— influence of 'process-work' on, 11.
—— earliest attempt of magazine, 16.
—— object of, 17.
—— to the early Victorian novels, 18.
—— to the *Cornhill,* 38, 39.
—— black and white, its requisites, 65, 66.
—— influence of photography on, 66.
—— preference of a drawing to a photograph, 67, 68.
—— in daily papers, 94.
—— new method employed in 'Pleasures of Memory' (1867), 137, 138.
—— regard for the older, 139.
—— comparisons of old and modern, 139.

Illustrator, position of the modern, 3, 9.
—— the popular artist of the period, 10, 134.
—— appreciation of, 10.
—— summary of the work of the sixties, 148, 149.

Ingelow, Jean, 'Poems' (1867, 4to), 4; illustrations to, by BOYD HOUGHTON, E. and T. DALZIEL, J. W. NORTH, E. J. POYNTER, G. J. PINWELL, and J. WOLF, 129, 130.

'Ingoldsby Legends,' The (1864), illustrations by CRUIKSHANK, LEECH, and TENNIEL, 123.

JACKSON, MASON, 'The Pictorial Press,' 92, 98.

Jackson's 'Engraving.' *See* Chatto.

Jerrold's 'Story of a Feather' (1867), illustrations by DU MAURIER, 133.

'Jingles and Jokes for Little Folks' (1866), illustrations by PAUL GRAY, 129.

JOHNSON, E. K., 57, 64.

Journalism, 55.

Judy, general poorness of its drawings, 90.
—— illustrated by MATT MORGAN and J. PROCTOR, 90.
—— value as representative of the 'eighties,' 90.

Junior Etching Club, 118, 151, 152, 153.

JUSTYNE, P. W., 64.

'Juvenile Verse and Picture Book' (1848), GILBERT, TENNIEL, R. CRUIKSHANK, WEIGALL, and W. B. SCOTT's illustrations to, 100.

'KAVANAGH' (1857), illustrations by BIRKET FOSTER, 108.

Keats's 'Poetical Works' (1866), illustrations by G. SCHARF, 129.

KEENE, CHARLES, 19.
—— quality of his work, 25; illustrations to:
  Once a Week, 25, 26, 36.
  Cornhill Magazine, 41.
  Good Words, 47.
  London Society, 59-62.
  Punch, 88, 89.
  'Voyage of the *Constance,*' 110, 111.
  'Lyra Germanica,' 113.
  'Sacred Poetry,' 115.
  'Mrs. Caudle's Curtain Lectures,' 124.
  'Ballads and Songs of Brittany,' 127.
  'Legends and Lyrics,' 128.
  'Touches of Nature,' 131.
  Thornbury's 'Legendary Ballads,' 146.
  Hood's 'Poems,' 152.
  'Passages from Modern English Poets,' 153.

KENNEDY, T., 129.

KEYL, F. W., 64, 114, 123.

'King Gab's Story Bag' (1868), illustrations by W. CRANE, 136.

Kingsley, C., 'Hereward,' 50.
—— 'The Water Babies' (1869), illustrations by PATON and SKELTON, 137.

Kingston's Annuals, 87.

'Krilof and his Fables' (1867), illustrations by BOYD HOUGHTON and ZWECKER, 135.

Krummacher's 'Parables' (1858), illustrations by CLAYTON, 109, 110.

'LAKE COUNTY,' THE (1864), illustrations by LINTON, 124.

LAMONT, T. R., 58, 65.

Landon (L. E.), 'Poetical Works' (1869), illustrations by W. B. SCOTT, 140.

Lasinio, his influence, 151.

Laurie's 'Shilling Entertainment Library' (1862), 118.

INDEX

193

INDEX

INDEX

INDEX

INDEX

ENGLISH ILLUSTRATION

Printed by T. and A. CONSTABLE, Printers to His Majesty,
at the Edinburgh University Press